WHICH BIBLE WOULD JESUS USE?

The Bible Version Controversy Explained and Resolved

Jack McElroy

© 2013 Jack McElroy
Which Bible Would Jesus Use?
The Bible Version Controversy Explained and Resolved

To learn more, go to:
www.whichbiblewouldJesususe.com or www.wbwju.com

All Scripture quotations, unless otherwise indicated, are taken from the King James Bible.

Scripture quotations marked NIV are taken from The Holy Bible, New International Version®, NIV®, Copyright ©1973, 1978, 1984, 2011 (New NIV) by Biblica, Inc.™ Used by permission. All rights reserved worldwide.

Scripture quotations marked ESV are taken from The Holy Bible, English Standard Version® (ESV®), Copyright © 2001 by Crossway, a publishing ministry of Good News Publishers. Used by permission. All rights reserved.

Scripture quotations marked NASB are taken from the New American Standard Bible®, Copyright ©1960, 1962, 1963, 1968, 1971, 1972, 1973, 1975, 1977, 1995 by The Lockman Foundation. Used by permission. (www.Lockman.org)

Scripture quotations marked NKJV are taken from the New King James Version®, Copyright ©1982 by Thomas Nelson, Inc. Used by permission. All rights reserved.

Scripture quotations marked RSV are taken from the Revised Standard Version of the Bible, Copyright ©1946, 1952, and 1971 National Council of the Churches of Christ in the United States of America. Used by permission. All rights reserved.

Scripture quotations marked HCSB are taken from the Holman Christian Standard Bible®, Used by Permission HCSB ©1999, 2000, 2002, 2003, 2009 Holman Bible Publishers. Holman Christian Standard Bible®, Holman CSB®, and HCSB® are federally registered trademarks of Holman Bible Publishers.

Scripture quotations marked NLT are taken from the Holy Bible, New Living Translation, Copyright ©1996, 2004, 2007 by Tyndale House Foundation. Used by permission of Tyndale House Publishers, Inc., Carol Stream, Illinois 60188. All rights reserved.

ALL RIGHTS RESERVED. This book contains material protected under International and Federal Copyright Laws and Treaties. Any unauthorized reprint or use of this material is prohibited. No part of this book may be reproduced or transmitted in any form or by any means, electronic or mechanical, including photocopying, recording, or by any information storage and retrieval system without express written permission from the publisher.

ISBN: 978-0-9860265-0-8 HB
ISBN: 978-0-9860265-1-5 PB

McElroy Publishing
Transforming Hearts and Lives Since 1992

27-33 Fredonian Street
Shirley, MA 01464
978-425-4055
978-425-6116
info@mcelroypublishing.com

Interior book layout and design: Sharon McElroy, SharonMcElroy.com
Copyediting: Kathleen Deselle, Freelance Editing Services

Then they that feared the Lord spake often one to another: and the Lord hearkened, and heard it, and a book of remembrance was written before him for them that feared the Lord, and that thought upon his name. (Malachi 3:16)

Other books by Jack McElroy:

How I Lost My Fear of Death and How You Can Too

Adoniram Judson's Soul Winning Secrets Revealed—An Inspiring Look at the Tools Used by "Jesus Christ's Man" in Burma, Co-authored with Daw Tin Tin Aye

Other titles from McElroy Publishing:

How to Be a Successful Camp Counselor

Mastering Leadership in the Christian Camp and Related Ministries

How to Be a Great Camp Counselor

The Camp Counselor's Handbook of over 90 Games and Activities Just for Rainy Days!

The Complete Encyclopedia of Christian Camp Directing and Programming

Contents

Dedication		v
Foreword	Dr. William P. Grady	vii
Preface	Want to settle the "Bible Version Controversy" once and for all?	xii
Introduction		1
Chapter 1	Why the Lord is forced to choose only one Bible	19
Chapter 2	Two "dirty little secrets" of modern textual criticism	35
Chapter 3	Proof—Prominent textual scholars believe God made mistakes when he wrote the Bible	55
Chapter 4	Why the Lord didn't preserve the original autographs	79
Chapter 5	Why the Lord can't choose the King James Bible without looking foolish to scholars	89
Chapter 6	Did the Lord make a monumental, multi-generational error by allowing the King James Bible to be published in the first place?	107
Chapter 7	Maybe the Lord Jesus Christ isn't a loser after all	117
Chapter 8	Why can't the Lord choose the ©1982 New King James Version?	127
Chapter 9	Where was the Bible before 1611?	151
Chapter 10	Which edition of the King James Bible is "The Bible"?	161
Chapter 11	What about the tens of thousands of differences between the 1769 edition (or any edition today) and the 1611 first edition?	179

Chapter 12	What about the differences between King James Bibles printed by the Oxford and Cambridge University Presses?	205
Chapter 13	Why "Which Edition?" is (quite often) a trick question	219
Chapter 14	The real reason for the fake question	227
Chapter 15	Inspiration of Scripture—What it is and what it isn't	233
Chapter 16	Inspiration—What it was and what they say it is now	245
Chapter 17	Who changed the definition of inspiration, and when did they change it?	259
Chapter 18	Did the Lord preserve error instead of truth in the extant biblical manuscripts?	275
Chapter 19	How to spot a standard Bible	289
Chapter 20	The Revelation 16:5 controversy	297
Chapter 21	Which Bible should you use?	305

About the Author   309

Bibliography   311

Index   323

Scripture Index   335

Image Credits   341

Dedication

This work is dedicated to the Lord Jesus Christ who gave himself for me. He gave me life and is my life. Without him I am nothing.

It's also dedicated to my family and fellow believers.

Like the Scripture says:

> Beloved, when I gave all diligence to write unto you of the common salvation, it was needful for me to write unto you, and exhort you that ye should earnestly contend for the faith which was once delivered unto the saints. (Jude 1:3)

Even as we are to contend for the faith we must also contend for the text and the book wherein that faith is found.

A handed down faith depends on a handed down text.

Foreword

It is an honor to contribute the Foreword to *Which Bible Would Jesus Use?* On a personal note, I am further blessed to pen these words on the twentieth anniversary of *Final Authority*, my own foray into the King James Bible controversy. While the battle was certainly intense back in 1993, Paul's end-day warning in 2 Timothy 3:13 that *"evil men and seducers shall wax worse and worse"* guarantees conditions will only deteriorate till the Rapture. For instance, in the second half of the last century, the "scholarship" arrayed against the A.V. 1611 ran the gamut from "Perhaps he is ... sitting on the toilet" (1971 Living Bible paraphrase of 1 Kings 18:27) to "Now the serpent was one bad dude" (1993 Black Bible Chronicles' Ebonics rendition of Genesis 3:1). In this new millennium, the four centuries-old King James Version must now "share the market" with the *Queen* James Version (2012) promoted as "A Gay Bible ... based on The King James Bible, edited to prevent homophobic misinterpretation."

Consequently, as intensified Satanic assaults call for emergency reinforcements, Jack McElroy's new book constitutes a timely addition to the Bible believer's arsenal. The novel thesis and wealth of fresh information (especially chapters two and three) combined with the author's lack of traditional "seminary credentials" (John 7:15) bear witness to the power of the Authorized Version itself; for implied in the command, *"Study ... the word of truth"* (2 Timothy 2:15) is the inspiring assurance that spiritual nuggets await the humble student in every generation (Isaiah 28:9; Matthew 11:25). To the consternation of the "scholars union," a diligent Christian businessman (Proverbs 22:29) has successfully reduced the rancorous "King James Only-ism" debate to a single, unconventional premise—"Which Bible would Jesus use?" The utter simplicity of Brother McElroy's question will undoubtedly render many in academia apoplectic. And yet, his unique approach is entirely Scriptural. As the human soul is composed of a *mind, emotion, and will,* believers are directed to emulate the Lord in all three areas: *"Let this mind be in you, which was also in Christ Jesus..."* (Philippians 2:5); *"...the* LORD *hath sought him a man after his own heart..."* (1 Samuel 13:14); and *"...Christ also suffered for us, leaving us an example, that ye should follow his steps..."* (1 Peter 2:21).

As the volume unfolds, one modern version after another is exposed for having a myriad of problems and subsequently disqualified from being "the Bible that Jesus would use." The author does this by demonstrating how various aberrations of the KJV text would be particularly offensive to the Lord. Such a "common sense" approach resonates with the "common man" (Mark 12:37). While composing this recommendation, I received a profound email from a brother who described himself as simply "...a dry land wheat farmer..." (i.e., a twenty-first-century version of the "ploughboy" William Tyndale was determined to liberate). Though unaware of this manuscript, he shared some good ol' horse sense ("stable thinking") that aptly speaks to the question at hand.

To paraphrase his comments, in the A.V. 1611 account of the adoration and prophecy of Simeon (occurring only eight days after Jesus' birth), Luke 2:33 is rendered, *"And Joseph and his mother marveled at those things which were spoken of him."* Conversely, nearly every modern "Bible" deletes Joseph, substituting the blasphemous reading, "And his *father* and mother..." (e.g., the ASV, RSV, NRSV, NASB, NIV, ESV, ERV, and HCSB). The problem here should be obvious; *if* Joseph *was* the father of Jesus, then Jesus could *not* be God, much less the Saviour of the world, etc. Thus, the question begs, as Matthew 1:18 and 19 shows that Joseph knew the child was not his and Luke 1:34 confirms that Mary knew the same, why do all the editors of the contemporary versions *lie* by making Joseph the father of Jesus? The greater question then becomes, *Why* would the Lord Jesus Christ endorse a "Bible" that invalidates both his divinity and ministry? (1 Corinthians 15:17–19; 2 Timothy 2:13)

Finally, as Ecclesiastes 12:13 declares, *"Let us hear the conclusion of the whole matter...,"* any doubt concerning "which Bible Jesus would use" can be settled by the litmus test of Jeremiah 10:5. Whereas the KJV reads, *"They are upright as the palm tree...,"* the 2011 NIV substitutes, "Like a scarecrow in a cucumber field...." (See similar readings in the RSV, NRSV, NASB, ESV, and HCSB.) The NIV's inane preference for "scarecrow" is made *scarier* yet by the fact that the same Hebrew word *is* translated "palm" in Judges 4:5 (*"palm tree"* in the KJV), constituting the only other appearance of this word. Would the Lord choose a "Bible" that morphs from a "palm tree" to a "scarecrow in a cucumber field"? With the celebrated (and calculated) publication of Zondervan's "newest" New International Version having coincided with the 400th anniversary of the "Old Black Book," should we laugh or cry at the finished product? As NIV spokesman Keith Danby assured the Body of Christ via *USA Today,* "...we'll make sure we get it right this time," we are left to conclude that "cucumber field" represents the corrected reading for "melon patch" in the 1984 edition. I wholeheartedly concur with Jack McElroy's astute pronouncement near the end of chapter three—"Oy vey, what a mess!"

"Ever learning, and never able to come to the knowledge of the truth."
(2 Timothy 3:7)

Dr. William P. Grady
Pastor, Macedonia Baptist Church
Swartz Creek, Michigan
February 14, 2013

William P. Grady, B.S., M.Ed., Th.M., Ph.D., D.D., "founded and pastored the Kootenai County Baptist Church in Post Falls, Idaho, from 1981 to 1986, at which time he returned to Hyles-Anderson College as a faculty member, continuing in that position through 1996. He then went into full-time evangelism, speaking in more than 500 churches over the next ten years.

He is a board member of the Baptist History Preservation Society of Rockwell, North Carolina.

Dr. Grady is also the author of four best-selling reference works: *Final Authority, What Hath God Wrought!, How Satan Turned America Against God,* and *Given by Inspiration.* Distributed by Ingram Books, these titles have generated twenty-eight printings to date. Dr. Grady's third book has maintained a five-star review at Barnes & Noble and was featured in *USA Today,* the Afterword written by the esteemed Jewish physicist Sam Cohen, "Father of the Neutron Bomb."

In the fall of 2006, while pursuing further studies at the University of Tennessee, Dr. Grady was called to the Flint, Michigan, area to start the Macedonia Baptist Church in Swartz Creek." (Grady Publications, "Dr. William P. Grady: A Biographical Sketch," accessed February 2013, http://www.gradypublications.com.)

Preface

Want to settle the "Bible Version Controversy" once and for all?

If so, read on…

You know how people get upset and sometimes even angry when someone talks about one Bible version being better than another? It happens a lot in Bible studies because the differences in versions are obvious to everybody.

The root of the problem stems from the fact that the teachers and leaders in evangelicalism and fundamentalism are still searching for the readings from a nonexistent book they define as "The Original Bible."

The wording of this "Original Bible" is a moving target. It changes depending on which textual expert you listen to. That's why there are so many "versions." And that's why new ones get printed all the time.

As a result, everyone has an opinion as to which Bible is best. The funny thing is, hardly anyone ever considers the opinion of the Lord Jesus Christ. Don't you think he has a preference?

Which Bible Would Jesus Use? will prove that the Lord himself has to choose among all the different Bible versions out there and is forced to pick just one of them.

Which one would he use? The evidence shows that it's the same brand he's been using for the past 400 years. And once you know for sure which Bible version the Lord has already chosen and why, you'll never again have any doubts about which Bible is truly God's Bible.

Introduction

... What have I now done?
Is there not a cause? (1 Samuel 17:29)

What would you do?

My friend's mother is dying and she doesn't know the Lord—neither does my friend. I've wanted to tell her about my Savior for months but just haven't had the opportunity—until now.

"Don't you ever think about dying?" I ask.

"Yes" she says, "but I try not to. I don't like to think about losing my husband or my kids, let alone my mother. I stay positive if I don't think about it."

"But you're ignoring the bus coming down the road," I counter.

"I know," she says, "but I function better this way if I don't focus on it."

So I begin to tell her about the Lord. The conversation quickly turns to the Bible, which is my only source of authority.

"Ahh!" she says, pointing her finger at me...

"But the Bible was written by men!"

We've all heard that one before, but what's really ironic is that professors in most evangelical and fundamental colleges and universities, as well as pastors of evangelical and fundamental churches, teach a version of the same doctrine. The shocking truth is that they believe and teach that "the Bible" as we have it today is actually a hybrid—a production of men and God.

I'll explain what I mean by that in a minute, but first...

When my friend used the word *Bible*, we both knew exactly what she meant—a book—and that's exactly what most people mean when they use the word. Common usage equates *Bible* with "a book."

Not so in fundamental and evangelical leadership circles. For over 130 years they've taught that *"the real Bible"* isn't a book you can hold in your hands, it's an ideal.

Oh, they'll swear on a stack of books with the word *Bible* printed on the spine that they believe in "the Bible." It's just that *"the Bible"* they're referring to never existed. It's not even a book.

Their *"Bible"* is one whose text is made up of an unavailable collection of original writings that comprise a book they call *"The Original Bible."*

But don't take my word for it...

Dr. Randall Price is Distinguished Research Professor and Executive Director of the Center for Judaic Studies at Liberty University. He wrote a book titled *Searching for the Original Bible*. The book is recommended by Kenneth L. Barker, ThM, PhD, General Editor of the NIV Study Bible; Dr. H. Wayne House, Distinguished Research Professor of Biblical and Theological Studies, Faith Evangelical Seminary, Tacoma, WA; Walter C. Kaiser Jr., President Emeritus and Colman M. Mockler Distinguished Professor of Old Testament, Gordon-Conwell Theological Seminary, Hamilton, MA; and the Foreword was written by Dr. Charles Ryrie, author of the *Ryrie Study Bible*.

Let's use the definition for *"The Bible"* given in Price's book...

> *Autograph* is the accepted term for the original edition of a particular work, written or dictated by the author.... In the case of the Bible,

the texts by biblical authors in their initial stage of composition are considered the *autographs or original manuscripts.*[1]

So, the words (text) that appeared in the original manuscripts comprise **"The Original Bible."**

What's odd is that *"The Original Bible"* is a Bible that nobody's ever seen, let alone read.

If such a "Bible" actually existed, consider what it would look like.

"The Bible" was written over a 1,600-year period by 40 men on 3 different continents. Do you really think all the original parchments, papyri, tables of stone, and so forth, were gathered into one book—one Original Bible? That would be a museum piece for sure! How could anybody collect all these pieces of history and assemble them into one book?

The original animal skins that Moses wrote on were replaced long before the time of the Lord Jesus Christ. And Moses broke the first tables of stone "written by the finger of God" on Mount Sinai shortly after they were made. And how do you retrieve Jeremiah's scroll delivered to King Jehoiakim. His servant Jehudi sliced it up and pitched it into the fire:

> And it came to pass, that when Jehudi had read three or four leaves, he cut it with the penknife, and cast it into the fire that was on the hearth, until all the roll was consumed in the fire that was on the hearth. (Jeremiah 36:23)

That original autograph got burned.

But Dr. Price is careful to say…

> Although neither the Hebrew nor the Greek original manuscripts ever existed in a form resembling our present Bible … their collective existence as original manuscripts constitutes the *autographa*, or the "Original Bible."[2]

From a born again believer's perspective, trusting in the lost *"Original Bible"*…

---
[1] Randall Price, *Searching for the Original Bible* (Eugene, OR: Harvest House, 2007), 33.
[2] Ibid, 34.

Doesn't make sense at best
and is tragically absurd at worst.

And yet just about all fundamental and evangelical leaders claim this unavailable collection of writings is their authority for all they believe, do, and teach.

They make bold proclamations like "I believe the Bible is the inspired and inerrant word of God!" and "The book is our only authority!" and yet it's "a Bible" they are still searching for.

They teach that the only "scripture" that **was** inspired and **was** without error is *"The Original Bible."* They say that the words we have today are inspired and inerrant only so far as they match the wording of *"The Original Bible."* But as to the exact wording of this unique "Bible" they are unsure.

Only in religious academia can this phenomenon occur.

Now, they won't come right out and tell you all this, but that's exactly what they teach. Think about it. The Lord supposedly inspires words but fails to deliver them to you. What kind of dysfunctional God are they selling you?

Plus, they teach that there is no book in existence today that contains all of God's words and only God's words. Worse yet, they believe all Bibles today contain errors, are defective translations, or have certain readings that may not be original at **all** but were added over the centuries by men.

Scary thought, isn't it?

They teach that some of the most highly recommended Bibles and versions (in any language including Hebrew and Greek) are a mixture of men's words and God's words and that it's up to textual critics to figure out which are which.

They teach that all Bibles and versions have errors in them. Moreover, the folks who translate, edit, and publish them actually know it and aren't doing anything about it.

They are positive that **only** *"The Original Bible"* is inspired—yet they are still searching for it.

They say that **any** representation of *"The Original Bible"* today is something they refer to as "The Word of God" to the extent it represents *"The Original Bible."*

This means **all** present representations of this top-shelf product are adulterated with uninspired words and errors of fact and, to varying degrees, are a deficient shadow of the real thing.

I can assure you that such statements would **never** fly in business. Nobody would buy such absurdity. In business there always is a known standard. Otherwise, no one can quote, contract for, deliver, or actually get paid for doing a job.

Imagine asking your plumber for an itemized bill and he tells you he's still "searching for it." Would you send him a check?

It's like a teacher asking a kid if he did his homework and the kid replies "absolutely." But when the teacher asks to see it, the kid says "I'm searching for it."

Likewise…

There has to be a book.

And that book has to be the standard for determining what God says. We all may disagree as to what the words mean, but first of all we have to know what the Lord says. And to do that, we need a book.

Multiple-choice standards don't work in business and neither do they work when it comes to determining what God says or which Bible is God's Bible.

Most all the men mentioned in this book believe in a nonexistent standard—*"The Original Bible"* that never was. Or, more precisely, they believe in readings in *"The Original Bible"* that they're still searching for.

This is all pretty pathetic when you consider that "the Bible" is the foundation for all we believe.

In this book, you'll learn that the errors in some of the most highly recommended modern versions are so bad that if the Lord Jesus Christ came to your church, he wouldn't give a second thought to using them.

Why would he ever want to use a Bible with errors in it? Why would you?

You'll learn why the Lord Jesus Christ **can't** use any modern Bible version without looking foolish.

But…

I understand why the professionals believe in the mythical *"Original Bible."*

There are so many variations in wording in the body of existing manuscripts that no one can prove which variations are authentic because no one has the original documents to compare them to.

And what's worse…

Many times the experts disagree.

Since there is no consensus of these readings, it's no wonder they take refuge in the position that only *"The Original Bible"* is completely inerrant and inspired.

I get it.

And if I only used inductive reasoning I would come to the same position that they have.

Yet deductive reasoning tells me that God is in charge of the project and that I should look for a book, not for a set of readings.

They defend *"The Original Bible"* they've never seen and admittedly are still searching for.

I have in my possession, defend, and promote one that not only exists but has had tangible results for the past 400 years.

Introduction

So we are in competition.

I believe in a real Bible—a book that exists—a book that's sold billions of copies and has a 400-year history of tangible results.

They believe in a theoretical Bible—a "book" that never existed and a "Bible" they readily admit that they're still looking for.

The Bible version issue can be very contentious.

Churches split up, pastors are let go, and folks get just plain nasty toward each other over this issue. And it's not surprising. Belief in the words contained in a book is all our faith is based on.

It's the only authority we have. We have no pope, no cardinal, no priest, no Watchtower Society, no Church in Salt Lake City. The book is our only and exclusive source of truth. It's our only and final authority.

The Bible (and when I say Bible I mean a book) is the foundational document for everything we believe. Our thoughts about God, about why we are here and what we are here for, and the reasons for our hope of eternal life are contained and defined for us in that book.

The legal record of the birth, death, and resurrection of our Savior is contained in that document. The Bible is the most important book on the face of the earth.

If we don't have a physical book that is without error containing only God's words, we have a defective foundation. Our arguments will stand or fall on our debating skills rather than on the living words of the living Savior.

Deductive reasoning tells me that there has to be a book—one book…

And it shouldn't be hard to find, either.

As a matter fact, God's book should be dripping with authority and should be obvious to any child of God. If it's the Lord's book, it should be a bestseller because of his blessing. Like him, it should have loving friends and fierce enemies.

- Like him, it will both unite and divide men.
- Like him, it should have the power to change men's lives.
- Like the Lord, who spoke with authority, even so his Bible should speak with authority. "The officers answered, Never man spake like this man" (John 7:46). Even so should his book speak like no other.
- Like him, it should be pure—containing all of God's words and not adulterated with men's words.
- Like him, it should have a name above all others.
- And like the Lord, unto whom all power in heaven and earth is given, it should be a powerful book.

I have such a book.

It's my privilege to present this book to you, but first…

Let me tell you about myself.

I was saved when I was 28 years old. I know personally the sickening despair and hopelessness of living in darkness, and I know the life-giving light of the Lord Jesus Christ.

I'm a Jesuit-trained (high school) former Roman Catholic. I know Catholic doctrine and I received all the sacraments except Extreme Unction and Holy Orders.

I'm a 62-year-old entrepreneur with 40 years of "in the trenches" business experience. I've been a CEO, manufacturer, distributor, publisher, and sales executive. I was even a roofing and siding contractor right after college.

I held Federal Communication Commission licenses to provide cellular telephone service in the Poughkeepsie, New York, and Minneapolis, Minnesota, markets. I was a limited partner in a cellular telephone system that served part of the Los Angeles market.

I've had two cases argued before the US Court of Appeals [McElroy Electronics Corp. v. FCC, 301 U.S.App.D.C. 81, 990 F.2d 1351 (1993) and McElroy Electronics Corp. v. FCC, 318 U.S.App.D.C. 174, 86 F.3d 248

Introduction

(1996)]. It's one thing to sue the United States government; it's another thing to win. We won both cases.

I've successfully negotiated deals totaling millions of dollars with some of the largest telecoms on earth; AT&T, Bell Atlantic Mobile, AirTouch Communications (now Verizon), and US Cellular.

Although I would prefer not to mention my experience, I only do so because it's important for you to know that I've been around "high-priced talent." I've spent hundreds of thousands of dollars on lawyers, engineers, and doctors, so I'm not awed or intimidated by men's titles and degrees. By the grace of God, I am what I am.

But I am **not**…

A theologian, professor, or pastor.

Although I've read through the Bible 17 times, taught it to all age groups, from preschoolers to adults, and served for years as a deacon at a Baptist church, the good news is that I never went to Bible College or Seminary.

This benefits you, dear reader, because you're getting a unique and informed slant on the issue, not someone else's repackaged teachings. You'll see the Bible version controversy from a different set of eyes. You'll see it from a business perspective.

But all this pales in comparison with the opportunity to represent my Savior and his book, the 1611 Authorized Version, popularly known as the King James Bible.

When it comes to the creation, manufacturing, and distribution of the Bible, I see the Lord Jesus Christ as the project manager. Getting a pure Bible into your hands is his job.

And truly…

He's the only one qualified for the job.

I expect more out of the Lord than some fundamentalists and evangelicals do when it comes to the Bible. I expect him to provide his own children with **a book** that contains all of his life-giving words and only his life-giving words. I expect that the Lord of Hosts would not leave us without a book.

In short...

There has to be a book.

I expect that the identity of that book would be clearly recognizable to his children.

Further, I don't believe that he requires his children to learn ancient Hebrew or Greek, Aramaic, Latin, Chaldean, or any other language, or become a textual critic in order to identify which Bible is the one he would use if he came to your church.

I believe that when it comes to what words the so-called *"Original Bible"* contained, the Lord Jesus Christ is the only one who can provide them. And when it comes to translation, he's the only one who can determine just how he wants his words translated. He's the author, and he's the only one who can determine what he wants said and how he wants it said.

But why should you even consider my opinion?

First of all, I've done my homework. I've been researching the Bible version issue for nearly 30 years. I've studied the history of the Bible, textual criticism, and translation theory. I've read books and articles by KJV-only and anti-KJV-only folks; Textus Receptus (TR) defenders; and Majority Text, Critical Text, and modern version supporters.

I have invested countless hours examining, comparing, and considering the differences between the 1611 King James Bible, and its subsequent reprints and modern versions.

I'm familiar with the arguments on all sides of the issue—from KJV only to TR only to Majority Text Preferred to Critical Text Preferred—as well as the strengths and weaknesses of each position, including my own. I've distilled this research into an easy-to-read book that not only tells you which Bible Jesus would use if he came to your church but also why.

Introduction

You'll find out which of the popular Bible versions the Lord absolutely would not use and why.

Most books on this subject compare verses and focus on variant readings, manuscript evidence, and opinions of scholars as to which readings are authentic.

This book is different. My presuppositions are that

1. There has to be a book—a physical book.
2. This book must contain all of God's words and only God's words. It can't be a mixture of men's words and God's words.
3. Most importantly, the work of providing this authentic, physical Bible is the responsibility of the Lord Jesus Christ.

I've combed through reams of research and scores of books for you.

I've combed through reams of research and scores of books for you.

The issue is focused by asking one simple "big picture" question:

"If he came to your church, which Bible would Jesus use?"

It's a question no one has ever dared to ask even though the answer should be easy. Although it may be politically incorrect, the Lord's Bible should be easy to recognize by its fruit. And the King James Bible has had more fruit than them all.

Proving it takes a little more work. That's what this book does.

This book will prove…

That the experts (who assembled the Greek text underlying the New Testaments of the NIV, NASB, ESV, HCSB, NLT, and a host of others) actually believe that the "original autographs" making up the so-called *Original Bible* **had errors in them.** They teach that the evangelists (Matthew, Mark, Luke, and John) made errors when they wrote the Gospels. You'll find the details in chapter 2. Plus, you'll learn:

- Why the Lord is actually forced to choose only one Bible. (Chapter 1)
- Why the Lord Jesus Christ would never use the English Standard Version (ESV) because of the known errors (admitted by experts) inserted into the text in Matthew 1:7, 8, & 10. (Chapter 3)
- Why the Lord wouldn't carry the New American Standard Bible (NASB) to church with him because of the known errors (admitted by experts) inserted into the text in John 7:8–10 and because of the way it refers to him in John 1:18. (Chapter 3)
- Why the Lord couldn't use the NIV, ESV, or the NASB because of the known geography error (admitted by experts) inserted into the text in Luke 4:44. (Chapter 3)
- Why the Lord can't use the NIV, ESV, or the NASB because of the known error (admitted by experts) inserted into the text in Mark 1:2. (Chapter 3)
- Why the Lord is hurt by how his character is besmirched in Mark 1:41 in the New International Version (NIV) and would never, ever use it. (Chapter 3)
- Why the Lord wouldn't bring the New King James Version (NKJV) into church with him because of how it undermines the historical integrity of his words in English. (Chapter 8)

This book goes on to answer other nagging questions like…

- Why didn't the Lord preserve the original autographs? (Chapter 4)
- Where was the Bible before 1611? (Chapter 9)
- Which edition of the King James Bible is "the Bible"? (Chapter 10)
- What about the tens of thousands of differences between the 1769 edition (or any edition today) and the first edition in 1611? (Chapter 11)
- What about the differences between King James Bibles printed by the Oxford and Cambridge University Presses? (Chapter 12)

Introduction

- What is the Bible's definition of inspiration? (Chapter 15)
- What was the commonly understood definition of inspiration in the late 19th century? (Chapter 16)
- Who is responsible for changing the Bible's definition of inspiration and when did they change it? (Chapter 17)
- Why do some conservative scholars say the Lord preserved error instead of truth in the extant biblical manuscripts? (Chapter 18)

You've probably heard that "all Scripture is given by inspiration of God" ever since you became a believer. But do you really know what that means?

Chapters 15–17 may be somewhat controversial.

You may be surprised to find out that the Bible's definition of *inspiration* is different from what's commonly taught today. And strange as it may seem, the word *inspired* isn't even in the King James Bible.

You can decide for yourself whether or not the King James Bible is "inspired" after reading chapters 15–17. Because when it comes to the word *inspiration*, even the experts disagree among themselves as to what *inspiration* really means. And they almost never define the word using the Bible to determine its meaning.

All I know is that the book contains all the words and only the words that my Savior wants us to have in English, and I know the words are alive and are life.

In John 6:63, the Lord said…

> … the **words** that I speak unto you, *they* are **spirit**, and *they* **are life**.

He spoke those New Testament words in Hebrew (even though some say Aramaic), and yet all the manuscript evidence we have for that statement is in Greek. This means that any Greek manuscript or printed text is a **translation** of the inspired original words of our Lord.

And if you believe that the "original" Greek, Hebrew, and Aramaic written words are inspired, then the "original" Greek is in fact an inspired translation of the Hebrew words spoken by our Lord in John 6:63.

As you think about inspiration, consider this…

Building the Bible (meaning a physical book) is just as important as writing it in the first place.

And so is making sure you get it without additions or subtractions. And so is how it's translated. It's the Lord's product and he's in charge of…

- Creating it—giving the words in the first place.
- Constructing it—assembling the component parts into books and assembling the books, letters, and other documents into A Book.
- Copying it—reproducing the text.
- Carrying it—translating the material into other languages.

The Lord is the owner of the words. The Holy Ghost is the General Contractor and overseer. He chooses the subcontractors that he will entrust the work to.

The Lord Jesus Christ is the living word. He is the Book. It's a living book able to impart life to its readers.

Every one of the Lord's words which he said "are life," transcending all language barriers. Otherwise, you can't get life from his words as you read them, memorize them, or quote them to a lost sinner hoping he or she will get "life" by believing them.

His life-containing, life-giving and living words aren't restricted to any language or any time period (i.e., when they were first written). All you have to do is find where he's displayed them.

I believe God has to provide his children with a book—a literal book; not a pile of variant textual readings that the experts are still "searching for."

I believe that although the Lord may have preserved his holy words through an assortment of manuscripts through the ages, he certainly would have gathered his words and placed them in one book after the invention of the printing press. And I believe that that book should be easily recognizable by his children.

Anything less doesn't fit the Lord's character. Anything less means textual critics care more about his words than he does.

It's 2013—**they're in a book** not scattered all over the place as some teach.

A quick note about literary devices used in this book.

My goal is to provide King James Bible believers and those folks who are on the fence reasons why they can have confidence in The Book. I'm very passionate about this.

I've used literary devices like hyperbole and sarcasm to evoke strong feelings and for emphasis. Hyperbole is an exaggeration for effect and sarcasm is a sharp, bitter, or cutting expression or remark; a bitter gibe or taunt. These figures of speech are also used in Scripture. The Lord Jesus Christ occasionally used both hyperbole and sarcasm.

Hyperbole:

- And if thy right eye offend thee, pluck it out, and cast it from thee: for it is profitable for thee that one of thy members should perish, and not that thy whole body should be cast into hell. (Matthew 5:29)
- If any man come to me, and hate not his father, and mother, and wife, and children, and brethren, and sisters, yea, and his own life also, he cannot be my disciple. (Luke 14:26)

Hyperbole and sarcasm:

- Ye blind guides, which strain at a gnat, and swallow a camel. (Matthew 23:24)

Sarcasm:

- Woe unto you, scribes and Pharisees, hypocrites! for ye are like unto whited sepulchres, which indeed appear beautiful outward, but are within full of dead men's bones, and of all uncleanness. (Matthew 23:27)
- Ye fools and blind: for whether is greater, the gift, or the altar that sanctifieth the gift? (Matthew 23:19)

And how about the sarcasm used by the Apostle Paul, the disciple Nathanael, and the Prophets?

- Ye did run well; who did hinder you that ye should not obey the truth? I would they were even cut off which trouble you. (Galatians 5:7, 12)
- For what is it wherein ye were inferior to other churches, except it be that I myself was not burdensome to you? forgive me this wrong. (2 Corinthians 12:13)
- And Nathanael said unto him, Can there any good thing come out of Nazareth? Philip saith unto him, Come and see. (John 1:46)
- And it came to pass at noon, that Elijah mocked them, and said, Cry aloud: for he is a god; either he is talking, or he is pursuing, or he is in a journey, or peradventure he sleepeth, and must be awaked. (1 Kings 18:27)

I have tried to keep my tone respectful of those who disagree with my position.

> ... *for we shall all stand before the judgment seat of Christ.* (Romans 14:10)

It's passion for the Lord, his name, his glory, and his word (which he has magnified even above his name) that motivates me.

I have settled in my own heart exactly which book the Lord would carry under his arm if he came to my church. It's easy to spot. It's the book he's been using for the past 400 years. It's the same book that's been printed billions of times and translated into over 760 languages.

It's the same book that has been woven into the fabric of my soul for the past 35 years. I had to write a book about the book. I am a man of the book.

> ... But *his word* was in mine heart as a burning fire shut up in my bones, and I was weary with forbearing, and I could not *stay*. (Jeremiah 20:9)

Why I wrote this book.

I wrote this book first of all for myself—to memorialize my own beliefs. I wrote the book secondly for my family and posterity. I want their faith to stand on the sure words of God as they appear in one book—a real book you can hold in your hands and believe and trust it contains all of God's words and only God's words.

And finally, I wrote this book for any and all whose faith in a book has been challenged by others (however well-meaning) whose "Bible" is a figment of some teacher's imagination.

I believe that "the Bible" is the 1611 Authorized Version—any edition—commonly known as the King James Bible. I believe that not only the first edition but also any and all of the subsequent editions are "the Bible."

Before you read the text, please understand three things.

First, I am a Bible libertarian, not a Bible fascist.

I believe that everyone has the right to use and believe whichever Bible version he or she wants. I'm into freedom of choice and association. I'm just trying to make the case for the King James Bible based on my own research.

Second, I am not personally against any man mentioned in this book. I'm just diametrically opposed to their view on the Bible version controversy.

Just remember…

> Great men are **not** *always wise*: neither do the aged understand judgment. (Job 32:9)

If they're saved, I'm glad for them.
If they're an unbeliever, I hope they come to know the Lord.
If they're dead, there is one who judges them, even the Lord Jesus Christ.

And finally, this book is written simply to extol **"The Book."**

Once you've read this book, I hope you'll be absolutely certain that "The Book" is his Book.

Jack McElroy
February 2013

**Please read the Introduction before you begin—
It's very important for understanding what follows.**

Chapter One

Why the Lord is forced to choose only one Bible

And there I will meet with the children of Israel, and the tabernacle shall be sanctified by my glory. (Exodus 29:43)

The Lord Jesus Christ comes to your church…

The crowd throngs the entrance so he uses the back door. You run to meet him. There stands your Lord. You fall at his feet and worship him. The Lord reaches down to lift you up. You see the nail prints in his hands. You can't stop crying because the wounds in his hands should have been yours.

He picks you up and looks into your eyes. You just want to tell him how much you love him. But you don't need to. One look into his eyes is enough. The Lord knows. He tells you he loves you but you already felt that.

He enters the auditorium with a Bible under his arm, so he's not using PowerPoint. Try as you might, you just can't make out which version it is as he takes the pulpit and prays. The crowd is hushed as he opens his Bible to read.

He came in with only one Bible, so he must have a preference. But which one is it?

Yes, dear reader, it's a question hardly anyone has ever thought to ask, but…

In this book you'll learn:

- Why he can't use them all,
- Why he can't use none,
- Why he can't use some, and
- Why he's already using one and which one it is.

First, he can't use them all because...

They don't all say the same thing.

For example, what's the Lord going to teach when he comes to...

The doctrine of the tabernacle in the wilderness?

There are literally thousands of doctrines in the Scripture. Nothing the Lord says is irrelevant or unworthy of our time to read it and heed it. He mentions the tabernacle 297 times in the Bible and goes into multi-chapter minute details of its construction, use, and operation. So it's pretty important to him.

	Exodus 36:19	
NIV (©1984)	Then they made for the tent a covering of ram skins dyed red, and over that a covering of **hides of sea cow.**[1]	
NASB (©1995)	He made a covering for the tent of rams' skins dyed red, and a covering of **porpoise skins** above.	
King James Bible (1611)	And he made a covering for the tent of rams' skins dyed red, and a covering of **badgers' skins** above *that*.	
ESV (©2001)	And he made for the tent a covering of tanned rams' skins and **goatskins.**	
New NIV (©2011)	Then they made for the tent a covering of ram skins dyed red, and over that a covering of the other **durable leather.**	

---

[1] When quoting Scripture throughout, boldface emphasis is mine.

But what did he say covered the tabernacle? "**Sea cows**," "**porpoises**," "**badgers**," "**goats**," or "**durable leather**"? It sure can't be all of the above.

What would happen if you raised your hand in class and ask him, "Lord, will you do a show-and-tell and bring in the animal whose hide covered the tabernacle?"

He's stuck. He can either

- Bring in a badger or
- A goat on a leash;
- Back up a furniture truck and drop off a sofa or
- Take you on a field trip to SeaWorld.

Only **one** of these readings is true. Only one can be true (although the New NIV ©2011's "other durable leather" is vague enough to be classified in the "we don't really know" category.)

This is a case where the **same** Hebrew word is translated five (5) different ways.

We assume the elite teams of biblical scholars, translators, and editors already went back to the Hebrew text and looked at the word in the "original Hebrew"—just to get a fuller understanding. After all, it's the 21st century and they have so many more resources at hand now than they had in 1611.

And yet, as you can see, there is still confusion regarding one of the most basic doctrines of the Bible.

Nonetheless, the Lord **must** pick the **one** Bible that **names** the **correct** animal. Any Bible that doesn't name the right animal is absolutely wrong. Only **one** can be correct. All the rest are nothing more than men's words and not God's words.

Even if he quotes the Hebrew word, it doesn't matter. He still has to reveal which animal provided the covering for the tabernacle.

When it comes to a "Bible," he has to pick **one**. And he's the **only one** who can make the right call.

Before we go further, some folks say...

"The Lord doesn't need a Bible because he IS the Bible!"

True. But it would sure be a lousy testimony if he instructs you to read the Bible and then walks into church without one. In the days of his flesh, he did read from a literal book (even if it was a scroll)...

> And there was delivered unto him the book of the prophet Esaias. And when he had opened the book, he found the place where it was written.... (Luke 4:17)

Let's look at another example of two Bibles saying and meaning two different things. The result is that they affect...

The doctrine of sin

What does the Bible say happens to the wicked after death?

Ecclesiastes 8:10	
ESV (©2001)	Then I saw the wicked buried. They ... **were praised** in the city....
NASB (©1995)	So then, I have seen the wicked buried ... they **are soon forgotten** in the city....

Each Bible is translating from a different text. Does the Lord use Ecclesiastes 8:10 to teach that the wicked "**were praised**" (as it says in the Septuagint and Latin Vulgate versions) or "**are forgotten**" (as it says in the Hebrew) after death? Which Bible contains the words of God?

One verse contains God's words, the other is counterfeit; nothing more than men's words added **after** the book of Ecclesiastes was written. Only the Lord knows for sure which verse belongs to him and which is the forgery.

The Lord **must** choose an inerrant Bible and dump the errant Bible. Will he choose the ESV or the NASB or some other?

Then there's Matthew 18:22...

The doctrine of forgiveness

How many times did Jesus say you should forgive your brother?

Matthew 18:22	
NIV (©1984)	Jesus answered, "I tell you, not seven times, but seventy-seven times." **[77 times]**
ESV (©2011)	Jesus said to him, "I do not say to you seven times, but seventy times seven." **[490 times]**

So how many times should you forgive your brother? What did the Lord say; 490 or 77? It can't be both. One is correct the other is an error. (Even if the Lord is using hyperbole, he could only have said one or the other at this particular time.) One verse contains God's words, the other is counterfeit; nothing more than men's words added **after** the book of Matthew was written. Only the Lord knows for sure which verse belongs to him and which is the forgery.

But isn't there any way to tell which version contains his words? There is, and we'll get to that later.

In the meantime, let's look at some more examples like…

The doctrine of inerrancy of the Scriptures

How many years does the Bible say Absalom waited to talk to King David?

2 Samuel 15:7	
ESV (©2011)	And at the end of **four years** Absalom said to the king, "Please let me go and pay my vow…."
NASB (©1995)	Now it came about at the end of **forty years** that Absalom said to the king, "Please let me go and pay my vow…."

There's quite a difference between 4 years and 40 years.

Which words are God's and which are men's? Which verse is the one the Lord wants you to "hide in your heart"?

Maybe it was 40 years as reported in the **NASB**, but just to be on the safe side…

Let's consult an expert.

Here's what Dr. R. Albert Mohler, Jr., president of the Southern Baptist Theological Seminary, said about the NASB:

> The New American Standard Bible has set the standard for faithful Bible translations for a generation. It is the favorite of so many who love the Bible and look for accuracy and clarity in translation. The New American Standard Bible should be close at hand for any serious student of the Bible. I thank God for this faithful translation.[2]

Dr. R. Albert Mohler Jr.
President of Southern Baptist Theological Seminary

Based on that glowing recommendation, maybe we should go with the 40-year NASB reading.

But wait! Here's what Mohler says about the ESV:

> The ESV represents a new level of excellence in Bible translations—combining **unquestionable accuracy in translation** with a beautiful style of expression. **It is faithful to the text**, easy to understand, and a pleasure to read. This is **a translation you can trust**.[3]

Here's a quick summary.

Version	Reading	Dr. Mohler's comments
NASB	40 years	"set the standard for faithful Bible translations" "the favorite of so many who love the Bible and look for accuracy and clarity in translation" "for any serious student of the Bible"
ESV	4 years	"unquestionable accuracy in translation" "faithful to the text" "a translation you can trust"

---

[2] Lockwood Foundation, "NASB Endorsements," http://www.lockman.org/nasb/endorsements.php.

[3] Crossway, "MacArthur Study Bible: ESV," http://www.esvmacarthurstudyBible.com/esv. (emphasis mine)

Which Bible contains the infallible, inerrant words of God? Which is legit and which is the imposter?

Dr. Mohler has endorsed **both** Bibles. Yet one of them is wrong. He can afford to be wrong and even recommend two **conflicting** authorities.

But…

The Lord can't.

The words are his. His honesty is at stake. He can't recommend them both. Soon you'll find out why the Lord can't recommend either. But…

If the president of the largest theological seminary in the world can't tell which is which, who can?

The Lord knows, and you can too. Keep reading and you'll learn how.

Bibles are a lot like newspaper reporters.

They both report historical facts, names, dates, locations, times; describe geography; relate events that happened; and most importantly, quote dialogue. Have you ever heard a reporter ask, "Can I quote you on that?" Good reporters even try to get the spelling straight.

You should hold any Bible to an even stricter standard than you'd require from a newspaper reporter. After all, the Bible is supposed to be the Holy Word of God. There is **NO** room for error. Speaking of good reporters, would a reporter from the *Washington Post* get the following FACT wrong?

Luke 10:1	
ESV (©2001)	After this the Lord appointed **seventy-two** others…
NASB (©1995)	Now after this the Lord appointed **seventy** others…

No matter how you cut it
70 ≠ 72.

These two "highly accurate" and true to the "originals" Bibles **report** two different things. Only ONE contains a TRUE report. The other is wrong.

This mismatch of fact **proves** that one is a translation you **might be able to trust**—the other, you **can't**.

Some folks say, "what difference does it make which Bible you use? They all say Jesus died for our sins and you need to be saved." But wait…

Don't all the facts we believe about Jesus dying for our sins come from the Bible? If the Bible can't be trusted because some of its facts are in error, how do you know Jesus' death did anything for you? That's where all your information comes from. If the book is faulty, isn't the message faulty as well?

And besides…

Don't you tell everyone that you believe "the Bible" is "God's word"?

Are you finally going to admit to friends and family that "the Bible" is **less accurate** than a big city newspaper? If the Bible is that corrupt, then you should focus on more important matters of life, like ESPN's "Pigskin Pick'em."

Let's face it, if you can't trust numbers and dates in the Bible, what makes you so sure you can trust the words around them?

If the Lord is the author of **both** the ESV and the NASB, then he can't even get his facts straight. If you can trust a reporter for the *Washington Post* **more** than you can trust your Savior, you should get a **new** Savior.

But don't be alarmed. The Lord is **not** the author of confusion.

He knows **exactly** how many men he appointed and sent out. The correct answer is in one book. Before we get to that, let's look at some more doctrinal issues…

The doctrine of plenary inspiration of the Scriptures

Plenary means complete in every respect. Doesn't the Bible say something about taking away or adding to the words of God?

Matthew 12:47	
NASB (©1995)	Someone said to Him, "Behold, Your mother and Your brothers are standing outside seeking to speak to You."
ESV (©2011)	————————————————

It's not a misprint. It's not "this page intentionally left blank."

The ESV doesn't contain Matthew 12:47. The NASB does. They **both** can't be the word of God unless your God is a schizophrenic.

This verse was either **taken away from** what the Lord said by the translators and editors of the ESV or it was **added to** what he said by the translators and editors of the NASB.

Now we're in a pickle. Everyone knows you can't add to or take away from the words of the Lord. Look at what the Scripture says.

- Ye shall **not add** unto the **word** which I command you, **neither shall ye diminish** *ought* from it, that ye may keep the commandments of the LORD your God which I command you. (Deuteronomy 4:2)

- What thing soever I command you, observe to do it: **thou shalt not add** thereto, **nor diminish** from it. (Deuteronomy 12:32)

- Every word of God is pure: he is a shield unto them that put their trust in him. **Add thou not** unto his words, lest he reprove thee, and thou be found a liar. (Proverbs 30:5–6)

Both Bibles can't be right. And that's a serious biblical problem because the Lord said **"Thy word is truth."** But which Bible contains all the true words?

If the Lord walks through the doors of your church, does he read Matthew 12:47 aloud or skip it because it's not there? The Lord himself **must choose** between these two Bibles. But how can we know which one He picks?

Let's check another expert.

Dr. Paige Patterson is president of Southwestern Baptist Theological Seminary in Fort Worth, Texas. [4] He's logged more than 50 years of faithful service and ministry as a pastor, evangelist, professor, college president, seminary president, and denominational leader.

Hopefully he can help us determine which Bible the Lord Jesus Christ uses.

Dr. Paige Patterson

Here are Dr. Patterson's comments on the ESV:

> For our churches and pulpits, as well as for our students, it is critically important to have a Bible translation that does not compromise orthodox theology or gender issues, and that is both faithful to the languages of the text and eminently readable. The ESV uniquely fulfills that prescription.[5]

Here are Dr. Patterson's comments on the NASB:

> The New American Standard Bible ... is still the most accurate translation of the Greek and Hebrew Scriptures available...."[6]

No help here. He says the NASB is "still the most accurate translation of the Greek and Hebrew Scriptures available" and it has Matthew 12:47, but he says the ESV is **"faithful to the languages of the text,"** yet it **doesn't have** Matthew 12:47.

What's funny is that both these Bibles are pitched to "serious students" of the Bible.

If they're BOTH "accurate and important resources," how come one is definitely WRONG?

What do we do now?

---

[4] Dr. Patterson preaches from the New King James Bible and believes it to be one of the best and by far the most elegant of all the translations. E-mail to author 6/15/13.
[5] Crossway, "ESV Endorsements," http://www.crossway.org/bibles/esv/endorsements.
[6] Lockwood Foundation, "NASB Endorsements," http://www.lockman.org/nasb/endorsements.php.

Let's try another professional.

John Piper is Pastor for Preaching and Vision at Bethlehem Baptist Church in Minneapolis, Minnesota. He recommends the ESV.

> My aim tonight is to help you be persuaded that exposing millions of people (pastors, teachers, students, laypeople) to the ESV would undo the dominance of the NIV and put in its place a more literal, and yet a beautifully readable, memorizable Bible—the English Standard Version. And this would be a good thing.[7]

Well-known author, Pastor John Piper

If the NASB is as accurate as they say, and if the ESV is defective, would the Lord encourage reading and memorizing error? Is that a good thing?

While we are on the topic, let's look at another doctrine affected by taking away from or adding to the word of God…

The doctrine of believer's baptism

Acts 8:36–38	
NASB (©1995)	36 As they went along the road they came to some water; and the eunuch said, "Look! Water! What prevents me from being baptized?" 37 [And Philip said, "If you believe with all your heart, you may." And he answered and said, "I believe that Jesus Christ is the Son of God."] 38 And he ordered the chariot to stop; and they both went down into the water, Philip as well as the eunuch, and he baptized him. [Note: The NASB includes verse 37 but places it in brackets and suggests that the verse was added later on. The editors add a footnote saying "(Early mss [manuscripts] do not contain this v[erse].)"

---

[7] John Piper, "Good English with Minimal Translation: Why Bethlehem Uses the ESV," January 1, 2004, http://www.desiringgod.org/resource-library/articles/good-english-with-minimal-translation-why-bethlehem-uses-the-esv.

ESV (©2011)	³⁶And as they were going along the road they came to some water, and the eunuch said, "See, here is water! What prevents me from being baptized?" **(Verse 37 missing)** ³⁸And he commanded the chariot to stop, and they both went down into the water, Philip and the eunuch, and he baptized him.
NIV (©2011)	³⁶As they traveled along the road, they came to some water and the eunuch said, "Look, here is water. What can stand in the way of my being baptized?" **(Verse 37 missing)** ³⁸And he gave orders to stop the chariot. Then both Philip and the eunuch went down into the water and Philip baptized him.

This is the one and only place where the Bible clearly states that you must first believe in order to be baptized. You could use this verse to prove that baptizing babies is "unscriptural" or not depending on which version you "prefer."

Which of the three versions do you think the Lord "prefers"? Or does anyone care what he thinks? Is it Scripture or not? Did the Lord inspire Acts 8:37 or was it added by men? The NASB thinks so and the other two are sure of it.

If it's some man's forgery, why print it in the first place? Why doesn't the NASB "man up" and just eliminate it like the NIV and ESV do? More importantly…

Should you memorize Acts 8:37?

If they're God's words, of course; if they aren't, of course not. Why waste your time?

By the way, if Acts 8:37 shouldn't be in the Bible, why not renumber the verses to "prove" it and be consistent?

Did God intend verse 37 to be in his word or not? Comparing versions doesn't help you—it only confuses you because you can't tell for sure what God said. You can't do any Bible study until you've determined **which** Bible is **the** Bible. One Bible says verse 37 might be the word of God, the others say it's not. What's worse is that influential Christian leaders recommend all three of them.

It's hard to tell someone you believe in **"The Bible"** when you don't even know what **"The Bible"** says—assuming your Bible is *"The Original Bible."*

Try witnessing to an intelligent Muslim and see how far that gets you.

At the end of the day, no man on earth can **prove** which Bible contains **all** of God's words. You're going to have to rely on the Lord for that.

Why? Because the only way to **prove** which Bible contains all of God's words beyond any doubt is to compare one of today's Bibles to the original manuscripts—which we don't have.

But the good news is the Lord knows which words are his and which Bible contains them. And the Lord hasn't kept his choice a secret. We're getting to that soon, but first…

Let's get the opinion of one of the most respected Christian leaders. **Dr. John F. MacArthur, Jr.**, is a well-known evangelical writer and pastor-teacher of Grace Community Church in Sun Valley, California. He is also president of The Master's College and The Master's Seminary. People listen to his radio program, *Grace to You,* in many countries. MacArthur has written and edited more than 150 books, most notably the *MacArthur Study Bible*. Surely a man of his acumen will help us determine which Bible the Lord would use.

Dr. John F. MacArthur, pastor-teacher of Grace Community Church

Dr. John MacArthur repeats one of the frequently stated "safe positions" on the Bible version controversy in a booklet called ***The Biblical Position on the KJV Controversy:***

> A believer should continue to use an accurate English translation which is personally most readable and understandable such as KJV, NASB, or NIV.[8]

Dr. MacArthur recommends **both** the NASB and the NIV. He says they're **both "accurate."** And yet one teaches believer's baptism and the other doesn't even mention it. How can they **both** be accurate?

Either the verse should be there or it **shouldn't**. If it shouldn't be there, then it was forged by men with an agenda. The book should be destroyed. Not recommended. They have "added to" God's words. Doesn't the Scripture call for severe judgment in that case?

The booklet also quotes Homer Kent, president of Grace Theological Seminary:

> In a few cases, we may not be certain **which of several variants is the original,** but our problem is an embarrassment of riches, not of loss.[9]

That doesn't sound bad; but you've already seen some of the differences. Unfortunately, they aren't few and they aren't trivial.

Plus, the Lord promised you could have the certainty of his words despite what Homer believes…

> Have not I written to thee excellent things in counsels and knowledge, That I might make thee know **the certainty of the words of truth;** that thou mightest answer **the words of truth** to them that send unto thee? (Proverbs 22:20–21)

The conclusion of the booklet quotes Homer Kent again as saying:

> It needs to be remembered that the differences between … text types are not nearly as great as might be supposed.… It is regrettable that an issue is being made over this matter in evangelical circles. The issue is forcing many Christians to make a choice **where they lack the necessary knowledge and skill to do so.**[10]

---

[8] Elders of Grace Community Church, "The Biblical Position on the KJV Controversy," accessed December 2012, http://jcsm.org/StudyCenter/john_macarthur/KJV.htm.
[9] Ibid. (emphasis mine)
[10] Ibid. (emphasis mine)

So now we find out that buying a Bible at Barnes & Noble takes "knowledge" and "skill." Who knew you needed a seminary education just to buy a Bible? This "Which Bible" business is getting *"curiouser and curiouser!"* as Alice would say.

"But what does one need to know in order to buy a bible around here?"

Alice in Christian Bookstore Wonderland

The good news is that your Lord has the necessary "knowledge" and "skill" to determine which "differences" are original and which are counterfeit, and he's already gathered his words into **one book.** All you have to do is find that book. And as we'll soon see, it's not that hard and you don't even need a seminary education to find it.

Here's the thing: if he doesn't put his words in **a book,** no one could ever know for sure which of the variant readings are his and which are not.

If he didn't put his words in **a book,** none of his children (most of whom don't have the time, ability, or inclination to study textual criticism and therefore judge the work of the men who assemble the Greek and Hebrew texts) could ever have the **"certainty of the words of truth"** the Lord promised. The good news is you don't have to swim with the textual criticism sharks. All you need is a "big picture view," which you'll get a little further along in this report. You don't even need to know Hebrew and Greek. And besides…

Knowing Hebrew and Greek makes you nothing more than a language technician.

There are plenty of language technicians who **can't** navigate the murky waters of Textual Criticism. It's a study unto itself. The propaganda is that Textual Criticism is a science. It's not; and there are agendas, personalities, paradigms, parsing of words, politics, and world views in the mix.

Learning the big picture of Textual Criticism is the key to knowing **which Bible** the Lord would use if he came to your church.

The big picture is that…

The textual critics who examine manuscripts for a living and have "the necessary knowledge and skill to do so" **disagree** as to not only which **words** appeared in the so-called *"Original Bible"* but also which **verses**.

Moreover, the men who do textual work for a living are surprisingly candid about the prospect of ever determining what the so-called *"Original Bible"* said.

Eldon J. Epp is Harkness Professor of Biblical Literature (Emeritus) at Case Western Reserve University (Cleveland, Ohio) and served as president of the Society of Biblical Literature in 2003–2004. He is the author of *Studies in the Theory and Method of New Testament Textual Criticism* (Eerdmans, 1993) and the editor of several works. He is a member of the Hermeneia commentary series editorial board. Epp is an expert and recognized authority in the field of New Testament textual criticism.

His viewpoint is startlingly honest:

> … we no longer think so simplistically or **so confidently about recovering "the New Testament in the Original Greek."** … We remain **largely in the dark** as to how we might reconstruct the textual history that has left in its wake—in the form of MSS and fragments—numerous **pieces of a puzzle that we seem incapable of fitting together** … we seem now to have no such theories and no plausible sketches of the early history of the text that are widely accepted. What progress, then, have we made? Are we more advanced than our predecessors when, after showing their theories to be unacceptable, **we offer no such theories at all** to vindicate our accepted text?[11]

Next, let's take a look at what the textual critics **really** believe, and see if they can help us figure out which Bible the Lord would use if he came to our church. It shouldn't be that hard to figure out, should it? After all, these folks are the experts…

---

[11] Eldon J. Epp and Gordon D. Fee, "A Continuing Interlude in NT Textual Criticism," *Studies in the Theory and Method of New Testament Textual Criticism* (Grand Rapids, MI: Eerdmans, 1993), 114, 115. (emphasis mine)

Chapter Two

Two "dirty little secrets" of modern textual criticism

For whosoever shall be ashamed of me and of my words, of him shall the Son of man be ashamed, when he shall come in his own glory, and *in his* Father's, and of the holy angels. (Luke 9:26)

If there's one thing all text critics believe in, it's the value of a couple of 4th-century manuscripts (handwritten documents, abbreviated MSS). They love these two relics because they are relatively complete and because they are old. They're known as **Vaticanus** (referred to as Codex **B**) and **Sinaiticus** (referred to as Codex **Aleph**, or the Hebrew letter א). A codex is a manuscript in the form of a book, rather than a scroll.

Vaticanus (so-called because it was found at the Vatican Library) is one of the oldest manuscripts of the Greek Bible.

Although Vaticanus' **variant readings** (different or alternative readings from what has been accepted as standard are called "variant readings") were known in the 16th century, it was not until the mid 19th century that the full text became available to scholars.

Sinaiticus (so-called because it was found at a monastery on Mt. Sinai) was discovered in the mid 19th century as well.

Current scholarship considers the **Codex Vaticanus** to be one of the best Greek texts of the New Testament with **Codex Sinaiticus** its only competitor.

These are the fabled "oldest and the best" manuscripts we've been told about.

Scholars love these two manuscripts so much that when they find variant readings in them, **they automatically default** to the variant and say that these readings are "original." No matter that these readings differ from what has commonly appeared since the church was founded. The truth is that...

They can't even come close to proving the variant readings are original, they just choose to believe it.

Jack McElroy with photographic facsmilies of the two famous "oldest and best" manuscripts, Codex Sinaiticus and Codex Vaticanus.

In short, the textual critics honestly **believe** that these two manuscripts are the closest representatives we have to the fabled *"Original Bible."*

These two manuscripts have had a tremendous influence on English versions of the Bible for the past 130 years. The whole Bible version controversy rises and falls on the trustworthiness of these two manuscripts.

It's the variant readings in these two manuscripts that cause all the controversy, especially when you are in a Bible study and the Bible versions say and mean different things. Believers have noticed that sometimes words and whole verses are missing.

Most times those different readings (or lack thereof) that you find in the NIV, ESV, NASB, NLT, HCSB, NRSV, *The Message,* etc., come from these two manuscripts. (For more detail on some of the variant readings found in these manuscripts, see Will Kinney's article, "The Character of Sinaiticus and Vaticanus Texts," at http://brandplucked.webs.com/an article. Kinney has done extensive research into the Bible version controversy and moderates a Yahoo! discussion group on the subject.[1])

Here's the point:

- The textual critics trust them.
- Big name Christian leaders trust them.
- Christian college and university professors trust them.

---

[1] http://groups.yahoo.com/group/whichversion.

But no one's asking the question…

Does Jesus trust them?

Some say we should thank God that he has delivered these wonderful manuscripts into the hands of textual critics who will help us find *"The Original Bible."*

Of course it raises the question, if these manuscripts are so important, how come God waited until the mid 19th century to deliver them to us? Why didn't he deliver them to us right after the invention of the printing press? But that's a question for another time.

Let's dig a little deeper and see how great these manuscripts really are and if the Lord trusts them as much as the experts.

First of all…

Are "the oldest" manuscripts really "the best"?

It's not well known, but it turns out that some of the biggest names in the field of textual criticism have openly admitted that a tremendous amount of corruption of Scripture took place before AD 200—well before Vaticanus and Sinaiticus were created.

Let's read some candid comments from Textual Criticism insiders.

Ernest Cadman Colwell (1901–1974) was past president of the University of Chicago, biblical scholar, textual critic, and paleographer. His many works include: *The character of the Greek of the Fourth Gospel. Parallels to the "Aramaisms" of the Fourth Gospel from Epictetus and the Papyri (1931); The Four Gospels of Karahissar, vol. I, History and Text (1936); An Ancient Text of the Gospel of Mark (1945); Some Unusual Abbreviations in ms. 2427 (1959); A Beginner's Reader Grammar for New Testament Greek (1965);* and *Studies in Methodology in Textual Criticism of the New Testament (1969).*

Dr. Ernest Colwell

So, Dr. Colwell's got the credentials to back up his opinions. He states:

The first two centuries witnessed the creations of the large number of variations known to scholars today ... in the manuscripts of the New Testament most variations, I believe, **were made deliberately**...

The majority of the variant readings in the New Testament were created **for theological or dogmatic reasons**. ... Most of the manuals and handbooks now in print (including mine!) will tell you that these variations were the fruit of careless treatment ... of the New Testament.... **The reverse is the case.** It was because they were the religious treasure of the church that they were changed.[2]

The overwhelming majority of variant readings were created **before the year 200.**[3]

Frederick H. A. Scrivener, LL.D (1813–1891), was an important New Testament textual critic and a member of the English New Testament Revision Committee, which produced the English Revised Version of the Bible (ERV). Scrivener edited several editions of the New Testament and collated (compared) the Codex Sinaiticus with the Textus Receptus.

Frederick Scrivener

Scrivener reveals:

> **The worst corruptions** to which the NT has ever been subjected, **originated within a hundred years after it was composed.**[4]

George Dunbar Kilpatrick (1910–1989) was Dean Ireland's Professor of the Exegesis of Holy Scripture at the University of Oxford from 1949 to 1977. He is well known for his work in textual criticism of the Greek New Testament and in source criticism. He was considered an innovative textual critic and wrote many articles about the subject. Kilpatrick

---

[2] E.C. Colwell, *What Is the Best New Testament?* (Chicago: University of Chicago Press, 1952), 52–53. (emphasis mine)

[3] E.C. Colwell, *Studies in Methodology in Textual Criticism of the New Testament Manuscripts* (Leiden, Netherlands: E.J Brill, 1969), 55. (emphasis mine)

[4] Quoted by Jack Moorman, *Forever Settled: A Survey of the Documents and History of the Bible* (Collingswood, NJ: Dean Burgon Society Press, 1999), 81. (emphasis mine)

was also editor of the second edition of the British and Foreign Bible Society's Greek New Testament (1958). He states:

> The **creation of new variants** ceased by 200 AD because it became impossible to sell them.[5]

It's not surprising that there was a lot of tampering going on (for whatever reason) when it comes to the words of the living God.

And it turns out that a lot of the mischief was being done in…

Alexandria, Egypt, home of Vaticanus and Sinaiticus.

As textual expert Wilbur Pickering said:

> It is generally agreed that all the earliest MSS, the ones upon which our critical/eclectic texts are based, come from Egypt.[6]

Here's what we know:

1. Paul made 3 missionary journeys, visited scores of cities, and **never** went to Alexandria, Egypt.

2. No original New Testament letters were ever written to anyone in Egypt.

3. The two main "oldest and best" Vaticanus (B) and Sinaiticus (Aleph) manuscripts originated in or near **Alexandria, Egypt**.

4. The best you could ever say about them is that they represent textual variations unique to that country.

---

[5] Ibid. (emphasis mine)
[6] Wilbur Pickering, *The Identity of the New Testament Text II*, 3rd ed. (n.p., 2003), 81. (Available: http://www.cspmt.org/pdf/Identity%20of%20the%20New%20Testament%20Text%20III.pdf).

5. There was a lot of creative editing for style (referred to as "Alexandrian trimming") and content instead of faithful copying going on in Alexandria.[7]

F.C. Burkitt (1864–1935) was a British theologian and scholar. He was Norris Professor of Divinity at the University of Cambridge from 1905 until shortly before his death.

Burkitt wrote that Tertullian (160–220) and Augustine of Hippo (354–430) both testified that the scribes in Africa were constantly **editing and revising the manuscripts.**[8]

Aren't you supposed to **copy** biblical manuscripts, not **edit** them?

Talk about crazy…

Take a look at this quote from the prestigious *Cambridge History of the Bible* stating that in Alexandria, Egypt (home of the "oldest" and the "best" manuscripts), there were **no fewer than 3 versions of the Gospel of Mark** in circulation.

> In 1960 Professor Morton Smith described a letter by Clement which he had discovered, and this letter makes plain the fact that at Alexandria **no fewer than three versions of the Gospel of Mark were in circulation.** First, there was the ordinary version known to all; secondly, there was a false version used by Carpocratian Gnostics;

---

[7] Philip W. Comfort, *New Testament Text and Translation Commentary* (Carol Stream, IL: Tyndale House, 2008), 42: "The variant is likely the original reading because of its presence in ℵ and B. This shorter reading cannot be discounted **as Alexandrian trimming** because the scribes of ℵ [a 6th-century manuscript of the Gospels] and B [Codex Vaticanus] did not shorten the same expression in any of the other five occurrences in Matthew (see 4:25; 8:1; 13:2; 15:30; 19:2). The NU [a 20th-century Greek text] reading, therefore, would have to be the result of scribal conformity to Matthean style."

[8] Geoffrey W. Bromiley, ed., *International Standard Bible Encyclopedia* (Grand Rapids, MI: Eerdmans, 1979), vol. IV, 970; F.C. Burkitt, *The Old Latin and the Itala* (Cambridge: n.p., 1896). "The latter is considered the standard source." As cited by Floyd Nolen Jones, *Which Version Is the Bible?* 17th ed. (The Woodlands, TX: KingsWord Press, 1999), 167. (Available: http://www.3bible.com/books/Which%20Version%20is%20the%20Bible. pdf. Also at http://www.scribd.com/doc/14110607/111/ANCIENT-TRANSLATIONS-SUPPORT-THE-RECEIVED-TEXT).

thirdly, there was a secret version, written by Mark himself at Alexandria and known only to the spiritual élite there.[9]

But what about the two "aces" in the hands of textual critics—Vaticanus and Sinaiticus?

Here's a shocking detail.

Textual expert Wilbur Pickering tells us that the "oldest and best" manuscripts **don't** agree with each other in over 3,000 places in the Gospels alone.

> Hoskier [textual researcher and analyst Herman Hoskier (1832–1904)], after filling 450 pages with a detailed and careful discussion of the errors in Codex B [Vaticanus] and another 400 on the idiosyncrasies of Codex Aleph [Sinaiticus], affirms that **in the Gospels alone** these two MSS **differ well over 3,000 times,** which number does not include minor errors such as spelling, nor variants between certain synonyms which might be due to "provincial exchange."[10]

Vaticanus is an edited text.

And how about this from British biblical scholar and textual critic B.H. Streeter (1874–1937):

> Now, whoever was responsible for it, the **B** [Vaticanus] text has been edited on the Alexandrian principle.[11]

Streeter's comment about "the Alexandrian Principle" of text editing echoes that of 19th century textual scholar Dean John Burgon who believed that:

> …words and clauses and sentences were **omitted** upon definitely understood **principles** in a small class of documents [the Alexandrian text] by careless or ignorant or prejudiced scribes.[12]

---

[9] P.R. Ackroyd and C.F. Evans, eds., *The Cambridge History of the Bible from the Beginnings to Jerome* (Cambridge University Press, 1989), 302. (emphasis mine)

[10] Pickering, *Identity of the New Testament Text,* 23. Pickering is citing H.C. Hoskier, *Codex B and Its Allies* (2 vols.; London: Bernard Quaritch, 1914), vol. II, 1.

[11] B.H. Streeter, *The Four Gospels: A Study of Origins* (London: Macmillan, 1951), 124.

[12] J.W. Burgon, *The Causes of the Corruption of the Traditional Text of the Holy Gospels,* (London: George Bell and Sons, 1896), p. 156.

Which Bible Would Jesus Use?

John W. Burgon (1813–1888) was Dean of Chichester from 1876 until his death. His biographer declared him to be "the leading religious teacher of his time" in England. "**Burgon was a masterful Greek scholar of the highest rank** who spent much of his life browsing through the museums and libraries of Europe examining the ancient Greek manuscripts."[13]

John W. Burgon

He was an incredible researcher. Burgon created an index of 16 folio volumes of more than 86,000 Scripture quotations and allusions to Scripture used by the church fathers.[13]

These 12 by 18 by 3 inch indexes are in London's British Museum and unfortunately have never been published. Dean Burgon and his associates not only cataloged them but color-coded each quotation or allusion to show exactly what page and version of the church fathers they were found.[14]

He did all this work by hand.

Burgon also personally collated the Sinaiticus and Vaticanus manuscripts.

In 1860, "he made a personal examination of Codex B (Vaticanus), and in 1862 he inspected the treasures of St. Catherine's Convent on Mt. Sinai [where Sinaiticus had been found 18 years earlier]. Later he made several tours of European libraries, examining and collating New Testament manuscripts wherever he went."[13]

Here's what Burgon said about Vaticanus and Sinaiticus in his 1881 book, *The Revision Revised*. One chapter is aptly titled:

"א B C D showed to be four of the most corrupt codices in existence."

---

[13] The Dean Burgon Society, "Who Was Dean John William Burgon?" accessed December 2012, http://www.deanburgonsociety.org/DeanBurgon/whowasdb.htm.
[14] The Dean Burgon Society, "Who Was Dean John William Burgon?" accessed December 2012, http://www.deanburgonsociety.org/DeanBurgon/whowasdb.htm.
[15] Loughran, "Bible Versions."

Two "dirty little secrets" of modern textual criticism

> ...B and ℵ [Vaticanus and Aleph], have within the last 20 years established a tyrannical ascendance over the imagination of the Critics, which can only be fitly spoken of as a **blind superstition**.[16]

And more...

> ...it is easier to find two consecutive verses in which the two MSS differ, the one from the other, than two consecutive verses in which they entirely agree. Now this is a plain matter of fact, of which anyone who pleases may easily convince himself.[17]

> Aleph, B [and] D are three of the most scandalously corrupt copies extant: ... exhibit the most shamefully mutilated texts which are anywhere to be met with: ... have become, by whatever process (for their history is wholly unknown), the depositories of the largest amount of fabricated readings, ancient blunders, and intentional perversions of Truth ... which are discoverable in any known copies of the Word of God.[18]

Note his comments:

- The most scandalously corrupt copies extant
- The most shamefully mutilated texts
- The largest amount of fabricated readings
- Ancient blunders
- Intentional perversions of Truth

None of this is good if you just want to know what the Lord said.

See the differences for yourself in just a few verses...

---

[16] John William Burgon, *The Revision Revised: A Refutation of Westcott and Hort's False Greek Text and Theory* (1881; reprint, Collingswood, NJ: Dean Burgon Society Press, September 2000), 11. (emphasis mine)

[17] John William Burgon, *The Last Twelve Verses of Mark* (1871; Reprint, Collingswood, NJ: Dean Burgon Society Press, 2008), 77–78.

[18] Burgon, *Revision Revised,* 16.

Verses	Vaticanus	Sinaiticus
Matthew 24:35	Includes	Omits
Matthew 12:47	Omits	Includes
Luke 10:32	Includes	Omits
Luke 17:35	Includes	Omits
Luke 23:17	Omits	Includes
Luke 23:34	Omits	Includes
John 9:38	Includes	Omits
John 16:15	Includes	Omits
John 21:25	Includes	Omits
1 Corinthians 2:15	Includes	Omits
1 Corinthians 13:1b–2	Includes	Omits

This chart doesn't show you the literally thousands of other differences in wording. Can you see why Dean Burgon said what he said?

And mind you, these manuscripts are the ones we are told are "ancient authorities," the "best witnesses" to the original text, the "earliest" and "the oldest and best" manuscripts. All this disinformation brings us to a couple of shocking truths...

Dirty little secret #1
The critics know their two "go-to" manuscripts are error-filled but believe in them anyway.

Dean Burgon's facts are not lost on modern textual critics. Everybody in the textual criticism business knows that these manuscripts contain errors of fact and errors in spelling, grammar, history, and geography. They know that they are missing words that are necessary to make a verse make sense, plus they know that there are missing words, phrases, and verses that appear in parallel passages or elsewhere in Scripture.

And this brings us to the second "dirty little secret" of modern textual criticism. Instead of just admitting their favorite manuscripts are corrupt...

Dirty little secret #2
The critics assert that God made those mistakes in the original autographs.

The textual critics won't dump these manuscripts even when they know they contain error. They choose error rather than truth and say that's what God originally wrote. Not a very high view of the Lord's integrity, is it?

They don't come right out and tell you, but most of them really believe that the Bible is a mere human book. No different than any of the classics. They know that the public believes that somehow God has something to do with the "Bible" so they are careful about their wording.

By subtly suggesting (or sometimes saying outright in their own publications) that the human authors of Scripture (i.e., Matthew, Mark, Luke, etc., made mistakes), they undermine the direct influence of the Holy Ghost in the production of the Bible.

And you'll soon see from their writings that they believe God made mistakes when he created his Bible.

They assert:

God made geography mistakes, God made history mistakes, God got his facts wrong, God made grammatical mistakes. He made doctrinal mistakes, and he left out important details of events that should have been there.

Why not just come right out and say that the Lord God of Hosts is incompetent?

This outrageous behavior was noted over 100 years ago by George Salmon, provost of Trinity College, Dublin, in his book *Some Thoughts on the Textual Criticism of the New Testament*:

> …but even more repulsive to conservative instincts was the number of cases in which these editors attribute to the **evangelists themselves erroneous statements** which their predecessors had regarded as copyists blunders. There was indeed but a little rhetorical exag-

geration in the statement that the Canon of these editors was **that Codex B was infallible and that the evangelists were not.** Nay, it seemed as if Hort [NT scholar] regarded it as a note of genuineness **if a reading implies error on the part of the sacred writer.**[19]

Notice what Provost Salmon said.

The textual critics believed that Vaticanus was infallible but the evangelists were not. The experts still do. They willfully choose the readings in Vaticanus and a few other manuscripts over the vast majority of manuscripts in existence.

Seems like an insult to God, but here's their logic:

They convinced themselves that these manuscripts (and especially Vaticanus) represent the text of *"The Original Bible."*

They do this based on a story that was concocted by an English New Testament scholar named Fenton Hort (1828–1892).

Hort's fable is still being repeated today even though there is still absolutely no evidence that it is true. We'll get to it shortly, but first we need a little background.

Fenton Hort

Hort was a man with an agenda. He was hired to "revise" the King James Bible but instead, along with a man named Brooke Westcott, substituted a newly created Greek New Testament based primarily upon the readings found in Vaticanus and Sinaiticus. Hort and Westcott published this critical edition of *The New Testament in the Original Greek* in 1881.

Their text is known as the Westcott and Hort Greek text and was the basis of the New Testament for the English Revised Version also published in 1881. It's the granddaddy of just about all the English versions/translations produced in the 20th and 21st centuries.

---

[19] George Salmon, *Some Thoughts on the Textual Criticism of the New Testament* (London: John Murray, Albemarle Street, 1897). (emphasis mine)

Two "dirty little secrets" of modern textual criticism

By the way, you'd fire both Westcott and Hort if they worked for you because they didn't do what they were hired to do or what they agreed to do.

Anyway, Hort made it his life's work to dethrone the Greek text (known as the Received Text or Textus Receptus) that had been used by the church for 1,800 years. When he was 23 years old, he referred to the Received Text as "vile and villainous."[19] That's an interesting comment coming from a 23-year-old kid.

Maybe he thought he'd get a prize at the judgment seat of Christ, or more likely, he really didn't care what the Lord thought.

The Received Text, also referred to as the Traditional text,[21] is represented by literally thousands of manuscripts whose readings in some places don't match up with the readings of Vaticanus and Sinaiticus. The critics simply ignore it.

Unlike Vaticanus and Sinaiticus, the text of this body of manuscript evidence does not contain errors of fact, or errors in spelling, grammar, history, or geography; it has no missing words that are necessary to make a verse make sense and no missing words, phrases, and verses that appear in parallel passages or elsewhere in Scripture.

The Received Text has a history of being used by the church throughout the centuries. The text based on the two Alexandrian manuscripts does not.

Elder David Loughran of the Stewarton Bible School in Scotland said:

> Burgon regarded the good state of preservation of B (Codex Vaticanus) and Aleph (Codex Sinaiticus) in spite of their exceptional age as proof not of their goodness but of their badness. **If they had been good manuscripts, they would have been read to pieces long ago.**[22] As another researcher has put it nicely:

---

[20] A.F. Hort, *Life and Letters of Fenton John Anthony Hort* (2 Vols.; London: Macmillan, 1896), I, 211. As cited by Pickering, *Identity of the New Testament*, 10.
[21] The Received Text is actually a subset of the Traditional Text. They are not exactly the same.
[22] Loughran, "Bible Versions."

In 1977 Pickering wrote that since there is only one existing copy of both B and Aleph [the] evident fact that they were not copied ... suggests that the early church rejected them.[23]

The Traditional text was used by the church because it was the original text given by God. The critics just don't want to believe it.

Dean Burgon wrote:

The history of the Traditional Text, on the contrary, goes step by step **in unbroken succession** regularly back to the earliest times...[24]

Wilbur Pickering cited textual critic and author Jacob Geerlings...

...who has done extensive work on certain branches of the "Byzantine" (also called the Majority Text) text-type, affirms concerning it: "Its origins as well as those of other so-called **text-types probably go back to the autographs.**"[25]

Considering the character of these manuscripts, it's no wonder these two manuscripts have no history of use in any of the churches after they were produced. The folks back then knew better.

The following graphic is designed to give you a quick and easy-to-understand overview. As you read it, remember that a handed-down text is needed for a handed-down faith.

---

[23] Russell Earl Kelly, "The King James Bible Controversy," September 2011, Acworth, GA, http://www.tithing-russkelly.com/theology/id34.html. Cf. Floyd Nolen Jones, *Which Version Is the Bible?* 17th ed. (The Woodlands, TX: KingsWord Press, 1999), 162; and Pickering, *Identity of the New Testament Text,* 127.

[24] Dean Burgon, *The Traditional Text of the Holy Gospels* (London: George Bell and Sons, 1896), 236.

[25] Pickering, *Identity of the New Testament,* 52, citing J. Geerlings, *Family E and Its Allies in Mark* (Salt Lake City: University of Utah Press, 1967), 1. (Available: http://www.cspmt.org/pdf/Identity%20of%20the%20New%20Testament%20Text%20III.pdf).

Two "dirty little secrets" of modern textual criticism

Text used by the church since its inception	Text not used by the church until 19th century
The New Testament text used by the church from the get-go is also known as: • The Byzantine Textform • Majority Text • Traditional Text • Ecclesiastical Text • Constantinopolitan Text • Antiochian Text or Syrian Text It is the form found in the largest number of surviving manuscripts and underlies: • The Received Text or Textus Receptus The Received Text is at the base of all Reformation Bibles in any language and appears today in any Bible bearing the name of King James (i.e., Authorized Version, 1611 KJV ©1984 NKJV, etc.). It is the New Testament text that has been handed down from one generation of believers to another in Greek and many other languages.	The Greek New Testament that predominates in the earliest surviving documents, as well as the text-type found in Egyptian Coptic manuscripts is known as: • The Alexandrian Textform (also called Neutral or Egyptian) The Alexandrian text never had any history of widespread use by the church until the late 19th century. The following texts were assembled and propagated in the late 19th–20th centuries by substituting the variant readings of Vaticanus and Sinaiticus (and a few other manuscripts) into the Traditional Text base. • Westcott & Hort text • Critical text • Nestle-Aland Text • UBS4 (United Bible Societies) • NU text (combination of Nestle's and UBS4) These texts are at the heart of the New Testaments of almost all modern versions: 1881 English Revised Version, 1901 ASV, 1984/2011 NIV, 2001 ESV, 1960/1994 NASB, NLT, etc.).

It is noteworthy that "the Coptic Orthodox Church prefers the Greek Textus Receptus, such as the New King James Version, for the New Testament."[26] If the Alexandrian textform was really their "historic text," then why aren't they using it today?

And all this raises an important question…

> **Why do textual critics and almost all Christian academics still reject the Received Text?**

They dump the readings of the vast majority of manuscripts based on Hort's cunningly devised fable about the history of the text even though it's been proven to be false.

How the Grinch Stole The New Testament!

Hort is the Grinch that stole the New Testament. But how did he do it? How could he get the church to abandon the text believed since the church's foundation to be the words of the living God?

> *The more the Hort thought on the vile Textus*
> *The more he purposed to destroy that Receptus.*
> *"But how shall it be and what shall I do*
> *To deceive those foolish and ignorant Whos?"*
> *But you know, that old Hort was so smart and so slick.*
> *He thought up a lie, and he thought it up quick!*
> *"Ahh!" said the Hort, "I know what I'll do;*
> *I'll fashion a fable their leaders think true."*
> *So he spun up a story about a recension*
> *He hoped would stop any and all Who dissension.*
> *And their leaders gave 'way their heritage without proof*
> *Based on a fairy tale, nothing more than a spoof.*

---

[26] Coptic Orthodox Church, Diocese of Los Angeles, "Orthodoxy: Holy Scripture," accessed December 2012, http://lacopts.org/orthodoxy/our-faith/the-holy-bible.

Hort's conspiracy theory

Hort knew that there was no history of the church using a Vaticanus style text so he simply made one up. He said that the Vaticanus style text was the original text but that there had been a conspiracy to revise it and replace it.

Hort claimed that there "**must**" have been an organized **revision** (known as a **Recension**, i.e., the practice of editing or revising a text based on critical analysis) of the text, executed and imposed upon the churches by some ecclesiastical authority. He claimed that the Traditional Received Text was fabricated between AD 250 and AD 350 or thereabouts.

He said that despite abundant evidence (i.e., thousands of manuscripts, versions, quotations by church fathers, and lectionaries in churches) to support the Traditional text of the New Testament.

So his major problem was to explain how this "traditional text" came into being, and above all how it came to dominate the field from the 5th century onward.

Hence the church and its leaders had been duped into accepting a new text that turns out to be grammatically, historically, and geographically correct. It gets the Gospel stories correct, spelling correct, names correct. All in all, this revision corrected all the readings that God got wrong in the first place.

And since it was so "good" it spread far and wide and was accepted by churches across Christendom.

This, of course, assumes that those believers and their leaders were idiots and the Holy Ghost couldn't lead a Christian out of a paper bag. That's the gist of the story.

The new conspiracy theory—an inside job

Fast-forward to today. After 130 years, the critics have finally quit looking for such a revision. Now everyone agrees that there never was a decree to produce a standard text.

So, today's textual insiders have come up with a new spin. The text was revised, but this time the culprits were…

People like you.

The culprits are now referred to as "orthodox" people. And just who are "the orthodox"?

Webster's 1828 dictionary defines orthodox as:

1. Sound in the Christian faith; believing the genuine doctrines taught in the Scriptures; opposed to heretical; as an orthodox Christian.
2. According with the doctrines of Scripture; as an orthodox creed or faith.

In short, "the orthodox" were people like you and your friends—well-meaning but misguided believers who were at the core of the conspiracy to "corrupt" (i.e., correct) the Scriptures as originally but faultily given by God.

So, Hort's fable is still repeated today but with a twist and told as if it were, pardon the expression, "gospel." It's kind of goofy, but here goes…

1. The original but faulty autographs were committed to paper (or parchment or papyri).
2. Then somewhere down the road "orthodox scribes" orchestrated a vast conspiracy to fix God's original errors. These pious scribes thus "corrupted" the originals in order to help God out.

Poor God.

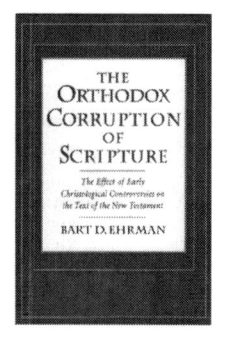

He just can't be relied upon to get his facts straight the first time.

Proof?

For starters, look at the book titles published by two key players in the field. *The Orthodox Corruption of Scripture* was written by premiere textual critic Dr. Bart Ehrman.

Two "dirty little secrets" of modern textual criticism

The title tells it all. The orthodox corrupted the Scripture.

Here's another.

The Text of the New Testament: Its Transmission, Corruption, and Restoration (4th edition) by Bruce M. Metzger and Bart D. Ehrman.

Notice that the text was **transmitted** then **corrupted** (by Bible believers) and then **restored** (by textual critics).

It's finally happened: George Orwell's *1984* has come to the church.

We've entered the age of Newspeak in the church of God.

War is peace, freedom is slavery, ignorance is strength, corrupt is correct, error is truth, orthodox is base and unorthodox is noble.

Hort died in 1892. But his dead hand lives on.

Textual expert E.C. Colwell writes:

> The dead hand of Fenton John Anthony Hort lies heavy upon us. In the early years of this century Kirsopp Lake [NT scholar] described Hort's work as a failure, though a glorious one. But Hort did not fail to reach his major goal. He dethroned the Textus Receptus. After Hort, the late medieval Greek Vulgate was not used by serious students, and the text supported by earlier witnesses became the standard text. This was a sensational achievement, an impressive success. Hort's success in this task and the cogency of his tightly reasoned theory shaped—and still shapes—the thinking of those who approach the textual criticism of the NT through the English language.[27]

British first edition cover, Secker and Warburg, 1949

---

[27] Pickering, *Identity of the New Testament Text,* 14; citing E.C. Colwell, "Scribal Habits in Early Papyri: A Study in the Corruption of the Text," *The Bible in Modern Scholarship,* ed. J.P. Hyatt (New York: Abingdon Press, 1965), 370.

Wilbur Pickering says:

> And that explains the nature and extent of the common divergence of the modern versions from the AV (King James Version)—they are all based essentially on the W-H theory and text whereas the AV is essentially based on the *Textus Receptus*.[28]

This would be nothing more than an amusement had not Christian academics been tricked into believing Hort's fable and its new incarnation.

Like they say, you can't just make this stuff up.

Why evangelicals and fundamentalists have "man crushes" on these textual critics is perplexing.

So why don't your teachers tell you the textual scholars who created the Greek New Testament text that underlies most modern versions of the Bible (i.e., ESV, RSV, NRSV, NIV, NASB, NIV, NLT, HCSB, etc.) believe there were **errors** in the Original Autographs?

They probably don't even know.

But let's look at some examples of how the known and acknowledged errors found in the Vaticanus and Sinaiticus manuscripts are preserved today in popular Bible versions.

As you read on, keep this in mind: just because some Christian leaders use the erroneous readings in these infamous manuscripts…

Does that mean the Lord Jesus Christ has to use them?

---

[28] Ibid., 15.

Chapter Three

Proof—Prominent textual scholars believe God made mistakes when he wrote the Bible

> … yea, let God be true, but every man a liar… Romans 3:4

It's hard to believe that men who work on the Bible text believe that God made errors when he wrote the Bible. But it turns out to be true. It's so hard, in fact, that you have to see what they've written with your own eyes. That's why scans of their work are provided for you.

Let's start out with a quote from New Testament Scholar of the University of Chicago Dr. Merrill M. Parvis:

> As long as men held to a belief in an absolute, faultless, unerring, verbally inspired Scripture, it was essential to that belief that they should have the original text of that Scripture before them. But that belief is no longer one that is generally accepted by most of us.[1]

Parvis wrote that in 1952. That's what the experts believed then and now. And he also said:

> "The Textus Receptus (also known as the Traditional Text and Ecclesiastical Text) is not the 'true' text of the New Testament…"

He went on to admit however, "The Textus Receptus is the text of the Church. It is that form of the text which represents the sum total and the

---

[1] Merrill M. Parvis, "The Nature and Tasks of New Testament Textual Criticism: An Appraisal," *Journal of Religion*, vol. 32, no. 3 (July 1952), 165–174. (Available: http://www.jstor.org/stable/1201165).

end product of all the textual decisions which were made by the Church and her Fathers over a period of more than a thousand years."[2]

Which is exactly what we saw in the last chapter.

None of this would matter much except that the supposed original errors actually show up in some of the most popular English Bibles on the market today.

Matthew 1:7–8 is a good example:

Matthew 1:7–8		
NIV (©1984) (©2011)	**ESV** (©2001)	**NASB** (©1995)
Solomon the father of Rehoboam, Rehoboam the father of Abijah, Abijah the father of **Asa, Asa** was the father of Jehoshaphat…	and Solomon the father of Rehoboam, and Rehoboam the father of Abijah, and Abijah the father of **Asaph** and **Asaph** the father of Jehoshaphat, and Jehoshaphat…	Solomon was the father of Rehoboam, Rehoboam the father of Abijah, and Abijah the father of **Asa. Asa** was the father of Jehoshaphat…

There is no one named "Asaph" in the Lord's genealogy and everyone knows it. "Asaph" is a known error. The spelling of a name may seem like a small thing to you, but in the world of biblical scholarship its significance is very well known.

Dr. Bruce Metzger (1914–2007) edited and provided commentary for many Bible translations and wrote dozens of books. He was an editor of the United Bible Societies' standard Greek New Testament, the starting point for nearly all recent New Testament translations. In 1952, he became a contributor to the Revised Standard Version (**RSV**) of the Bible, and was general editor of the

Dr. Bruce Metzger

---

[2] David L. Brown, "More Proof the Traditional Text (Textus Receptus) Is of Apostolic Origin," King James Bible Research Council, accessed November 2012, http://www.kjbresearchcouncil.com/Pages/Articles/More_Proof.htm.

Reader's Digest Bible (a condensed version of the RSV) in 1982. From 1977 to 1990, he chaired the Committee on Translators for the New Revised Standard Version (**NRSV**) of the Bible and was "largely responsible for ... seeing [the NRSV] through the press. Dr. Metzger claims:

> "...the evangelist [Matthew] may have derived material for the genealogy not from the Old Testament directly, but from subsequent genealogical lists, in which the erroneous spelling occurred.."[3]

The evangelist is supposed to be getting his information from the Holy Spirit.

Why does the ESV include the error in its Bible? Because that's what it says **in both of the "oldest and best" manuscripts**. Evidently, they followed the scholarship of the men who believe that Matthew made a mistake. These are the same men that prepared the Modern Greek New Testaments.[4]

The reading is so obviously wrong that the NIV and NASB **dump** the two "oldest and best" and go with the reading from the vast majority of manuscripts that get the facts straight.

Dr. Metzger is telling you that Matthew got his information from a **corrupted** genealogy and then blundered while penning the original autograph. So the Apostle Matthew got his information from **a lousy source *and* he can't spell either.**

Instead of admitting that the oldest aren't necessarily the best, the textual critics make lame excuses for the defective manuscripts by charging God with error.

How do you like what a "go to" modern Greek scholar believes about the "inspiration" of *"The Original Bible"*? Evidently, these scholars must believe that the Lord is an inspirer of a defective Bible. Which is fine for them; they can believe anything they want. But why do the ESV folks go along with it? The NIV and NASB folks didn't.

---

[3] Bruce M. Metzger, *Textual Commentary on the Greek New Testament* (Stuttgart: German Bible Society, 1994), 1.

[4] Nestle-Aland 27th edition (NA27) and United Bible Societies Greek New Testament (UBS4).

Where is the adult supervision in all of this?

If you were the editor of the ESV and you **knew "Asaph"** was an error, would you put it in your Bible? Would you assume Matthew made a mistake or that the mistake must be in the manuscript the experts were using?

If you wouldn't use it, then why does the ESV use it?

And besides…

How many mistakes does it take to wreck a Bible?

Maybe there should be a **warning** label on the ESV.

The position of the guys who worked on the Modern Greek New Testament (the one everyone tells you is based on manuscripts that are "closest to the Original Autographs") is that **Matthew made a mistake when he wrote the gospel.**

Is this a Jedi mind trick?

Remember the scene in *Star Wars Episode IV: A New Hope,* when Obi-Wan Kenobi used The Force to influence the thoughts of sentient creatures to coerce them into agreement through voice manipulation?

Obi-Wan: "These aren't the droids you're looking for."

Storm trooper: "These aren't the droids we're looking for."

Obi-Wan: "He can go about his business."

Storm trooper: "You can go about your business."

Obi-Wan: "Move along."

Storm trooper: "Move along … move along …"[5]

Dr. Metzger: "It doesn't matter that Matthew made a mistake … Move along…"

---
[5] Internet Movie Database, s.v. "Memorable Quotes for *Star Wars* (1977)," http://www.imdb.com/title/tt0076759/quotes.

Proof—Prominent textual scholars believe God made mistakes when he wrote the Bible

Christian Scholars: "It doesn't matter that Matthew made a mistake ... Move along ..."

No matter what any "oldest and best" manuscripts say, wouldn't you assume Matthew didn't make an error since he was writing under the guidance of the Holy Ghost? Wouldn't you conclude that the manuscripts are **wrong**—no matter how old they are?

And they're not even that old considering that they were written nearly 300 years after the New Testament was finished.

Moving along, we find the same type of problem pops up again in Matthew 1:10. This time Vaticanus and Sinaiticus confuse King Amon with someone named Amos. Again Dr. Metzger notes the error:

> the textual evidence for the reading "**Amos**," [is] **an error** for "**Amon**," the name of the king of Judah…[6]

In spite of this known error, the ESV handles the passage exactly the same way it handled Matthew 1:7–8—it prints the error—on purpose.

Matthew 1:10		
NIV (©1984) (©2011)	ESV (©2001)	NASB (©1995)
Hezekiah the father of Manasseh, Manasseh the father of **Amon, Amon** the father of Josiah, …	and Hezekiah the father of Manasseh, and Manasseh the father of **Amos**, and **Amos** the father of Josiah, …	Hezekiah was the father of Manasseh, Manasseh the father of **Amon**, and **Amon** the father of Josiah.

You need to see more detail on Dr. Metzger's comments to fully appreciate the gravity of the situation.

Dr. Metzger clearly tells us:

1. Asaph is the name appearing in the "oldest and best" manuscripts and it is an error.

---
[6] Metzger, *Textual Commentary on the Greek New Testament*, 1. (emphasis mine)

2. The error was subsequently corrected by later Scribes.
3. The evangelist, Matthew made the error by referring to some random genealogical lists instead of the Old Testament.

Notice how he phrases it in his *Textual Commentary on the Greek New Testament*:

> "it is clear that the name "Asaph" is the earliest form of text preserved in the manuscripts...Furthermore, the tendency of scribes, observing that the name of the psalmist Asaph... was confused with that of Asa the King of Judah (1Kgs 15.9 ff.), would have been to correct the error..."[7]

And then the bombshell...

> "...the evangelist [Matthew] may have derived material for the genealogy not from the Old Testament directly, but from subsequent genealogical lists, in which the erroneous spelling occurred."[8]

He tells us that the error is repeated in Matthew 1:10 as well...

> The textual evidence for the reading "Amos," an error for "Amon," the name of the King of Judah, is nearly the same as that which reads Asaph in verses 7 and 8.[9]

So Matthew made the same kind of "genealogical" mistake in verse 10 of his original autograph. Maybe we're supposed to believe that Matthew was good at collecting taxes but bad at writing the bible.

Kind of tragic, wouldn't you say?

How about some more comments on Matthew 1:10?

Dr. Roger L. Omanson was the United Bible Societies' Consultant for Scholarly Editions and Helps. He worked as a translation consultant for UBS for nearly thirty years, working with translators in nearly 130 lan-

---

[7] Ibid.
[8] Ibid.
[9] Ibid.

guages in Africa, Asia, Europe, the Caribbean, and Latin America. He also taught New Testament studies for eight years.[10]

Here are his comments on the verse:

> According to Davies and Allison … the name Amos "may represent a corruption in Matthew's source or in the post Matthean textual tradition, Or **perhaps Matthew simply made an error."**[11]

"…or perhaps Matthew simply made an error."

Wow—

Has anybody told the Lord that Matthew, writing under the inspiration of the Holy Ghost, made an error?

Roger Omanson is quoting from *A Critical and Exegetical Commentary on the Gospel According to Saint Matthew* (International Critical Commentary, vol. III) by Professors W. D. Davies and Dale C. Allison. Here is what one commenter said about the book on Amazon:

> [Davies and Allison] … also stress forcefully that even though the story of Christ's birth in Matthew 1:18–2:20 is powerful and evocative, **most of it must be regarded as myth.**[12]

Not exactly the fellows you want teaching Vacation Bible School, are they?

It's one thing if Matthew made a mistake, but maybe Mark did better. Sadly, the experts tell us Mark wasn't up to the job either.

We're taught that…

Mark made a mistake in his "original autograph"

Look at the comments on Mark 1:2 from Roger Omanson's book, *A Textual Guide to the Greek New Testament*. He cites commentator R. T.

---

[10] Union Theological Seminary, New York, http://www.utsnyc.edu/Page.aspx?pid=2526.
[11] Roger L. Omanson, *A Textual Guide to the Greek New Testament* (Stuttgart: German Bible Society, 2006), 2.
[12] Dr. Marc Axelrod, comment on W. D. Davies and Dale C. Allison, *A Critical and Exegetical Commentary on the Gospel According to Saint Matthew* (International Critical Commentary, vol. III), Amazon.com post, September 8, 2006. (emphasis mine)

France as saying Mark's error was obviously **corrected by copyists at a later date.** Everyone knows the O.T. quotation is from two prophets; Malachi 3:1 and Isaiah 40:3.

> **THE GOSPEL ACCORDING TO MARK**   57
>
> **1.2** ἐν τῷ Ἠσαΐᾳ τῷ προφήτῃ (in Isaiah the prophet) {A}
>
> The quotation in vv. 2 and 3 comes from two different OT texts. The first part comes from Mal 3.1 and the second part is from Isa 40.3. It is easy to see, therefore, why copyists would have changed the words "in Isaiah the prophet" to the more general reading "in the prophets" (ἐν τοῖς προφήταις). France (*The Gospel of Mark*, p. 60) calls this "an obvious 'correction.'" The reading in the UBS⁴ text is also supported by the earliest representative witnesses of the Alexandrian and the Western text-types.
>
> *"CORRECTIONS" ARE MADE TO FIX ERRORS*

Roger L. Omanson, *A Textual Guide to the Greek New Testament,* p. 57

So the "orthodox" people are at it again. Trying to help God out by fixing what God fouled up in the first place.

Even textual critic Philip W. Comfort in his work, *New Testament Text and Translation Commentary,* admits the same:

> … or perhaps Mark was using an early Jewish collection of texts relating to the Messiah (Cole 1961, 57). Whatever his source, Mark attributed the text to Isaiah only. It may be that he was more familiar with Isaiah, or that he thought Isaiah's name was the one which his readers would most often associate with prophecies about the Messiah.[13]

So Mark, writing under the influence of the Holy Ghost, may have omitted the Malachi reference because he was more familiar with Isaiah or perhaps because he was using a source that omitted the prophet Malachi. Do you suppose Mark just wasn't up to the job? Or maybe the Holy Ghost just didn't feed him the proper information?

This is just another lame excuse for the two **defective** "oldest and best manuscripts" while blaming the Holy Spirit for a subpar job of inspiration. This wouldn't be half bad if the NIV, ESV, and NASB didn't follow the reading—but they do…

---

[13] Philip W. Comfort, *New Testament Text and Translation Commentary* (Carol Stream, IL: Tyndale House, 2008), 93.

Mark 1:2	
NIV (©1984): As it is written in **Isaiah** the prophet… **ESV** (©2001): As it is written in **Isaiah** the prophet… **NASB** (©1995): As it is written in **Isaiah** the prophet…	**NKJV** (©1982): As it is written in **the Prophets**: *"Behold, I send My messenger before Your face, Who will prepare Your way before You."*

The rest of verse 2 is a quote from Malachi 3:1 while verse 3 is from Isaiah 40:3.

Now that we've learned that Matthew and Mark both made mistakes, how about Luke? Turns out textual critics think he wasn't on the ball when it came to **geography**.

Remember the '90s kids' TV show *Where in the World Is Carmen Sandiego?* It was great for teaching geography. Too bad Dr. Luke didn't live in the 20th century. He'd at least have learned that Galilee and Judea are about 30 miles apart at their closest point and they are **separated by Samaria**.

The good doctor made a geography mistake according to Dr. Bruce Metzger.

He and his committee (again following the oldest and best manuscripts that they're convinced represent *"The Original Bible"*) testify to the geography error in their Greek New Testament.

What's even more mysterious is that the NIV, ESV, and NASB **boldly include the error** in their Bibles.

Look at Luke 4:44 and the parallel passages…

63

Which Bible Would Jesus Use?

	Luke 4:44	Matthew 4:23	Mark 1:39
NIV (©1984)	And he kept on preaching in the synagogues of **Judea**.	Jesus went throughout **Galilee**...	So he traveled throughout **Galilee**...
ESV (©2001)	And he was preaching in the synagogues of **Judea**.	And he went throughout all **Galilee**...	And he went throughout all **Galilee**.
NASB (©1995)	So He kept on preaching in the synagogues of **Judea**.	Jesus was going throughout all **Galilee**...	And He went into their synagogues throughout all **Galilee**...
Holman HCSB (©2003)	And He was preaching in the synagogues of **Galilee**...	Jesus was going all over **Galilee**...	So He went into all of **Galilee**...

Here's the thing: everybody knows from the context as well as the parallel passages that Jesus was in **Galilee** (and continued there), not in **Judea**.

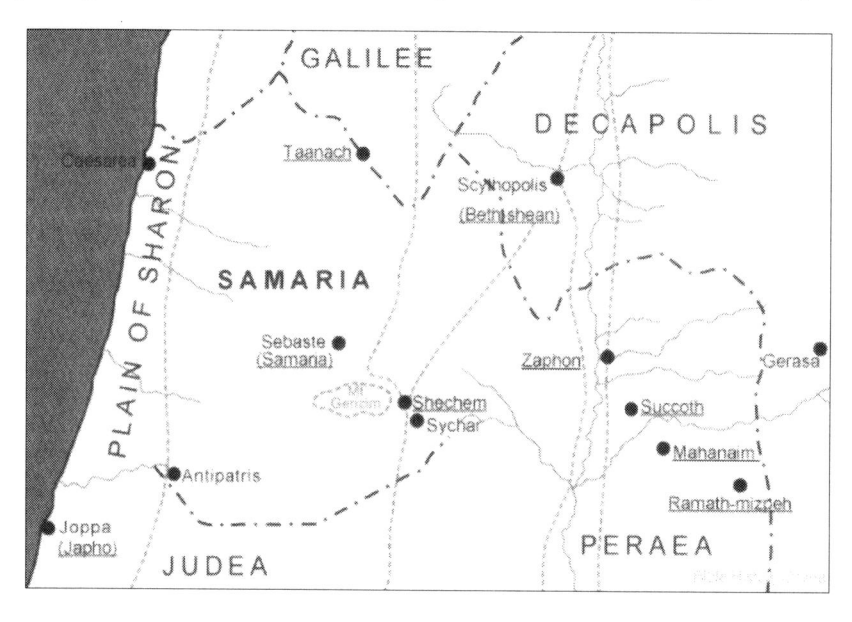

64

Proof—Prominent textual scholars believe God made mistakes when he wrote the Bible

The Southern Baptists over at Holman must have been fans of *Carmen Sandiego* because they flat out **ignored the Greek text** they used as a base for their Bible. Good for them. Because in this instance, any Bible version that chooses "Judea" in Luke 4:44 is trashing the doctrine of inerrancy.

Here's a discussion by textual expert Wilbur Pickering:

> In the parallel passage, Mark 1:35–39, all texts agree that Jesus was in Galilee. Thus NU [NA27 and UBS4] contradicts itself by reading Judea in Luke 4:44. Bruce Metzger makes clear that the NU editors did this on purpose when he explains that their reading "is obviously the more difficult, and copyists have corrected it … in accord with the parallels in Mt 4.23 and Mk 1.39."[14]

What the NIV, ESV, and NASB editors are saying is that Luke made a geography error. They even allow the contradiction to stand in their own Bibles as the previous chart attests. Either they weren't paying close attention to the biblical narrative or they just closed their eyes and trusted in the genetically modified text provided to them by the textual critics.

But…

"Does the Lord want geography mistakes in his Bible?

How do you think the Lord feels about this "on purpose" error in a book that's supposed to represent his integrity?

And they're willing to call God incompetent just to protect Vaticanus and Sinaiticus.

But what's really telling is that one of the experts that was on the committee that assembled the Greek New Testament that underlies almost all modern versions…

---

[14] Wilbur Pickering, *What Difference Does It Make*, citing Metzger, *A Textual Commentary on the Greek New Testament* (New York: United Bible Societies, 1971), 137–138. (Available: http://www.google.com/url?sa=t&rct=j&q=&esrc=s&source=web&cd=1 &ved=0CD8QFjAA&url=http%3A%2F%2Fsomehelpful.info%2FNT%2FMajority-text%2FPickering-other%2FWhat_difference_does_it_make.doc&ei=ddHCUOuYNpT V0gHfmoCACw&usg=AFQjCNFk5tQQ5EGEYWc6uK11LL-FdR4VeQ).

Doesn't necessarily believe that the oldest manuscripts are the best.

Despite what we were taught about the "oldest and best" manuscripts, Kurt Aland knows otherwise. Aland, one of the most respected men in the textual criticism business, was a key member of the committee along with Metzger that assembled the Greek New Testament (UBS4), which is the basis for the NIV, ESV, NASB, and a host of other new Bible versions. Aland said:

Kurt Aland (1915–1994), German theologian and founder of the Institute for New Testament Research and Church History, Münster, Germany

> We need not mention **the fact** that the **oldest manuscript does not necessarily have the best** text. P^{47} is, for example, by far the oldest of the manuscripts containing the full or almost full text of the Apocalypse, but it is certainly not the best.[15]

Be sure not to raise your hand in class and challenge the dogma of the oldest-is-the-best, however, because it won't matter. You'll be labeled a crazy conspiracy theorist.

Even with these **known and blatant errors** here's the pitch for the ESV by the publisher, Crossway Publications:

> The ESV Bible was created by a team of more than 100 leading evangelical scholars and pastors. Since its publication in 2001, the ESV has gained wide acceptance and is used and trusted by church leaders, numerous denominations, and millions of individuals around the world.[16]

Do you think that the team of "more than 100 leading evangelical scholars and pastors" knew about these errors in the originals **before** they put their names on the Bible? Look at the A-list of endorsements.[17]

---

[15] Wilber Pickering, *Identity of the New Testament Text II*, 86. (Available: http://www.enigstetroos.org/pdf/PickeringWN_TheIdentityofTheNewTestament%20II.pdf); citing Kurt Aland, "The Significance of the Papyri for New Testament Research," in *The Bible in Modern Scholarship*, edited by J.P. Hyatt (Nashville, TN: Abington, 1965), 333. (emphasis mine)

[16] Crossway, "The ESV Bible," http://www.crossway.org/esv.

[17] Crossway, ESV.org, "Endorsements," http://www.esv.org/esv/endorsements/all. (emphasis mine)

Proof—Prominent textual scholars believe God made mistakes when he wrote the Bible

R.C. Sproul	Al Mohler	Paige Patterson
John Piper	Erwin Lutzer	Vicki Courtney
Carolyn Mahaney	Philip Graham Ryken	Tom Schreiner
Ravi Zacharias	Darrell Bock	Bryan Chapell
Jerry Bridges	John Walvoord	Steve Green

And look at some of the words they're using to endorse it:

- "A new standard in **accurate** Bible translations"
- "**The most accurate** English translation of the Bible ever completed"
- "Unquestionable **accuracy**"
- "**The standard** translation for the English-speaking world"
- "**Surpasses all** other English translations"
- "The Bible of the future"[18]

Calling something **"accurate"** that misrepresents God brings Bible promotion to a new level of disinformation.

And what about "church leaders, numerous denominations, and millions of individuals around the world" who are using and trusting the ESV?

Has anybody told them?

No matter who recommends it, if he taught in your Sunday school class, would the Lord use the ESV with these gigantic blunders? What do you think?

What a dilemma…

Maybe we should just go back to the trusted NASB?

After all, the Lockman Foundation's copywriters have pumped sales using "ego appeal" by selling it as **the Bible** for "**serious students**" to do "**serious**" Bible studies since it came out in 1971. Unfortunately for sales, their pitch also limited the market to a special class of Bible enthusiast.

Not surprisingly, the copywriters' appeal is mirrored by…

---

[18] Terry Watkins, "The Truth About the English Substandard Version," http://www.av1611.org/kjv/ESV_Intro.html.

More influential Christian leaders' endorsements:

I want to know God's Word in the deepest and richest ways possible. I use the Updated NASB for all my personal study, since it is so close to the original text.—**Joseph Stowell**, Former President, Moody Bible Institute

I believe the NASB is the most accurate translation thus far. It's my Bible of choice, and I highly recommend it for all pastors and seminary Bible students.—**Dr. Charles Stanley**, Pastor, First Baptist Church, Atlanta; President, In Touch Ministries

The New American Standard Bible has set the standard for faithful Bible translations for a generation. It is the favorite of so many who love the Bible and look for accuracy and clarity in translation. The New American Standard Bible should be close at hand for any serious student of the Bible....—**Dr. R. Albert Mohler, Jr.**, President, Southern Baptist Theological Seminary, Louisville, KY

Better than any other English translation, the Updated NASB represents the writings of the original Hebrew and Greek authors. For private study and public readings, it's unsurpassed!—**Bruce A. Ware**, Ph.D., Associate Dean, School of Theology Professor of Christian Theology, Southern Baptist Theological Seminary, Louisville, KY

The NASB is an excellent translation that seeks the closest possible verbal equivalency.—**Dr. R.C. Sproul**

The NASB is "my" Bible, the finest and clearest of translations for inductive study. You can be sure this is the translation I recommend above all others.—**Kay Arthur**, Cofounder, Precept Ministries International[19]

Pretty solid recommendations—but...

What does the Lord do with a "most accurate" Bible that assails...

---

[19] Lockman Foundation, "NASB Endorsements," http://www.lockman.org/nasb/endorsements.php.

The doctrine of
the sinlessness of Christ (round 1)?

Would the Lord use a Bible that calls him a liar? Lying used to be a sin...

John 7:8,10	
NASB (©1995)	"Go up to the feast yourselves; I do not go up to this feast because My time has not yet fully come." ... But when His brothers had gone up to the feast, **then He Himself also went up**...

Notice the Lord clearly said He was not going up to the feast. Then **he went. Which means he just flat out lied to his brothers.**

Maybe it was just a "white lie." White lies must be okay because Jesus told them. By the way, not all Bibles report him to be a liar.

Here's what the NIV (©1984) says:

John 7:8,10	
NIV (©1984)	You go to the Feast. I am **not yet** going up to this Feast, because for me the right time has not yet come." ... However, after his brothers had left for the Feast, **he went also**, not publicly, but in secret.

Notice the ©1984 NIV claims Jesus said "**not yet**." Then he went up.

Close call. Nice to see there is a Bible out there that accurately reports exactly what the Lord said. You know, that he actually told the truth to his brothers.

Where did the NASB translators and editors get this reading? Right out of the very same Greek New Testament text that the ESV got its erroneous readings.

Did the NASB editors and translators know leaving out "yet" is considered an error in the Original Autographs by the United Bible Societies' Greek New Testament committee? They did if they read Dr. Metzger's commentary—which they all should have...

> THE GOSPEL ACCORDING TO JOHN   185
>
> ἤθελεν more than counterbalances any considerations bearing on the more difficult versus the less difficult reading.
>
> 7.8 οὐκ {C} [handwritten: NOT ORIGINAL – I DO NOT GO UP YET] [handwritten: NOT ORIGINAL – I GO NOT UP YET]
>
> The reading οὔπω was introduced at an early date (it is attested by 𝔓⁶⁶, ⁷⁵) in order to alleviate the inconsistency between ver. 8 and ver. 10.

Bruce M. Metzger, *Textual Commentary on the Greek New Testament*, p. 185.

Here's Dr. Metzger saying someone tampered with the "original autograph" to fix what the beloved apostle John supposedly "originally" wrote so Jesus wouldn't be lying. But he calls it an "inconsistency."

So the Lord wasn't really lying; he was being "inconsistent." That one wouldn't fool your teacher if you "lost" your homework.

Sad. And that's the reading the translators and editors of the NASB chose to put in their Bible.

How can the Lord use the NASB? It calls him a liar. Would you use a book that called you a liar?

In case you were wondering, here's what the ESV reports about…

The doctrine of the sinlessness of Christ (round 2)

John 7:8,10	
ESV (©2001)	⁸You go up to the feast. I am not going up to this feast, for my time has not yet fully come." … ¹⁰But after his brothers had gone up to the feast, then he also went up, not publicly but in private.

You'd have to question the Lord's honesty with his brothers, wouldn't you? First he says he's not going to the feast in verse 8, and then he goes up two verses later! Surely he knew in advance exactly what he was planning to do.

How can the Lord use the ESV? Now the ESV and the NASB both report him to be a liar. (Would you use a book that made you out to be a liar?)

Maybe the Lord should use the New International Version?

Even though evangelicals are starting to dump it for the ESV, the NIV is still a bestseller—over 400 million sold.[20] And talk about endorsements...

> The NIV is wonderfully accurate according to the manuscripts of the Scriptures. It is reliable. And because it is accurate, it holds up under close scrutiny. It clearly is the Bible of choice for English speaking and reading people around the world.
> —**Charles Swindoll**, Chancellor, Dallas Theological Seminary[21]

Charles Swindoll, founder and Chairman of the Board of Insight for Living and author of more than 70 books

Alas, despite the glowing recommendations, look what happens if the Lord uses the NIV to teach...

The doctrine of inerrancy of the Scriptures

2 Samuel 21:19	
400 million **NIVs** (©1984) say:	In another battle with the Philistines at Gob, Elhanan ... killed Goliath ...
All the new **NIVs** (©2011) say:	In another battle with the Philistines at Gob, Elhanan...killed the brother of Goliath...

Every kid knows David killed Goliath, and yet Dr. Swindoll recommends the ©1984 NIV, which has **Elhanan** killing Goliath. **Four hundred million** of these NIV Bibles were printed this way.

But in 2011 it turns out that **Elhanan** killed **the brother of** Goliath.

---

[20] Amazon.com book description, *Holy Bible: New International Version* (hardcover), http://www.amazon.com/The-Holy-Bible-International-Version/dp/1444701533.

[21] WORDsearch, "New International Version (NIV)," Critical Reviews, https://www.word-searchbible.com/products/12533. (emphasis mine)

Talk about a three-ring circus!

Same verse ... Same Bible ... Saying **two DIFFERENT things.**

We assume the first 400 million were in error. Has the publisher issued a recall? Can you get a prorated refund? If the Lord's going to use the NIV, how does he deal with this problem?

This isn't good. Both Bibles are supposed to be the "word of the Lord." But how can they be?

Crazy isn't it?

It gets worse; the New ©2011 NIV assails...

The doctrine of Jesus Christ

Just what kind of man was the Lord? That depends on which Bible you believe.

Take a look...

Mark 1:41	
NIV (©1984)	Filled with compassion, Jesus reached out his hand and touched the man. "I am willing," he said. "Be clean!"
NIV (©2011)	**Jesus was indignant.** He reached out his hand and touched the man. "I am willing," he said. "Be clean!"

The Lord went from being **"filled with compassion"** to **"indignant"** in 26 years.

If you're upset by this reading, can you imagine how the Lord feels?

USA Today published an article on the NIV Bible update prior to its 2011 release. The paper quoted Keith Danby, president and chief executive officer of Biblica (which owns the rights to the NIV), who said...

> And we'll make sure we get it right this time...[22]

---

[22] Cathy Lynn Grossman, "Update of Popular 'NIV' Bible Due in 2011," *USA Today*, September 1, 2009, http://www.usatoday.com/news/religion/2009-09-01-Bible-translation_N.htm.

You know the Lord. Do you think they "got it right this time"? Maybe they should try again.

And you aren't going to believe what else the ©2011 NIV translators and editors did.

Remember the verse in John 7:8 where Jesus said he wasn't going up to the feast "**yet**"? You know, the one where Bruce Metzger has the apostle John calling the Lord a liar?

Well, take a peek at this…

John 7:8,10	
NIV (©1984)	You go to the Feast. I am **not yet going** up to this Feast, because for me the right time has not yet come." … However, after his brothers had left for the Feast, **he went also**…
NIV (©2011)	You go to the festival. **I am not ___ going** up to this festival, because my time has not yet fully come." … However, after his brothers had left for the festival, **he went also**…

The ©1984 NIV reports the Lord telling the truth to his brothers. Twenty-six years later the ©2011 NIV reports that **he lies** to them. This means…

The NIV contradicts the NIV … (again).

How odd. This is an absolute disaster for the NIV.

You'd think the Lord might not condemn a Bible that sold 400 million copies, but then you find out that it's got a verse that adversely affects…

The doctrine of the sinlessness of Christ (round 3)

If the Lord was a sinner, we're all doomed. How shall one sinner die in place of many sinners?

Matthew 5:22	
NIV (©2011)	But I tell you that **anyone who is angry** _____ with a brother or sister **will be subject to judgment**…
NKJV (©1982)	But I say to you that whoever **is angry** with his brother **without a cause** shall be in danger of the judgment…

OOPS … The NIV doesn't have the exception "**without a cause.**" (Maybe they were following one of the "oldest and best manuscripts" that contains this error.) Here's the problem…

If the NIV is true, then the Lord broke his own command here…

Mark 3:5	
NIV (©2011)	**He looked around at them in anger** and, deeply distressed at their stubborn hearts, said to the man, "Stretch out your hand." He stretched it out, and his hand was completely restored.

Does any of this really matter or is it just nitpicking over nonessential details? You be the judge…

There's a site called www.freethinkersbooks.com. The site is run by a guy who says he "had a 'born again' experience in high school." He says his goal is to help Christians "make better informed decisions about their religious beliefs." He goes on to say:

> Many Christians have been programmed to read the Bible **without ever seeing what it really says.**… We can help you help them understand their own book, because seriously studying the Bible has turned more Christians into Atheists than anything else.

He also says:

> There are many things about your beliefs that "professional Christians"—ministers, pastors, preachers, priests, seminary professors

and Bible college teachers—**know and are not telling you** [like] Jesus sinned by breaking his own command."[23]

And he's right if you believe the NIV quoted the Lord correctly.

But if the Lord actually used the words **"without a cause"** like it says in the NKJV, this guy is wrong.

How can the Lord use the NIV when it presents him as breaking his **own** commandment?

What's the Lord supposed to do?

1. How can the Lord possibly use either the ©1984 or ©2011 NIV? The '84 edition has Elhanan killing Goliath. The ©2011 edition calls him a liar.
2. How can the Lord use the NIV when it makes him out to be a sinner?
3. How can the Lord use the ESV, NASB, or NIV if they contain errors in the "originals"?
4. How can we follow a Lord who, according to the NASB, ESV, and NIV, lied to his brothers

Let's face it. The Lord taught against lying and then, according to the ©2011 NIV, ESV, and NASB versions of the Bible, he goes and does it.

They're reporting that your Savior is a dishonest hypocrite.

Would you use a book that describes you as a dishonest hypocrite? If you wouldn't, why would he?

Maybe he shouldn't use any Bible. After all, The Lord IS the Bible.

He knows it perfectly—100% without any errors or additions or subtractions. Why bother to bring any book to class with him? He should just teach the class without one.

Oh, wait, he can't do that either.

---

[23] Freethinker's Books, accessed August 2011, http://www.freethinkersbooks.com. At of the time of publication the website was under construction. (emphasis mine)

1. He's still got to quote words that appear in a book. A book called A Bible. Like we saw in Chapter 1, he's got to be able to tell us which animal skin covered the tabernacle and a whole lot more.
2. What kind of example would he set if the author of the book didn't show up with the book he wants you to read every day?

Maybe the Lord should just end the madness by bringing the Original Autographs to class with him?

Maybe he should just resurrect the Original Autographs and use those. Maybe the Lord is an "OA Onlyist." Most Christians are these days. We're told that's the one and only Bible that's inspired and inerrant.

Speaking of the "Original Autographs," they tell us that **all** Greek and Hebrew manuscripts, printed texts, and translations have errors in them. But you've already seen with your own eyes that the real experts (who assembled the Greek New Testament text from which the NIV, ESV, and NASB were translated) believe the "Original Autographs" contain errors as well.

Oy vey, what a mess.

So maybe the Lord will just use the originals—you know, the parchment that Moses and the prophets wrote on. It would be really cool if the Lord showed up hauling the two tables of stone written by the finger of God that he gave Moses. Maybe the Lord could even resurrect the "original" Jeremiah told Seraiah to pitch into the Euphrates River.

> And it shall be, when thou hast made an end of reading this book, *that* thou shalt bind a stone to it, and cast it into the midst of Euphrates. (Jeremiah 51:63)

If anyone could resurrect these pieces of history and somehow **assemble them** into **one book** called The Bible, which would be the hypothetical Bible everyone says is **inspired** and **inerrant**, surely the Lord could do it.

The question is, how does he bind the 4 tables of stone (Moses busted one set and the Lord had to make another), 39 multi-foot long scrolls, and literally hundreds of pieces of papyri into a book called "**The Bible of the Original Autographs**"? If he came to your church, maybe that's what he'd bring with him. It would be quite a **Bible**—all squashed between two gigantic covers.

He'd have to put it in a wheel barrel. He'll have a real tough time finding a passage in the pile, but that's the Bible he'd have to use **if only** the **originals** are **inspired** and **inerrant** like we are taught.

Somehow this just doesn't sound like something the Lord would do, does it?

With all the controversy, don't you wonder why the Lord didn't preserve the originals?…

Chapter Four

Why the Lord didn't preserve the original autographs

> But without faith it is impossible to please him: for he that cometh to God must believe that he is, and that he is a rewarder of them that diligently seek him. (Hebrews 11:6)

Everybody knows the original parchments and even the tables of stone the Lord gave Moses are long gone.

But look at how haphazardly the Lord treated them…

Originals burned:

> And it came to pass, *that* when Jehudi had read three or four leaves, he cut it with the penknife, and cast *it* into the fire that *was* on the hearth, until all the roll was consumed in the fire that *was* on the hearth. **(Jeremiah 36:23)**

Originals added to:

> Then took Jeremiah another roll, and gave it to Baruch the scribe, the son of Neriah; who wrote therein from the mouth of Jeremiah all the words of the book which Jehoiakim king of Judah had burned in the fire: and there were added besides unto them many like words. **(Jeremiah 36:32)**

Originals thrown into the river:

> And it shall be, when thou hast made an end of reading this book, *that* thou shalt bind a stone to it, and cast it into the midst of Euphrates: **(Jeremiah 51:63)**

Who knew?

But maybe there's a reason the Lord didn't preserve them.

Maybe he didn't preserve them because **he forces** men to **believe** his **promises** to **preserve** his words. The scripture says:

> "without faith *it is* impossible to please *him*." **(Hebrews 11:6)**

Take a look at these verses and see what you think…

- The words of the Lord are **pure** words: as silver tried in a furnace of earth, purified seven times. Thou shalt **keep them**, O Lord; thou shalt **preserve them** from this generation **for ever.** (Psalm 12:6–7)
- The counsel of the Lord standeth for ever, the **thoughts of his heart to all generations.** (Psalm 33:11)
- For the Lord is good; his mercy is everlasting; and **his truth *endureth* to all generations.** (Psalm 100:5)
- Thy word is **true** from the beginning: and **every one** of thy righteous judgments **endureth for ever.** (Psalm 119:160)
- But he answered and said, It is written, Man shall not live by bread alone, but by every word that proceedeth out of the mouth of God. (Matthew 4:4)
- For verily I say unto you, Till heaven and earth pass, one jot or one tittle **shall in no wise pass** from the law, till all be fulfilled. (Matthew 5:18)
- Heaven and earth shall pass away, **but my words shall not pass away.** (Matthew 24:35)
- Heaven and earth shall pass away: **but my words shall not pass away.** (Mark 13:31)
- Heaven and earth shall pass away: **but my words shall not pass away.** (Luke 21:33)

If you **believe** what he said, you will find that he has kept his word to keep his words.

If you don't **believe** his promise to keep his words, you'll never find them.

Some Textual Critics **believe** God inspired the original writings and then either lost them or scattered them across many manuscripts. They make a living trying to retrieve them—although some of the experts admit it's impossible.

Some **believe** you can't find all of God's words without error in any language, in any book on earth.

Others believe that we have 110% of the words—and they think this is a good thing.

For example, Professor Daniel Wallace of Dallas Theological Seminary says:

> Though textual criticism cannot yet produce certainty about the exact wording of the original, this uncertainty affects only about two percent of the text. And in that two percent support always exists for what the original said—never is one left with mere conjecture. In other words it is not that only 90 percent of the original text exists in the extant Greek manuscripts—rather, 110 percent exists. Textual criticism is not involved in reinventing the original; it is involved in discarding the spurious, in burning the dross to get to the gold.[1]

He doesn't get it. Having 110% of the words is really terrible because it means **men's words are mixed with God's words**. Even after more than 100 years the experts are still trying to determine which are which.

And if Textual Critics really have 110% of the words like he says, then how come they're still searching for *"The Original Bible"*?

Speaking of which, Dr. Randall Price, in *Searching for the Original Bible,* informs us:

> In regard to the New Testament, for over four-fifths of it, the Greek text is considered 100% certain ... Moreover, regarding the entire Bible, through the science of textual criticism at least 95% of the

---

[1] Daniel B. Wallace, *The Majority Text and the Original Text: Are They Identical?* Bible.org, accessed December 2012, http://Bible.org/article/majority-text-and-original-text-are-they-identical.

original text of the Old Testament has been recovered, and 99% of the New Testament.[2]

In summary, he claims...

Ninety-nine percent of the New Testament has been found and something over 80% of that is 100% certain but they're still looking for 1% of the text.

Evidently, we're supposed to be happy that they've actually recovered 99% of the New Testament. It would be interesting to see how they derived that data.

First of all, wouldn't you think the Lord would have provided those missing words by now? After all, it's been nearly 2,000 years since the New Testament was completed.

And secondly, how do you know that you have 99% of something that is unknown? It's not until you have determined the exact number of words or verses or whatever you're looking for that you can determine what percentage you don't have.

Maybe Price should have run that one past the math department at Liberty University before making that statement.

The strange thing is that even though they don't have all the parts, textual critics are sure that over 80% of it is good. But what about the other 15–20%?

None of this seems very scientific, does it? And yet they claim textual criticism is a "science."

Depending on whose books you read, some believe they've determined anywhere from 87–99.5% of God's original words. Dr. Daniel Wallace thinks 98%.

Dr. Maurice Robinson, associate professor of Greek at Southeastern Baptist Theological Seminary in Wake Forest, North Carolina, is an expert in textual criticism and coauthor of *The New Testament in the Origi-*

---

[2] Randall Price, *Searching for the Original Bible* (Eugene, OR: Harvest House, 2007), 208.

nal Greek: Byzantine Textform (2005). Dr. Robinson asserts that in the New Testament:

> ...over 85% of the text found in all manuscripts is identical.[3]

No one's arguing over the 85%...

It's the other 15% that's in question.

Assuming he's been awake and has paid attention to what's been going on in the Bible production business, we should fully expect that the Lord has intervened to make sure **all** of the verses and **all** of his original words made it into print. And, more importantly, made it into print in **one book**.

- **Even though** we are taught that the only "**inspired**" and "**inerrant**" Bible is the one made up of the Original Autographs, and
- **Even though** there is no Bible on earth containing the Original Autographs and **never was**, and
- **Even though** this is the politically correct position in most churches and schools today, and
- **Even though** it's called **heresy** to believe that the Lord **gathered the original readings** after the invention of the printing press and put them into **one book** in any language anywhere on earth,

Three questions remain...

1. Does it make any sense for the Lord to require you to believe in a "Bible" that doesn't exist?

2. Was the Lord unable or unwilling to deliver all of his words and only his words into a book?

3. Did he fail to deliver the last 15%?

To which we respond...

---

[3] Maurice A. Robinson, "The Case for the Byzantine Textform: A New Approach to 'Majority Text' Theory." Paper presented at the Southeastern Regional Evangelical Theological Society Meeting, Toccoa Falls, GA, March 8–9, 1991. (Available: Theological Research Exchange Network, www.tren.com).

- Is he a quarterback who gets the ball to the 15-yard line and chokes in the red zone?
- Is he an ace reliever who blows the save in the ninth?
- Is he the go-to shooter with the hot hand that misses the shot at the buzzer?
- Is he a gymnast who performs a great routine but fails to "stick" the landing?

Does that sound like your Savior?

No way. Your Lord was willing and able. We're getting to that soon.

The game changer was the invention of the printing press.

By the time Gutenberg invented the printing press, around 1440, biblical manuscripts had become adulterated with men's words. Among the 400,000 variants there are literally thousands of men's words maliciously and **purposefully inserted** into the manuscripts and masquerading as the very words of God.

What kind of Bible do you think God wants you to have? One that mixes his words with men's words or a Bible that contains only his holy words—only his words of truth?

The true Bible **cannot** be adulterated with men's words. It cannot contain errors. Because…

The Lord God of heaven and earth doesn't do mistakes.

He doesn't build a product with defective parts to hand down to his children.

And yet that's exactly what Christian educators teach when they say that only *"The Original Bible"* is/was inspired and inerrant. They claim that all physical Bibles (i.e., books) are not without error.

This claim is not new. For the past 250 years, the authenticity and reliability of the Holy Bible (meaning a real book) has been challenged by the doctrine of *"The Original Bible."* The *"Original Bible"* doctrine has permeated Christian culture today to the point where souls are lost because the only authority (i.e., The Book) has been stripped from the flock by teachers who leave them realizing that their Book is a mix of men's words and God's words.

Consider this book by Daniel Joseph Malane. He holds a bachelor's degree in religious studies from Santa Clara University. In *The Bible: "Word of God" or words of men? Truth versus the myths of Christian Fundamentalism,* Malane says:

> This work reviews the findings of modern Bible scholarship today, weighing the *facts* we know to be true about the Bible, against the claims made by its Christian Fundamentalist adherents.[4]

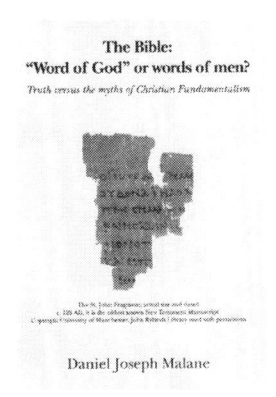

He then goes on to use "modern" Biblical scholarship to trash the Book. He points out **variant readings and contradictions** and concludes the Book is unreliable because it's adulterated.

This same scholarship is generally taught in fundamental and evangelical schools, colleges, and universities. They just don't bring it to the same conclusion.

They tell you that (a) the variants, contradictions, and errors don't affect doctrine, and (b) even though you don't have an infallible, inerrant Bible today, don't worry—because *"The Original Bible"* was all these and more.

But Malane asks:

> Can the Bible be used as a basis … that billions of people who follow other faiths will go to hell forever because they had not made Jesus their Lord and Savior? Is the Bible the one and only "Word of God," or do the scriptures of other world religions have an equal standing?[5]

Malane goes further…

> The original, autographed copies have been lost or destroyed…. We do not have the original manuscripts, and the ones that we do have

---
[4] Daniel Joseph Malane, *The Bible: "Word of God" or Words of Men? Truth Versus the Myths of Christian Fundamentalism* (Bloomington, IN: Xlibris, 2007), 8. (emphasis mine)
[5] Ibid., 7.

do not agree with each other. In light of these facts, how can we honestly believe that the New Testament is the inerrant, inspired Word of God?[6]

His summary is chilling:

> Since it has been established that our Bible is not inerrant and infallible, it follows that our Scripture is not greater than those of other religions, and our scripture does not contain the only one true way to God.[7]

It sounds like Mr. Malane understood what he was taught. The Bible, as error-filled as we have it, is a mix of men's words and God's words. And he brings the doctrine of *"The Original Bible"* to its logical conclusion—you can't trust The Book.

Since you can't trust The Book, it loses its authority and joins a happy parade of other religious books—no better, no worse.

The Lord to the Rescue

The only one who knows which words are authentic and which are imposters is the Lord. Who else is qualified to separate the wheat from the chaff?

After the invention of the printing press, his true words had to be gathered into **a book**. There has to be a corpus. Even as God prepared a body for the Lord Jesus Christ, so also he has located his words in **a book**.

It wasn't up to Erasmus (editor of the first printed edition of the Greek New Testament) in 1516 to find the true words, or even up to the King James translators in 1611. Nor did the Lord lose his words when the original manuscripts perished; and he did not become dependent upon textual critics of the 17th–21st centuries to find them.

---

[6] Ibid., 41–42. (emphasis mine)
[7] Ibid., 133.

The mission was far too important to leave up to mere men.

The words had to be assembled by the one who inspired them in the first place. Only he knows which words are his and which words are men's. Once he assembled his words into **one Bible**, all that's required for the Christian is to find the book of the Lord, then read it and believe it.

If the Lord cares about the number of hairs on your head, how much more must he care about you getting a copy of all his holy words?

Think about it. If he didn't preserve all his words in a book you can read, then maybe they weren't important enough for him to inspire in the first place.

So where does this leave the Lord?

If the Lord can't use or recommend the heavy-hitting NASB, ESV, or NIV, then he's stuck with the **one book** the Lord **absolutely cannot** choose.

You'll find out which one and why this is so next…

Chapter Five

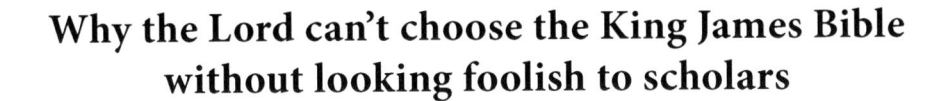

Why the Lord can't choose the King James Bible without looking foolish to scholars

> Let us go forth therefore unto him without the camp, bearing his reproach. (Hebrews 13:13)

If the Lord believes in the King James Bible **to the exclusion** of the rest, he'll have an august body of Christian leaders against him. He even risks being called a heretic—a spiritual criminal.

Consider this…

- **Dr. Jerry Falwell** [former Chancellor of Liberty University] announced that he had hired Dr. Harold Rawlings to "refute the 'King James Only' **cultic movement** that is **damaging** so many good churches today."[1]

- **William W. Combs, Th.D.**, Academic Dean and Professor of New Testament at Detroit Baptist Theological Seminary says that anyone who asserts "that the KJV, or any edition of it, could be infallible and inerrant" … "is not just wrong but **spouting heresy**."[2]

- **Dr. Robert Sumner** [editor of The Biblical Evangelist] warns about the "veritable fountain of **misinformation** and **deceptive double talk** on the subject of 'King James Onlyism.'"[3]

---

[1] David J. Stewart, "Is the King James Bible Inspired or Preserved?" Jesus-is-savior.com, accessed December 2012, http://www.jesus-is-savior.com/Bible/inspired_or_preserved.htm. (emphasis mine)

[2] Bill Combs, "Is the Preface to the King James Version Really an Embarrassment to the KJV-Only Movement?" *Theologically Driven* (blog), May 16, 2012, http://dbts.edu/blog/?p=2985. (emphasis mine)

[3] Stewart, "Is the King James Bible Inspired or Preserved?" (emphasis mine)

- Dr. James B. Williams [general editor of *From the Mind of God to the Mind of Man*] characterizes those who advocate a King James Only position as "**misinformers**" and as a "**cancerous sore.**"[4]

- Dr. James R. White [author of *The King James Only Controversy*] warns that King James Bible proponents are "**undercutting the very foundations of the faith itself.**"[5]

- Dr. Kevin Bauder [former president of Central Seminary Minneapolis, MN] in comparing hyper-fundamentalism and new evangelicalism says, "If anything, **King James Onlyism is worse**, for it shows **contempt** for the **Word of God**. It attacks the heart of Christianity by sitting in judgment over its source of authority."[6]

The Lord would have to be out of his mind to choose a King James Bible **to the exclusion** of the others as "**The**" Bible that contains **all** of his words and only His words without error.

According to "The World's Most Unusual University,"[7] that's blasphemy.

Consider this from Bob Jones University…

> The university requires use of the King James Version (KJV) of the Bible in its services and classrooms, but it does not hold that the KJV is the only acceptable English translation or that it has the same authority as the original Hebrew and Greek manuscripts.
>
> The King James Only Movement or more correctly, movements, since it has many variations—became a **divisive** force in fundamentalism only as conservative modern Bible translations, such as the New

---

[4] Thomas Strouse, "A Review of the Book *From the Mind of God to the Mind of Man*," StudytoAnswer.net, accessed December 2012, http://www.studytoanswer.net/bibleversions/mind_review.html. (emphasis mine)

[5] James R. White, *The King James Only Controversy: Can You Trust Modern Translations?* (Minneapolis, MN: Bethany House, 2009), 17. (emphasis mine)

[6] Kevin Bauder, "Now, About Those Differences, Part Twenty Three: Sinister Et Dexter," Central Seminary, accessed December 2012, http://www.centralseminary.edu/resources/nick-of-time/in-the-nick-of-time-archive/100-now-about-those-differences/229-now-about-those-differences-part-twenty-three-sinister-et-dexter

[7] "The World's Most Unusual University" was a former promotional slogan of Bob Jones University.

American Standard Bible (NASB) and the New International Version (NIV) began to appear in the 1970s. BJU has taken the position that orthodox Christians of the late nineteenth and early twentieth centuries (including fundamentalists) agreed that while the KJV was a substantially accurate translation, only the original manuscripts of the Bible written in Hebrew and Greek were infallible and inerrant. Bob Jones, Jr. called the KJV-only position a "**heresy**" and "in a very definite sense, **a blasphemy**."[8]

Looks like Dr. Bob's really upset. It makes you wonder which verse Dr. Bob Jr. used to prove that believing in a particular Bible is a heresy and blasphemy.

Now these fellows aren't **against** the King James Bible. They're just not completely **for** it. They all recommend you use it in conjunction with the rest. They are politically correct.

Anyway, Dr. Bob says "orthodox Christians" in the late 19th and early 20th centuries agreed that the KJV was a "substantially accurate" translation. Evidently anybody who thinks better of the King James Bible is unorthodox.

Don't you wonder who made the cut and got to be called "orthodox"? And who gets to make the call on what exactly "substantially accurate" means? Who gets to be the judge? And better, who appoints the judges?

Dr. Jones may have gotten this idea from the famous fundamentalist W.B. Riley, who said in 1917:

> … The accepted versions of the Bible are all substantially correct.[9]

What's interesting is that Riley didn't believe in a literal six-day creation.[10] Kind of a goofy position for a fundamentalist fighting the "menace of modernism," wouldn't you say?

---

[8] *Wikipedia*, s.v. "Bob Jones University," last modified November 30, 2012, http://en.wikipedia.org/wiki/Bob_Jones_University#King_James_Bible.
[9] William B. Riley, *The Menace of Modernism* (New York: Christian Alliance, 1917), 25.
[10] Ibid., 14. Cf. Ken Keathley, "What I've Been Reading (6)—Creationism Is Evolving," Between the Times, September 7, 2012, http://betweenthetimes.com/index.php/2012/09/07/what-ive-been-reading-6-creationism-is-evolving.

You'd think Dr. Bob Jr. and the others would have noticed this quote from Philip Schaff (1819–1893), Protestant theologian, church historian, author of *History of the Christian Church*, and president of the committee that translated the 1901 American Standard Version of the Bible:

...to the great mass of English readers King James's Version is virtually the inspired Word of God.[11]

Philip Schaff said that in 1891.

Sounds like there was a **"great mass"** of average Christians who believed the King James Bible was **the inspired word of God**. That was then. You were allowed to believe that then and only gentlemen like Philip Schaff and other academics who were promoting competing Bibles would make fun of you.

And it goes back even further…

David Daniell, professor of English at University College London and Honorary Fellow of Hertford and St. Catherine's Colleges, Oxford, wrote:

> From 1769, effectively, there grew the notion that the KJV was peculiarly, divinely, inspired.[12]

That's quite a lofty view of the Scripture in English, but this would be among the common people. And it's not surprising, for the Scripture says:

> …the common people heard him gladly. (Mark 12:37)

Certainly, the intelligentsia would never have shared that opinion. Looks like the Lord would have to condescend into the ranks of "the great unwashed" if he chooses the King James Bible.

Referring to the King James Bible, Anglican archbishop and famous philologist Richard Chenevix Trench (1807–1886) wrote in 1858…

---

[11] Philip Schaff, *A Companion to the Greek Testament and the English Version*, 4th ed. rev. (New York: Harper & Brothers, 1903), 413, as referenced in "Excerpt from *Double Jeopardy: The NASB Update*," chap. 1, by Laurence M. Vance, http://www.Biblebelievers.com/Vance3.html.

[12] David Daniell, *The Bible in English: Its History and Influence* (New Haven, CT: Yale University Press, 2003), 619.

> We must never leave out of sight that for a **great multitude** of readers the English Version **is not the translation** of an inspired Book, **but is itself the inspired book**....[13]

Evidently, there was "**a great multitude**" of readers back in 1858 who thought pretty highly of the King James Bible. But...

You're no longer allowed to believe the **King James Bible** is the inspired word of God like Christians did in 1858 and 1891. They call it heresy now.

W.B. Riley noticed the same kooky thing in his day. He wrote:

> Is the King James version absolutely inerrant? On this point we are inclined to think that, even unto comparatively recent years, such a theory has been entertained. The result of course, is to make a sort of fetish of the book.[14]

That was in 1917. Looks like there were a bunch of crazies back then who thought their Bible didn't have any mistakes in it.

If the Lord musters up enough courage to believe in the King James Bible in lieu of **any** other version, he'll be forced to admit that it's only "a substantially accurate translation" or he'll be accused of being a heretic, a deceptive misinformer, showing contempt for the Word of God and undercutting the very foundations of the faith itself.

Unfortunately, the Lord can't be politically correct. He can't please everybody by being "big tent inclusive." Unlike the professional Christian leaders, he **must** choose.

Why? Because the **Bible** is his **book**.

If the Lord chooses the King James Bible, he risks being called ignorant.

Schaff, Riley, and Trench weren't the only ones to observe the love many Christians had for that book.

---

[13] Richard Chenevix Trench, *On the Authorized Version of the New Testament in Connection with Recent Proposals for Its Revision* (New York: J.S. Redfield, 1858), 174. (Available: http://ia600308.us.archive.org/35/items/authorizedversio00trenrich/authorizedversio00trenrich.pdf).

[14] Riley, *Menace of Modernism,* 11–12.

Twentieth-century lecturer, Presbyterian minister, and author of *The Bible in America,* Reverend P. Marion Simms said:

> Unfortunately the King James Version came finally to be considered **as itself divinely inspired**, and the idea is not entirely gone even today. In fact, many people, who ought to be more intelligent, seem to think that the King James Version is the original Bible which God handed down out of heaven, all done up in English by the Lord himself.[15]

Simms wrote that in 1936.

He went on…

> Millions of men and women … who know absolutely nothing about how the Bible was originally written; … inevitably corrupted …; how the text has been revised again and again in scholarly efforts to eliminate the corruptions and recovered the original text; … This widespread ignorance is the chief explanation of the continued use of … the King James version … **only ignorance can deliberately prefer a Bible** with a known corrupted text, with numerous mistranslations that mislead, with many obsolete words that are not understood, and with frequent words, … so changed in meaning that the reader can have no idea what many texts teach.[16]

The Lord takes a great risk if he hauls a KJB into church.

By the way, the real issue isn't so much the translation. You can argue about how to translate a word, but the real issue is **what words** get translated. That's known as **"the text."**

You've already seen some textual differences where the professionals disagree and don't know which words are authentic and which are counterfeit. You've also seen how those differences materially harm Christian doctrine. But…

---

[15] P. Marion Simms, *The Bible in America: Versions That Have Played Their Part in the Making of the Republic* (New York: Wilson-Ericsson, 1936), 96.
[16] Ibid., 216.

It gets really wild when you get to the King James Bible.

That is a Bible the Lord absolutely can't bring to class with him.

Here's why…

Professor of New Testament Studies Daniel B. Wallace from Dallas Theological Seminary says:

> The problem is that the King James Bible is filled with readings which have been created by overly zealous scribes.[17]

Finally, someone is bold enough to tell it like it is. Dr. Wallace doesn't mince words. He gives it to you straight. The KJB is "filled" with "**created**" readings. There you have it. It's "**filled**" with **counterfeit** words "**created**" by men.

It would be nice if Dr. Wallace would inform Bob Jones University, which has been requiring the "use of the King James Version (KJV) of the Bible in its services and classrooms." They have unwittingly been exposing their "preacher boys" to these fabricated readings for over 80 years without a warning label. You'd think the BJU Bible department would be on top of this and call a halt to the travesty.

After all, what Dr. Wallace said **must** be true because he's taught Greek and New Testament courses on a graduate school level since 1979. He's written nine books, and his *Greek Grammar Beyond the Basics: An Exegetical Syntax of the New Testament* has become a standard textbook in colleges and seminaries. He is the senior New Testament editor of the NET Bible, and he's executive director for the Center for the Study of New Testament Manuscripts.

At least **16 complete verses** in the King James Bible caused Dr. Wallace to be concerned with "overly zealous scribes." These 16 verses are not in

---

[17] Daniel B. Wallace, "Why I Do Not Think the King James Bible Is the Best Translation Available Today," Bible.org, accessed December 2012, http://Bible.org/article/why-i-do-not-think-king-james-Bible-best-translation-available-today.
[18] Bible.org, "Daniel B. Wallace," http://Bible.org/users/daniel-b-wallace.

Codex Vaticanus or Codex Sinaiticus, and thus not in the NIV and ESV. The NASB brackets these verses with a note indicating that the verses were not in *"The Original Bible"* but **added** later, just like Dr. Wallace says.[19] Here's the list of verses as they appear in the King James Bible...

1. Matthew 17:21: Howbeit this kind goeth not out but by prayer and fasting.

2. Matthew 18:11: For the Son of man is come to save that which was lost.

3. Matthew 23:14: Woe unto you, scribes and Pharisees, hypocrites! for ye devour widows' houses, and for a pretence make long prayer: therefore ye shall receive the greater damnation.

4. Mark 7:16: If any man have ears to hear, let him hear.

5. Mark 9:44: Where their worm dieth not, and the fire is not quenched.

6. Mark 9:46: Where their worm dieth not, and the fire is not quenched.

7. Mark 11:26: But if ye do not forgive, neither will your Father which is in heaven forgive your trespasses.

8. Mark 15:28: And the scripture was fulfilled, which saith, And he was numbered with the transgressors.

9. Luke 17:36: Two men shall be in the field; the one shall be taken, and the other left.

10. Luke 23:17: For of necessity he must release one unto them at the feast.

11. John 5:4: For an angel went down at a certain season into the pool, and troubled the water: whosoever then first after the troubling of the water stepped in was made whole of whatsoever disease he had.

---

[19] "Early mss do not contain this v[erse]." See, for example, footnote to Matthew 17:21: http://www.Biblegateway.com/passage/?search=Matthew%2017:21&version=NASB.

12. Acts 8:37: And Philip said, If thou believest with all thine heart, thou mayest. And he answered and said, I believe that Jesus Christ is the Son of God.

13. Acts 15:34: Notwithstanding it pleased Silas to abide there still.

14. Acts 24:6b–8a: and would have judged according to our law. But the chief captain Lysias came upon us, and with great violence took him away out of our hands, Commanding his accusers to come unto thee.

15. Acts 28:29: And when he had said these words, the Jews departed, and had great reasoning among themselves.

16. Romans 16:24: The grace of our Lord Jesus Christ be with you all. Amen.

Here's an intriguing aside. All these verses are also omitted by...

The 1985 Roman Catholic New Jerusalem Bible

Carlo Maria Martini, S.J.

Of course, this isn't so surprising since a Jesuit cardinal was on the committee that assembled the Greek New Testament from which all these versions were translated. His name is **Carlo Maria Martini** (1927–2012). He was a Jesuit and Archbishop emeritus of Milan, Italy, a member of the College of Cardinals of the Roman Catholic Church, and was once was considered as possible successor to Pope John Paul II.

The Vatican said:

One must remember that he was the only Catholic member of the ecumenical committee that prepared the New Greek edition of the New Testament.[20]

---

[20] Holy See Press Office, College of Cardinals Biographical Notes, "Martini, Card. Carlo Maria, S.I.," updated January 9, 2012, http://www.vatican.va/news_services/press/documentazione/documents/cardinali_biografie/cardinali_bio_martini_cm_en.html.

It's also important to remember that the Roman Catholic hierarchy has "had it out" for the King James Bible and other English Bibles of the Reformation.

That's why they published their own competing version—The Douay-Rheims Bible (New Testament in 1582 and Old Testament in 1610).

The committee Martini served on is the one that selected the variant readings that make the NIV, NASB, ESV, NLT, and HCSB different from the King James Bible.

What's also fascinating is that...

The text ... was adopted internationally by Bible Societies, and following an agreement between **the Vatican** and the United Bible Societies it has served for the basis for translations and revisions made under their supervision. This marks a significant step with regard to **interconfessional** [read "ecumenical"] **relationships**.[21]

Do the fellows who recommend the NIV, NASB, ESV, and HCSB, etc., **even know** that a Jesuit priest helped to assemble the Greek New Testament text that underlies these versions? Shouldn't they be concerned?

Dr. Phillip G. Kayser, senior pastor of Dominion Covenant Church in Omaha, Nebraska, and author and textual expert Dr. Wilbur N. Pickering make these comments about the members of the UBS committee that assembled the Greek New Testament used by modern translations:

> Kurt Aland, Matthew Black, Carlo M. Martini, Bruce M. Metzger and Allen Wikgren are **not evangelicals, but liberals**. And it is surprising to see the degree of trust that evangelicals have placed in these men.

---

[21] Bobby Adams, Samuel C. Gipp, Eberhard Nestle, and Kurt Aland, *The Reintroduction of Textus Receptus Readings in the 26th Edition and Beyond of the Nestle/Aland Novum Testamentum—Graece* (Miamitown, OH: DayStar, 2006), 24, citing Aland et al., Introduction of the NA27, page 45, referring to the textual union between the UBS *Greek New Testament* and Nestle's *Novum Testamentum—Graece*. (emphasis mine)

Gordon Clark in *Logical Criticisms of Textual Criticism* has done good work in showing many of their unbelieving presuppositions.[22]

All this is bizarre enough, but it gets even more intriguing when you discover that there is a **Roman Catholic NIV Psalms**.

Who knew? The NIV text and words must be acceptable to the Church, otherwise they wouldn't publish it.

The goal of the Church of Rome has always been to eliminate competition.

They know the only authority claimed by Protestants is "the Bible." If they can eliminate the renegade Bible (i.e., The King James Bible), they go a long way to eliminating the competition and eventually bringing "the separated brethren" (referring to Protestant and Orthodox) back under the control of the Vatican.

Father Martini "in committee" working on the Greek New Testament that was used for the NIV, ESV, and NASB

Ideally, in their eyes there should be **One Bible**—the one approved by the Vatican that displays the "Imprimatur" (from Latin, "let it be printed"), which is a declaration authorizing Roman Catholic publication of a book. That's the goal.

But we're getting off track. The King James Bible has a real problem.

According to the experts, it contains...

---

[22] Phillip G. Kayser and Wilbur N. Pickering, *"Has God Indeed Said?" The Preservation of the Text of the New Testament* (Omaha, NE: Biblical Blueprints, 2009, 2004), footnote 34, 24. From the back cover: "*Wilbur Pickering* is a graduate of Dallas Theological Seminary and a proponent of the Majority Text. He is author of *The Identity of the New Testament Text* and was in charge of public relations for Wycliffe Bible Translators/Summer Institute of Linguistics in Brasilia. He is a missionary in Brazil. Phillip Kayser is the Senior Pastor of Dominion Covenant Church in Omaha, NE. He holds a M.Div. from Westminster Theological Seminary (California) and a Ph.D. from Whitefield Theological Seminary (Florida)."

16 verses NOT found in *"the Original Bible."*

We notice that these **16 verses are not** found in "the oldest and best" manuscripts (except Luke 23:17, which is found in one but not the other manuscript) and so don't show up in the NIV, ESV, and are bracketed by the NASB.

Imagine, 16 entire verses added to *"The Original Bible."*

NIV Psalms, Saint Joseph Catholic Edition, 1996

Dr. Wallace joins other scholars who say these verses were added to God's Word by **"pious scribes"** and **"orthodox"** (i.e., "born again") Christians who **corrupted the New Testament text** during the manuscript period in an effort to help God out—just like we saw in chapter 2.

You can read more about it in Dr. Bruce Metzger's book, *The Text of the New Testament: Its Transmission, Corruption, and Restoration,* or Dr. Bart Ehrman's book, *The Orthodox Corruption of Scripture: The Effect of Early Christological Controversies on the Text of the New Testament.* To these men, your beliefs are "orthodox."

Metzger and Ehrman claim the spurious words and verses eventually made their way into the King James Bible because the KJB translators followed a different Greek text (the Received Text) than is used by the NIV, ESV, and the NASB (which followed *UBS4* and *NA27*, whose different readings come from Vaticanus and Sinaiticus).

It was this **Received Text** that was printed by the Protestant reformers in the 16th century.

And yet fundamental and evangelical academics teach that the authentic Greek words underlying modern translations were **hidden for centuries** in libraries, monasteries, and holes in the ground.

They tell us that this true text was not restored until the mid to late 19th century when the two "oldest and best manuscripts" were discovered and used to reconstruct it. Codex Vaticanus was hidden by the popes and Codex Sinaiticus was hidden by the monks at St. Catherine's Monastery on Mount Sinai.

But why the Lord would **hide the true text of the Bible for 1,500 years** is still a mystery since he promised that every generation would have access to his holy words.

> For the Lord *is* good; his mercy *is* everlasting; and his truth *endureth* to all generations. (Psalm 100:5)

You would have thought that the Lord would have been more considerate. Notwithstanding, this is what they teach.

Here's another odd thing, most professors at most evangelical and fundamental colleges and universities know about the "added" verses, and yet they somehow recommend the King James Bible, New King James Version, the NIV, ESV, HCSB, and/or the NASB.

If the textual critics and fundamental and evangelical proponents of modern versions **actually believe** there are gross corruptions and additions in the King James Bible, then they should never, ever recommend it as an acceptable translation. More than that, they should warn the flock against it! How "good" can a translation be that translates men's words in place of God's words?

They'll tell you that it's a "good translation" of the underlying text. But they're reticent to inform you that they believe the text stinks.

If what they really believe is true, then…

No one should read it. It's a fraud. It should be burned. Get rid of it. It's a book masquerading as the Word of God when it's loaded with mistakes and the fraudulent words of "overly zealous scribes."

At the very least, if the King James Bible is no good, they should just keep their mouths shut and **not recommend it**. But they do.

Conversely, if the verses **should** be there and were **deleted** by men, then the modern translations are corrupt. Textual critics and fundamental and evangelical leaders should **never** recommend Bibles like the NIV, ESV, HCSB, and NASB because men **deleted** the very words of God.

You have to choose...
only one Bible or the many versions

You can't **honestly** recommend the King James Bible **and** the rest. And yet that's what is done *in From the Mind of God to the Mind of Man: A Layman's Guide to How We Got Our Bible...*

Bible believers can read, for example, the King James Version, the New American Standard Version, or the New King James Version and believe with all confidence that they are reading God's preserved word.[23]

By the way, here's what Dr. Bob Jones III said about *From the Mind of God...*

When it is written, the history of the American church will surely reveal this to be one of the 10 most important books published for believers in the 20th century.[24]

Pretty hefty recommendation, isn't it? Think about how many books were published for believers in the 20th century. Is this really one of them?

Here's the Statement about
Bible Translations from the BJU website...

Although Bob Jones University does not hold to a King James Only position, we continue to hold the widely-used King James Version (KJV) **as the campus standard** in the classroom and in the chapel pulpit. The position of the University on the translation issue has not changed since the founding of the school in 1927.

We believe in the verbal, plenary inspiration of the Bible **in the original manuscripts**, and we believe that God has supernaturally preserved every one of His inspired words for us today. However, from the founder to the present administration, we have never tak-

---

[23] James B. Williams and Randolph Shaylor, eds. *From the Mind of God to the Mind of Man: A Layman's Guide to How We Got Our Bible* (Greenville, SC: Ambassador-Emerald International, 1999), 216.

[24] Ibid., back cover.

en the position that there can be only one good translation in the English language.[25]

If the folks at BJU know that modern scholarship on the whole claims that the King James Bible has been adulterated with the words of men even to the point where **16 entire verses** have been wantonly and maliciously added to the corpus of God's Holy words, why do they hold it as "the campus standard"?

Here's a thought…

Why not let the Lord be our guide?

The Lord is honest and dependable. In him is no guile. He won't take the politically correct route. He will judge righteous judgment. And he won't misrepresent the facts.

So which Bible will the Lord choose? Before we get to that, consider…

He's got the most to lose.

Think about it; the Bible is supposed to be his book. He's the one who claims the words are his and won't pass away—"Heaven and earth shall pass away, but **my words** shall not pass away" (Matthew 24:35). He's the one who claims the words are important to him. You have to assume he cares about **which book** those words are found in.

He's the one who has magnified his word even above his name; "… thou hast magnified thy word above all thy name" (Psalm 138:2). And he has a name "which is above every name" (Philippians 2:9). His name is so important to him that anyone who blasphemed it "bought the farm." See Leviticus 24:11–16.

And speaking of his name…

---

[25] Bob Jones University, "Statement about Bible Translations," accessed November 2012, http://www.bju.edu/communities/ministries-schools/position-statements/translation.php. (emphasis mine)

He's the one who's staked his reputation on the words contained in a book.

The Lord said:

> A *good* name *is* rather to be chosen than great riches... (Proverbs 22:1)

His words represent him. They are a reflection on his good name. His truthfulness, character, honor, integrity, honesty, reliability, counsel, wisdom, glory, and all the rest of his glorious attributes **depend on** the truthfulness, accuracy, and dependability of each and "**every word that proceedeth out of the mouth of God**" (Matthew 4:4).

He's the one who claims his words are true: "**Thy word is truth**" (John 17:17).

Your eternal destiny is staked on the fact that every single word that comes out of his mouth is **true**. Your whole life and any hope you have of life beyond this one depends on the words that are written in **a book**.

He's the one who claims his words give you eternal life: "**Being born again ... by the word of God**" (1 Peter 1:23).

He's the one who claims "Man shall ... live by ... **every word** that proceedeth out of the mouth of God" (Matthew 4:4).

He's the one who says you will be judged by his words: "He that rejecteth me, and receiveth not **my words**, hath one that judgeth him: **the word that I have spoken,** the same shall judge him in the last day" (John 12:48).

He's the one who's on record as saying he's **honest**...

> God is not a man, **that he should lie** ... And also the Strength of Israel **will not lie** nor repent ... which **God, that cannot lie,** promised before the world began ... **it was impossible for God to lie.** (Numbers 23:19; 1 Samuel 15:29; Titus 1:2; Hebrews 6:18)

Take it to heart, beloved, your Lord...

- **Should not,**
- **Will not, and**

- **Cannot lie.**

It's simply impossible.

The preservation of the Scriptures has to be the work of God, not the work of men. It's a big job, and he's the only one you can trust to get the job done right.

God's words are so important that he put you on notice that there would be attempts to change and corrupt them.

- **Men pervert God's words…**

"And the burden of the LORD shall ye mention no more: for every man's word shall be his burden; for **ye have perverted the words of the living God**, of the LORD of hosts our God." (Jeremiah 23: 36)

- **Men corrupt God's words…**

"For we are not as **many**, which **corrupt the word of God**: but as of sincerity, but as of God, in the sight of God speak we in Christ." (2 Corinthians 2:17)

- **Men wrest** (to twist or turn from the proper course, application, use, meaning) **the words of God…**

"As also in all his epistles, speaking in them of these things; in which are some things hard to be understood, which they that are unlearned and unstable **wrest, as they do also the other scriptures**…" (2 Peter 3:16)

If what the Christian academic elites say is true, and if the Lord picks the **NIV, ESV, HCSB,** or **NASB** because they really contain **all** of his words and only his words, then you should …

1. Dump the King James Bible because it was defective from the get-go and
2. Blame the Lord Jesus Christ because he's responsible.

Think of what he's done…

Chapter Six

Did the Lord make a monumental, multi-generational error by allowing the King James Bible to be published in the first place?

"… What hath God wrought!" (Numbers 23:23)

Consider this: if the King James Bible doesn't contain **all his words without error** and is filled with counterfeit readings like Professor Daniel Wallace says, then…

The Lord messed up big time by allowing it to be published in the first place.

And he deserves the blame. You'd never want him on your payroll. What a gaffe.

Worse—he's been making a multi-generational mistake. You'd think after centuries of work he'd get it right.

What do I mean?

Think of it this way…

He allowed literally billions of copies of a defective Bible to be published over a 400-year period that had a cocktail of **16 verses added** by some unknown group of random men over the centuries.

Imagine—**16 whole verses**. You'd like to think better of him. What kind of God is that?

Plus, in addition to the 16 verses, the King James Bible has over 8,000 readings (i.e., words and/or phrases) that critics claim have been **added by men** over the centuries.

You can find the details in Dr. Jack Moorman's book *8,000 Differences Between the N.T. Greek Words of the King James Bible and the Modern Versions.*

Christian writer and author Leslie R. Keylock said in a 1985 article in *Moody Monthly*:

> Few people realize, for example, that thousands of errors have been found in the KJV.[1]

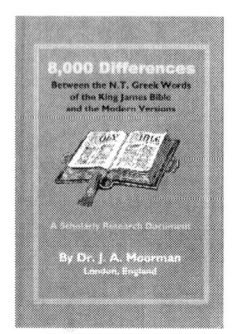

Jack Moorman's book detailing over 8,000 differences between the Greek texts of the KJB and NIV, ESV, and NASB

You would think that the Lord would have realized centuries ago that, as Professor Wallace says, "the Greek text which stands behind the King James Bible is **demonstrably inferior in certain places**"[2] than the text behind the NIV, ESV, HCSB, NASB, and a host of new versions.

So, those 16 verses and thousands of other readings must be forgeries—nothing more than the words of men instead of the words of God. It also makes you question what kind of God doesn't even know how many verses should be in his book.

You would think he would have made sure of the number of verses before he put it out.

And look at how the Lord really confused everybody's theology. He allowed 1 John 5:7 to be put in this corrupted Bible. Turns out, it's the only verse that can be used as a "proof text" for the Trinity and it's not found in the NIV, ESV, or NASB.

---

[1] The Old Time Gospel Ministry, "The Authorized King James Version of the Bible," 4, citing Leslie R. Keylock, "The Bible that Bears His Name," *Moody Monthly* (July–August 1985), accessed December 2012, http://www.theoldtimegospel.org/about/akjvb4.html.

[2] Daniel B. Wallace, "Why I Do Not Think the King James Bible Is the Best Translation Available Today," Bible.org, accessed December 2012, http://Bible.org/article/why-i-do-not-think-king-james-Bible-best-translation-available-today.

Did the Lord make a monumental, multi-generational error by allowing the King James Bible to be published in the first place?

	1 John 5:7–8
King James Bible (1611)	⁷For there are three that bear record in heaven, the Father, the Word, and the Holy Ghost: and these three are one. ⁸And there are three that bear witness in earth, the Spirit, and the water, and the blood: and these three agree in one.
New International Version (©2011)	⁷For there are three that testify: ⁸the Spirit, the water and the blood; and the three are in agreement.
English Standard Version (©2001)	⁷For there are three that testify: ⁸the Spirit and the water and the blood; and these three agree.
New American Standard Bible (©1995)	⁷For there are three that testify: ⁸the Spirit and the water and the blood; and the three are in agreement.

Notice that the King James Bible **adds** 24 words:

… the Father, the Word, and the Holy Ghost: and these three are one. 8And there are three that bear witness in earth … in one.

Let's hear from an expert. Dr. Charles Caldwell Ryrie (b. 1925) is a Christian writer and theologian. You may be familiar with him as the author of the Ryrie Study Bible, available in versions such as the KJV, NASB, and NIV.[3]

Dr. Ryrie says that there is no "proof text" in the Bible for the triunity of God.

Here's what Ryrie said in his book *Basic Theology*:[4]

> The N.T. contains no explicit statement of the doctrine of the triunity of God (since "these three are one" in 1 John 5:7 *is apparently not a part of the genuine text of Scripture*). (p. 60)

---

[3] Theopedia, s.v. "Charles C. Ryrie," accessed December 2012, http://www.theopedia.com/Charles_C._Ryrie.

[4] Charles Ryrie, *Basic Theology: A Popular Systematic Guide to Understanding Biblical Truth* (Chicago: Moody Publishers, 1999). (emphasis mine)

> But many doctrines are accepted by evangelicals as being clearly taught in the Scripture for which **there are no proof texts**. The doctrine of the Trinity furnishes the best example of this. It is fair to say that *the Bible does not clearly teach the doctrine of the Trinity. In fact, there is not even one proof text*, if by proof text we mean a verse or passage that "clearly" states that there is one God who exists in three persons. (p. 89)

He teaches us that "apparently" **"the Father, the Word, and the Holy Ghost: and these three are one"** is not **"genuine"** Scripture.

1 John 5:7 **would have been** a proof text **if** it was **in** the Bible. But it isn't.

It is in the King James Bible, **but** "apparently" this is an error. The words were **added** by men. More fraud.

Now the Lord **should** know what genuine Scripture is and what it is not. So why did he allow **"more than 5 billion copies"**[5] of this fraudulent, corrupt Bible to be distributed over the last 400 years?

Think of it. This has to be the biggest gaffe in the history of the earth.

In addition to this phony insertion to **prove the doctrine of the trinity**, God also allowed the forged 16 verses, thousands of other "flawed readings," errors in translation, and readings not based on "the oldest and best" manuscripts to be printed **billions of times**.

Maybe the Lord should be taken off the Bible job.

First, he allowed men to corrupt his words and then disseminate those corruptions into thousands of manuscripts all over the known world. Then after this monumental millennium mishap, he made matters worse when he had the opportunity to redeem himself **after** the invention of the printing press.

---

[5] Adam Nicholson, interview with Gwen Ifill, December 24, 2003, PBS Online NewsHour. (Available: http://www.pbs.org/newshour/bb/entertainment/july-dec03/nicolson_12-24.html). Historian Adam Nicholson is author of the national bestseller *God's Secretaries: The Making of the King James Bible*. Also see:
http://www.huffingtonpost.com/timothy-beal/happy-400th-birthday-king_b_836538.html; http://www.sltrib.com/sltrib/home/51258251-76/Bible-james-english-king.html.csp; http://www.calvarychurch.com/site/files%5Clookingup%5CLU05-08-2011.pdf.

Did the Lord make a monumental, multi-generational error by allowing the King James Bible to be published in the first place?

Wouldn't his "foreknowledge" tell him that the Greek text on which the perennial best-selling King James Bible stands...

"was not based on early manuscripts, not reliably edited, and consequently **not trustworthy**," according to popular apologist and author Dr. Norman Geisler?

And he ought to know. Dr. Norman Geisler is

> the author or co-author of some 70 books and hundreds of articles. He has taught theology, philosophy, and apologetics on the college or graduate level for 50 years. He has spoken or debated in some 26 countries on six continents. He has a B.A, M.A., Th.B., and Ph.D (in philosophy). ... He has taught at some of the top Seminaries in the United States, including Trinity Evangelical and Dallas Seminary and currently he is Distinguished Professor of Apologetics at Veritas Evangelical Seminary in Murrieta, CA.[6]

What's even more outrageous is why the Lord allowed William Tyndale (who produced the first printed N.T. in the English language in 1525) and John Rogers (Matthew's Bible, 1537) to be burned at the stake. He let Miles Coverdale (editor of the Coverdale Bible—the first complete Bible in English, 1535) lose three houses all in the struggle to ultimately produce an English New Testament whose underlying text, according to Dr. Geisler, is "**not trustworthy**."

Did the Lord know that the Greek New Testament he was providing to believers during the Reformation was "**not trustworthy**"? Dr. Geisler knew.

Why wasn't the Lord more on the ball than that?

The Lord **could have** trotted out the "oldest and best manuscripts" so that they could be used in the production of the early English and foreign language Bibles including the Greek New and Hebrew Old Testaments right after the invention of the printing press. But no; he missed his chance.

---

[6] Norman L. Geisler and William E. Nix, *A General Introduction to the Bible* (Chicago: Moody Bible Institute, 1968), 384.

Only after he put out the **defective** product **first** did he finally wake up 400 years later and allow men to "find" the "oldest and best" manuscripts so that all modern versions could be translated from them.

Evidently, the Lord turned out to be a choke artist.

What's really criminal about this is that the Lord **knew** where the two "oldest and best" manuscripts were hidden all along. And he let error and confusion multiply.

He **finally** delivers these manuscripts up to have their readings included in the critical Greek New Testament that underlies the NIV, ESV, HCSB, and NASB text published in 1881. That's over 430 years from the invention of the printing press.

How can you trust someone who makes these kinds of blunders?

After a move like that, if the Lord Jesus Christ was on *Celebrity Apprentice,* Trump would have to say: "You're fired!"

But it gets worse. Why on earth did the Lord allow this defective book to be directly...

Translated into more than 760 languages?

Sir Winston Churchill said that the King James Bible...

> superseded all other versions ... [and] **has been translated into more than seven hundred and sixty tongues.**[7]

Why did he allow the King James Bible to become "**the best-selling book of all time**"?[8] All he did was expose more people to more error.

---

[7] Winston Churchill, *Churchill's History of the English-Speaking Peoples,* edited by Henry Steele Commager (1958, reprint, New York: Barnes and Noble Books, 1995), 160.
[8] Ward Allen, *Translating for King James* (Nashville, TN: Vanderbilt Press, 1969), back cover.

Did the Lord make a monumental, multi-generational error by allowing the King James Bible to be published in the first place?

According to publishing giant Thomas Nelson, Inc., he let this error-strewn book become "the most influential book ever published in the English language."[9]

And worse, he let this monstrosity become "**the Bible for the masses, or 'the people's Bible,'**" again according to Thomas Nelson, Inc.[10]

Because he allowed this imposter of a Bible in print for so long, he even faked out Dr. Henry Morris, founder and president emeritus of Institute for Creation Research.

Morris was so deceived that he said:

> I believe, therefore, after studying, teaching, and loving the Bible for over 55 years, that Christians—especially creationists!—need to hang on to their old King James Bibles as long as they live.
>
> **God has uniquely blessed** it in the history of England and America, **in the great revivals, in the worldwide missionary movement, and in the personal lives of believers more than He has through all the rest of the versions put together.**
>
> The King James Bible is ... **the most reliable of any that we have or ever will have**, until Christ returns.[11]

Then there's that other deluded believer, John Bunyan

A university man who met Bunyan on the road near Cambridge said to Bunyan…

> "How dare you preach, not having the original Scriptures?" "Do you have them—the copies written by the apostles and prophets?" asked Bu-

John Bunyan
(1628–1688)

---

[9] Nelson KJV, "About the Translation," accessed November 2012, http://www.kjv400celebration.com/about_the_translation.php.
[10] Ibid.
[11] Henry M. Morris, "A Creationist's Defense of the King James Bible," Institute for Creation Research, accessed December 2012, http://www.icr.org/home/resources/resources_tracts_kjv/. (emphasis mine)

nyan. "No," replied the scholar. "But I have what I believe to be a true copy of the original." "And I," said Bunyan, "believe the English Bible to be a true copy too."[12]

Poor John Bunyan; he actually thought the **King James Bible** was a true copy of the original.

And the Lord completely hoodwinked **Queen Victoria** of England. She told…

> an African chieftain to whom she presented a copy of the 1611 Holy Bible: *"That Book accounts for the supremacy of England."*[13]

Here's a fodder for real political laugher.

Supposedly, the Lord provided a Bible based on an inferior text that came from late-model manuscripts that were loaded with errors and as a consequence…

> Public officials on all levels of governments, including presidents, have taken their oath of office with the King James Bible.[14]

Evidently the Lord wasn't too concerned about the testimony of his words when he allowed many US presidents to swear an oath on this defective Bible.

Whether it's swearing an **oath** to uphold the Constitution or to tell the "**whole** truth and nothing but the truth," if you are swearing on a King James Bible that **does not** contain the "**whole** truth and **nothing** but the truth," your oath is ludicrous.

If God doesn't care enough to give you the **whole** truth and **nothing but** the truth in his Book, then why should you worry about lying under an oath taken on a defective, dishonest Bible?

---

[12] Sarah's Albion Blog, "The KJB Story 1611–2011, The Word of a King," quoting W. Burgess McCreary, *John Bunyan, The Immortal Dreamer*, February 5, 2011, http://sarahmaidofalbion.blogspot.com/2011/02/kjb-story-1611-2011-word-of-king.html.
[13] Ibid., quoting Henry H. Halley, *Halley's Bible Handbook* (New York: Regency, 1965), 18.
[14] The Official King James Bible Online, "King James Bible News," April 12, 2011, http://www.kingjamesbibleonline.org/King-James-Bible-News/.

Did the Lord make a monumental, multi-generational error by allowing the King James Bible to be published in the first place?

He should have shut production down from the get-go—as soon as he saw the first disgusting units roll off the press. At the very least, he should have done what any reputable and responsible manufacturer would do; he should have issued a recall. Car manufacturers do it, so why shouldn't it be required of him?

What the Lord Jesus Christ should have known and when should he have known it?

Let's face it, he should never have put such a publication on the market to begin with. The Lord should have known that many readings in the King James Bible were "created by overly zealous scribes." Professor Dan Wallace knew. Evidently the Lord didn't.

It's unconscionable that he even allows it to exist today, especially when he's got the power to stop this madness

It makes him look foolish to have published and marketed **billions of copies** of such a defective book, seeded with the fraudulent words of men in literally thousands of places for 400 years with his name all over it.

You should vomit the King James Bible out of your mouth. It's worse than lukewarm. It's unclean, impure, and most heinous of all, it's been masquerading as God's truth when there are versions closer to *"The Original Bible."*

Every Christian leader recommending a modern version believes the King James Bible is **defective** or they wouldn't be endorsing a competing book. And who's to blame for this shameful state of affairs in the Bible world?

The blame lies squarely at the feet of the Lord Jesus Christ. He, his Father, and the Holy Spirit have made a terrible misjudgment.

Could any of this be true? Or…

Chapter Seven

Maybe the Lord Jesus Christ isn't a loser after all

> Wherefore God also hath highly exalted him, and given him a name which is above every name… (Philippians 2:9)

Maybe there's a reason the King James Bible is the "**most influential and revered English Bible that has ever existed**," as Wheaton College Professor Leland Ryken says.[1]

Maybe there's a reason it "is probably the most beautiful piece of writing in all the literature of the world," according to newspaperman and famous agnostic H. L. Mencken.[2]

Maybe there's a reason that "the English language was largely shaped by one book—the King James Version of the Bible," according to historian Paul Cross.[3]

Maybe there's a reason the King James Bible was "the very greatest literary achievement in the English language," according to historian Alister McGrath.[4]

Maybe there's a reason "[p]riests, atheists, skeptics, devotees, agnostics, and evangelists, are generally agreed that the Authorized Version of the

---

[1] Leland Ryken, *The Legacy of the King James Bible: Celebrating 400 Years of the Most Influential English Translation* (Wheaton, IL: Crossway Books, 2011), 13. (emphasis mine)
[2] David Sorenson, "The Most Influential Book in the World: How the King James Version Has Changed the World," Ministry 127, May 4, 2011, http://ministry127.com/christian-living/the-most-influential-book-in-the-world.
[3] Ibid.
[4] Ibid.

English Bible is the best example of English literature that the world has even seen," according to Williams Lyon Phelps of Yale University.[5]

Maybe there's a reason it's "rightly regarded **as the most influential book in the history of English civilization**," according to Compton's Encyclopedia.[6]

Maybe there's a reason it "has **contributed 257 idioms** to English, **more than any other single source**, including Shakespeare," according to Oxford University Press (China).[6]

Maybe there's a reason that "**more than 1,000 churches** worldwide subscribe to a statement of faith that this 400-year-old translation '**preserves the very words of God in** the form in which He wished them to be represented in the universal language of these last days: **English**,'" as reported by Gordon Campbell, author of *Bible: The Story of the King James Version 1611–2011.*[8]

Maybe there's a reason "[o]n a historical scale, the sheer longevity of this version is a phenomenon, without parallel … '**King James' is still the best-selling book in the world** … In the story of the earth on which we live, its influence cannot be calculated," according to Professor David Daniell.[9]

Maybe there's a reason that it "**lives on the ear, like music that can never be forgotten**, like the sound of church bells," according to British theologian and hymn writer (Faith of Our Fathers) F.W. Faber (1814–1863).[10]

Maybe there's a reason that the King James Bible is **the only** Bible whose words were heard simultaneously by **25% of the earth's population**

---

[5] Ibid.
[6] Compton's Online Edition, downloaded from America Online, May 26, 1995.
[7] Oxford University Press (China), "In the beginning was the Word," OUP China 50th Anniversary Exhibition, April 18, 2011, http://www.oupchina.com.hk/50thanniversary/exhibition_press.asp. (emphasis mine)18.
[8] Cited in Ron Grossman, "For Some Christians, King James Is the Only Bible," *Chicago Tribune,* March 12, 2011, http://articles.chicagotribune.com/2011-03-12/news/ct-met-king-james-20110311_1_king-james-Bible-translation-Bible-study-class. (emphasis mine)
[9] David Daniell, *The Bible in English: Its History and Influence* (New Haven, CT: Yale University Press, 2003), 427. (emphasis mine)
[10] *Wikipedia,* s.v. "Frederick William Faber," accessed December 2012, http://en.wikipedia.org/wiki/F._W._Faber. (emphasis mine)

when the Apollo 8 crew made a Christmas Eve 1968 television broadcast in which they read the first 10 verses from the Book of Genesis.

> According to TV Guide (10–16 May 1969), the live television broadcast on Christmas Eve was watched by a quarter of the people on Earth, **1 billion people** in 64 countries. The U.S. Postal Service issued a stamp commemorating the event.... To date; no other English Bible translation has been read from outer space.[11]

Maybe there's a reason its "influence goes beyond the land of English-speaking people and extends to many parts of the world through the vigorous ministries of English-speaking missionaries. If any Bible translation activity took place in these mission fields, the KJB was often found to be the model text or even the source text from which the local translation was made."[12]

If the King James Bible isn't **THE Holy Bible**, then it's the best imposter in the history of mankind.

Maybe the Lord Jesus Christ isn't a loser after all.

Maybe the inconceivable happened.

Maybe the Lord is a brilliant wordsmith, master publisher, and professional marketer who gathered his words found in manuscripts and early printed texts, polished them, and assembled them into the text of an English Bible 160 years after the invention of the printing press.

And maybe some Christian leaders just missed the move because they were searching for *"The Original Bible"* instead.

---

[11] Helen Moore and Julian Reid, eds., *Manifold Greatness: The Making of the King James Bible* (Oxford, England: Bodleian Library, University of Oxford, 2011). (emphasis mine)

[12] Cited in Ron Grossman, "For Some Christians, King James Is the Only Bible," *Chicago Tribune*, March 12, 2011, http://articles.chicagotribune.com/2011-03-12/news/ct-met-king-james-20110311_1_king-james-Bible-translation-Bible-study-class. (emphasis mine)

Maybe the book of the LORD IS the King James Bible to the **exclusion of all** others.

Maybe we've been taught to look through the wrong end of the looking glass. Doesn't it make sense that the Lord must be the author and promoter of the "best-selling" Bible ever printed?

The Lord actually did what no man on earth could do.

Maybe he assembled the words of the original inspired autographs into **one book** in o**ne language after the invention of the printing press,** all the while knowing that this new technology would disseminate billions of copies of his life-giving words to the far reaches of the planet.

Maybe he gathered all the authentic variant readings that were scattered throughout the manuscripts, sifted through them in a moment of time and gradually fed them to the editors and printers of his word during the 16th and early 17th centuries.

Maybe he assembled a database of authentic readings and published them in **one book**. He had to do it; no one else could because no one else is certain which readings are authentic.

The primary difference in Bible versions and the whole "King James Only" controversy is a debate over which **variant readings** are authentic, and **not** so much the way the text is translated. It's about the text. It's about which words are authentic and which are forgeries.

Once you have determined **which words** are authentic, then and only then can you decide how to translate them. Critics talking about which "translation" someone "prefers" is simply an issue avoidance technique. It's great for controlling the conversation, but it's always at the expense of the Lord's integrity.

So the Bible version issue and the ensuing arguments over the past hundred years really have been over which variants (differences in words and verses) are authentic and which are fake; which words are the "pure" words of God and which are the words of men.

All textual critics know **"it's all about variants."**[13]

Luke 13:35 gives us an example of how textual variants in the Greek text affect the translation of different versions.

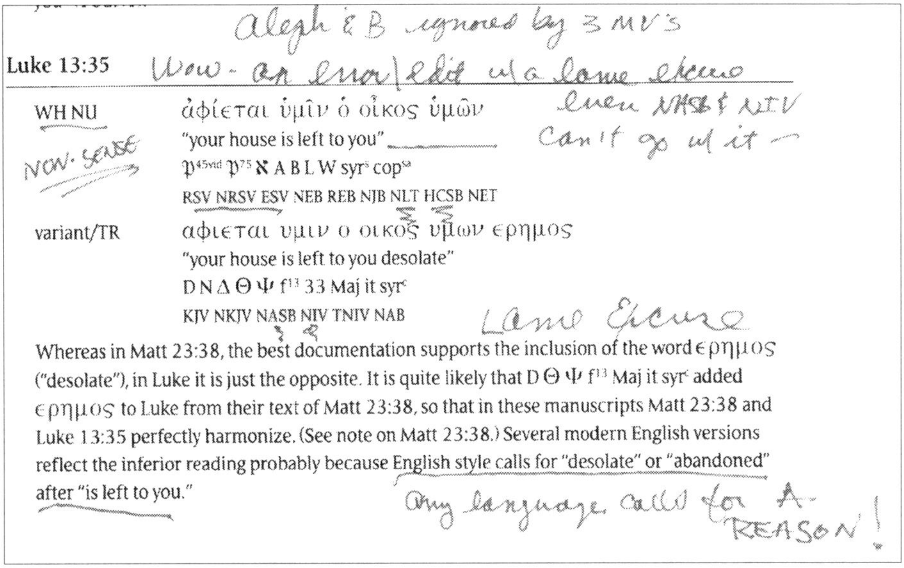

> Luke 13:35
>
> *[handwritten: aleph & B ignored by 3 MV's]*
> *[handwritten: Wow - an error/edit w/ a lame excuse]*
>
> **WH NU**
> ἀφίεται ὑμῖν ὁ οἶκος ὑμῶν
> "your house is left to you"
> 𝔓45vid 𝔓75 ℵ A B L W syr^s cop^sa
> RSV NRSV ESV NEB REB NJB NLT HCSB NET
>
> *[handwritten: even NASB & NIV can't go w/ it]*
> *[handwritten left margin: NOW-SENSE]*
>
> **variant/TR**
> ἀφίεται υμιν ο οἶκος υμων ερημος
> "your house is left to you desolate"
> D N Δ Θ Ψ f[13] 33 Maj it syr^c
> KJV NKJV NASB NIV TNIV NAB *[handwritten: Lame Excuse]*
>
> Whereas in Matt 23:38, the best documentation supports the inclusion of the word ερημος ("desolate"), in Luke it is just the opposite. It is quite likely that D Θ Ψ f[13] Maj it syr^c added ερημος to Luke from their text of Matt 23:38, so that in these manuscripts Matt 23:38 and Luke 13:35 perfectly harmonize. (See note on Matt 23:38.) Several modern English versions reflect the inferior reading probably because English style calls for "desolate" or "abandoned" after "is left to you."
>
> *[handwritten: Any language calls for A REASON!]*

Philip W. Comfort, *New Testament Text and Translation Commentary*, p. 213.

Note that the RSV, NRSV, ESV, NLT, and HCSB include one variant in their Bibles and the KJV, NKJV, NASB, NIV, TNIV, and NAB put the other in theirs.

So, …

On the one hand, there is **a complete set** of variants that has remained unchanged for the past 400 years as presented in the King James Bible.

On the other hand, there is **a competing set** of **unstable, uncertain, and not finalized** textual variants that have been popularly in print since 1881.

This competing set of variants is not set in stone because nobody has the authority to do it or the **power** to enforce it.

---

[13] Eldon Jay Epp, "It's All about Variants: A Variant-Conscious Approach to New Testament Textual Criticism," *Harvard Theological Review,* vol. 100, no. 3 (July 2007): 275–308 (DOI: http://dx.doi.org/10.1017/S0017816007001599). (emphasis mine)

What applies to the **16 verses** cited earlier also applies to **thousands** of other words and verses as well. The propaganda that these variants **do not affect Christian doctrine** has already been shown to be false, as you have seen with your own eyes.

At the end of the day, the only one who's qualified and who has the authority to select the authentic variants and put them in print is our high priest, the Lord Jesus Christ.

It's precisely because of the competing variant readings that the Lord is **forced** by his own integrity to drop his authentic words into **a book—One Book**. If he doesn't then he's a defective God.

After all, he's the one who promised you could know "the **certainty of the words of truth**; that thou mightest answer **the words of truth** to them that send unto thee" (Proverbs 22:21).

Modern textual critics would have us believe that although God thinks his words are really important, they aren't important enough for him to gather them in one place where they can be put on display for the whole world to see.

No way. This whole idea that the true readings are "out there" and that "they're working on it" is absurd on its face. It's illogical and unreasonable.

Consider Ezra, Chapter 2.

When the children of Israel, who had been carried away by Nebuchadnezzar, came again unto Jerusalem and Judah, a question arose as to who could be reckoned a priest. They had a register, and if your name was not found in it, you were "**as polluted, put from the priesthood**" (see Ezra 2:62).

Even so, any words or verses found in the Bible that are not "found in the register" must be put away "**as polluted**" from the rest of the holy words of God. If God did this to the priests, wouldn't he be just as zealous for his holy words?

When it came to verifying who really was a priest, they had to wait "till there stood up a priest with Urim and with Thummim" (Ezra 2:63).

When it comes to the holy words of God, the only one who knows 100% which are and which are not his words is the Lord Jesus Christ. He is the high priest with the Urim and with Thummim.

When it comes to **his children, "The Lord knoweth them that are his"** (2 Timothy 2:19).

When it comes to variant readings, the same truth applies: "The Lord knoweth them that are his."

He's made his selection, and he's been displaying the same text **unchanged** for the past 400 years. In fact, he's so confident in it that he's had it produced billions of times.

And think about this…

The Bible is one book.

It's a combination of the Hebrew Old and Greek New Testaments.

The two Testaments **had to be** combined into one book.

The one book **had to be** in one language to qualify as "**The Bible.**" Remember, *bible* means book.

You can't **honestly** tell people you **believe** in the Bible and not be able to show them **the book** you believe in.

The Lord joined the two testaments into one Book, and just like man and woman, "and they twain shall be one flesh … Wherefore they are no more twain, but one flesh. What therefore God hath joined together, let not man put asunder" (Matthew 19:5–6).

Why is one Bible necessary?

After the invention of the printing press, the Lord picked English as his language of choice. What other language would you suggest?

Didn't they teach us that proper Bible study is to "compare Scripture with Scripture"? If the Old Testament is Scripture and the New Testament is Scripture, how else can you compare Scripture with Scripture unless it can be done in one language?

Sure, you can compare New Testament Greek words to other New Testament Greek words (assuming you even buy the theory that the New Testament was originally written completely in Greek, which we'll examine in more detail later) and you can compare Old Testament Hebrew words with other Old Testament Hebrew words, but you can't compare words in the whole Bible unless it's been translated into one language.

Does it sound like your God to manufacture a fragmented Bible?

No engineer or developer would do that. And no businessman is stupid enough to put a product like that on the market. It's an insult to the Lord of Hosts to even suggest that he would do such a thing.

What about readability? One of the common arguments for using the NIV is that it's easier to understand. But look…

The KJB outperforms the NIV 5 to 1 in "taste tests."

A 1998 Barna Research Group poll of adults 18 years old and up found that:

> The King James Version is **more likely to be the Bible read** during the week than is the NIV **by a 5:1 ratio.**[14]

How about this from *USA Today*?

> Although there are two dozen English-language Bibles in many contemporary translations, **the King James Version reigns even more supreme among those who actually read their Bibles: 82% of those who read the Good Book at least once a month rely on the translation that first brought the Scripture to the English-speaking masses worldwide.**[15]

That's funny; Dr. Norman Geisler in his *Notes on Bible Versions* says…

---

[14] Barna Research, "Data and Trends: Answers to Frequently Asked Questions," data collated from several surveys through 1998, accessed December 2012, http://web.archive.org/web/19990508110144/http://www.barna.org/PageStats.htm. (emphasis mine)

[15] Cathy Lynn Grossman, "Bible Readers Prefer King James Version," *USA Today,* updated April 21, 2011, http://www.usatoday.com/news/religion/2011-04-21-king-james-Bible.htm. (emphasis mine)

> The King James Version (1611) ... died of "old age," including (1) outdated language, (2) an outdated text, (3) an outdated knowledge of the languages by the translators.[16]

Why hasn't anyone informed Christian bookstores that they're selling a zombie Bible that nobody wants?

A Gallup Poll for the American Bible Society found that...

> in households with a Bible, 54 percent owned the King James, followed by 15 percent for the New International Version and single-digit responses for the [rest].[17]

So how do you know which "Brand" of Bible the Lord would walk into church with?

That's easy...

Just look for the one he's been using for the past **400 years**; the one he produced billions of copies of and that's been translated into over **760 languages**, that's **read more** than any other Bible, and has influenced more people than any other book on the face of the earth.

We'll get to the question of which edition/printing of the King James Bible is "the Bible" soon. But first, ...

What about just updating the KJB language?

Maybe the Lord will bring the New ©1982 King James Version into church with him. After all, everyone believes it's pretty much the same as the King James Bible but with updated English for easier reading.

Let's see if he will...

---

[16] Norman Geisler, *Bible Translations: Which Ones Are Best?* Complete PowerPoint Library CD © 2008.

[17] "Poll: Americans Have Contradictory Desires in Choosing Bibles," *Peninsula Clarion* (Alaska), May 4, 2001, http://peninsulaclarion.com/stories/050401/rel_050401rel0100001.shtml.

Chapter Eight

Why can't the Lord choose the ©1982 New King James Version?

If any man will do his will, he shall know of the doctrine, whether it be of God, or whether I speak of myself. (John 7:17)

Here's a question about the ©1982 NKJV that nobody asks…

Why did it need to be produced?

Did the Lord decide that the 1611 Authorized Version he'd been blessing for 371 years just didn't cut it anymore? When did the best-selling, most read Bible of all time become insufficient to meet the needs of his people?

Here's a theological question:

Do you believe that just because someone publishes a book with the title "Bible" on it that it has to be "God's will"?

How many things have you done that were definitely "God's will"?

Likewise, just because some academic, scholarly Christian contracts his translation services to a businessman, does it automatically follow that it's "God's will" just because he's agreed to work on a book titled "Bible"?

There have been well over 100 English Bible versions published in the last hundred years. Do you think the Lord was behind them all? Even if their publishers and committee members did, that doesn't make it so.

Consider this…

If the Lord chooses the ©1982 NKJV then he would be **undermining the integrity of the brand** that he established over 400 years ago.

Top brands distinguish themselves by setting **a standard of quality** that all pretenders to the throne must meet or be forever lost in the ordinary.

You always get what you expect from top brands because they consistently prove themselves dependable. Their quality doesn't change over time. They give you confidence. That's why you trust them.

It's why people buy jewelry from Tiffany's, luxury automobiles from Mercedes, and landmark residential condominiums from Trump.

Love 'em or hate 'em, the Trumps are some of the most successful entrepreneurs on earth.

From left: Jack McElroy, Eric Trump, Susan McElroy, J.T. Foxx

The Trump name is synonymous with some of the most prestigious projects around the world—from deluxe residential condominiums and world-renowned architecturally significant hotels to premier golf courses and luxury resorts.

The Trump brand stands at the forefront of global real estate providing the highest level of exclusivity. They have branded prestigious landmarks around the world; from New York, Toronto, Chicago, and Los Angeles to Istanbul, Panama City, Seoul, and Manila.

> The Trump Organization is owned and managed by the Trump family with Donald Trump as its CEO and three of his eldest children—Donald Trump Jr., Ivanka Trump, and Eric Trump serving as Executive Vice Presidents within the organization.[1]

---

[1] *Wikipedia*, s.v. "The Trump Organization," last modified November 29, 2012, http://en.wikipedia.org/wiki/The_Trump_Organization.

Their properties exude luxury and stand for everything that the Trump brand signifies—something they are proud of when their projects are completed.

Is the Lord any less proud of his landmark book—a book that shaped and molded a language, a people, and a nation?

It's no wonder that the King James is more likely to be the Bible read during the week than the NIV by a 5:1 ratio.[2] **The King James Bible stands alone.** Its position is **firmly established by a 400-year history** of market domination and billions of copies sold.

The reason there is such a thing as "King James Onlyism" is because the King James Bible is the only brand millions of folks insist on. In marketing, this is known as "**brand insistence.**" It didn't happen by accident. The Lord is the "brand manager."

The Trumps jealously guard their brand—which is also their name. Their "brand" can be trusted. Financiers, bankers, developers, and other entrepreneurs are anxious to do business with them because of their reputation.

Do you think the Lord is any less jealous for the King James Bible brand and the integrity and purity of the words he's been using for the past 400 years? His King James brand is proven. The words can be trusted.

Bearing this in mind, here's another question…

Was the Lord even behind the production of the ©1982 NKJV?

Let's take an under-the-hood assessment to find out…

What was the publisher's motive?

Do you assume Sam Moore, former CEO and president of Thomas Nelson, Inc., prayed and fasted before he came up with the idea that we

---

[2] Barna Research, "Data and Trends: Answers to Frequently Asked Questions," data collated from several surveys through 1998, accessed December 2012, http://web.archive.org/web/19990508110144/http://www.barna.org/PageStats.htm.

desperately needed a "revision" of the King James Bible? Did the Lord lay a "burden" upon his heart?

Alas, the "burden" came, first of all, from...

His son.

Dr. Kenneth Barker, one of the original translators of the New American Standard Bible and New International Version, relates this story about Sam Moore and the origin of the NKJV:

> However, when his son Joe asked, "Why can't you make a Bible I can understand?" Moore decided to use the resources of his company to produce another translation.[3]

That's just great. It's laudable to do good things for your kids.

But...

Building a new Bible isn't one of them.

Barker continues...

> The year was 1975. The *Living Bible and the New American Standard Bible* were already commercial successes. The New Testament of the *New International Version* was also selling well. Like those translations, the new version Moore envisioned would be produced by conservative and evangelical scholars. It would, however, have an important difference. While every major English Bible translation from 1885 to 1975 was based on a critical or eclectic text, only the King James was based on the traditional text. Moore proposed a new revision of the *King James* based on the same Hebrew and Greek text used by the *KJV* translators themselves.
>
> In a series of meetings in Chicago, Illinois; Nashville, Tennessee; and London, England, Moore explained his proposal and solicited the support of conservative evangelicals. His idea even won the praise

---

[3] Kenneth Barker, "The American Translations of the Bible," Helpmewithbiblestudy.org, accessed December 2012, http://helpmewithBiblestudy.org/5Bible/TransTheAmericanTranslations_Barker.aspx.

of many fundamentalists who previously had been suspicious of any attempt at revision of the *King James*.[4]

All successful businessmen test the water temperature before they leap into the pool. So Mr. Moore floated a trial balloon. He saw he could get leadership acceptance and invested $4 million in the project.[5]

He knew that if he could convert even a small percentage of King James Bible users to his new product then, like the marketers say, he'd absolutely "crush it." With the backing of leadership to use in promotion of the book, Moore was ready to dive in.[6]

Did any conservative evangelicals and fundamentalists wonder if the Lord had an opinion? Or did they just think it was a "good idea"?

Moore is a Christian and an outstanding entrepreneur.[7] He had been publishing Bibles since 1963. Thomas Nelson, Inc., sells books; some of them have the name Bible on them. The brand of Bibles isn't the issue.

They sell Bibles; more than 6 million copies annually—**any brand**. So the question of whether or not it was the Lord's will that a "**competing**" Bible should be produced probably never crossed his mind. They're all good.

But let's consider…

The translation committee.

Did the fellows that agreed to be on the committee to "revise" the translation of the 1611 King James Bible do so because they just had to…

---

[4] Ibid.
[5] Funding Universe, "Thomas Nelson, Inc. History," accessed December 2012, http://www.fundinguniverse.com/company-histories/thomas-nelson-inc-history.
[6] More than 60 million units have been sold in the past 30 years. Lighthouse Christian Bookstore, "NKJV Study Bible: Second Edition," accessed December 2012, http://www.thelighthousechristianbookstore.com/product.asp?sku=9781418548674.
[7] Thomas Nelson Corporate web site, accessed December 2012, http://www.thomasnelson.com/consumer/dept.asp?dept_id=1118916&TopLevel_id=100000.

sensitively polish the archaisms and vocabulary of the 1611 King James version in order to preserve and enhance its originally intended beauty and content[8]

… or did they logically justify their decision after they emotionally decided that it was in their personal interest to be on the committee? Was the idea of memorializing themselves in a printed work of such great import as translating the Bible what compelled them?

The ©1982 NKJV was a wonderful business opportunity for both the publisher and the committee who worked on it.

But this isn't some ordinary product. When it comes to the Bible, you've stepped into another realm. You're dealing with the eternal words of the living God. That's a scary thought; and a great responsibility before God.

He knows the hearts of men. He knows all our motives. And he knows the hearts and motives of the men who were involved in the project.

But let's give the benefit of the doubt and suppose the committee really was burdened because they felt the body of Christ desperately needed a clearer and more understandable Bible.

Elmer Towns, a member of the NKJV oversight committee, said Mr. Moore's burden was to…

Modernize the King James word forms and spelling.

> Some time ago my good friend Mr. Sam Moore of Thomas Nelson Publishing Co. in Nashville, Tennessee, shared with me his burden to publish the King James Version of the Bible in an updated translation that would retain the text, the dignity and the beauty of the 1611 version and yet provide modernization of the word forms and spellings as they are now used in the twentieth century.[9]

---

[8] *Holy Bible: The New King James Version*, Old Time Gospel Hour edition (Nashville, TN: Thomas Nelson, 1982), 1234.
[9] Holypop, "What Does the Bible Say? New King James Bible Translation," accessed December 2012, http://www.holypop.com/answers/New_King_James_Bible_Translation.

This all seems like "stuff and nonsense" because we're still using virtually the same spelling and word forms used back in 1762 and 1769 when the spelling and grammar of the 1611 King James Bible was modernized. You'll read more on this later.

Nevertheless, they made it a point to dump the "thees and thous" even though such wording is quite familiar to us from hymnals and even from TV reruns like *Little House on the Prairie* and *The Waltons*.

But (and this is even more telling) why does the ©1982 NKJV still contain difficult words?

Wrap your brain around these:

> Alighting; Allays; Armlets; Befalls; Belial; Bleat; Bray; Buffet; Burnished; Caldron; Carrion; Chalkstones; Circumspect; Citron; Dainties; Dandled; Daubed; Dappled; Enmity; Entrails; Fallow; Festal; Fowlers; Fuller; Furlongs; Jackdaw; Mammon; Matrix; Paramours; Parapet; Pilfering; Pinions; plaited; Potentate; Potsherd; Poultice; Prattler; Prow; Pyre; Quadrans; Raze; Retinue; Rivulets; Rogue; Satiate; Shards; Sistrums; Skiff; Supplanted; Tamarisk; Terebinth; Timbrel; Tresses; Verdure; Verity; Waifs; Wane; Wend; and woof

And these aren't "theologically significant" words either, like "propitiate," "atonement," and "reconciliation." So it's not like they had to translate them that way to maintain doctrine. Anyway, it's kind of hard to believe that the only reason the ©1982 NKJV was published was because the 1611 KJB is too difficult to read.

Dr. James Price, former professor of Hebrew and Old Testament at Temple Baptist Seminary (1972–2005), said:

> In my early days, it never entered my mind that the King James Version needed revision into modern English because I cut my teeth on that edition of the Bible, memorizing it from early childhood. Consequently, I understood King James English as well as modern English and did not know some people had trouble comprehending it. It was not until I began teaching in seminary that I discovered I was investing a worthwhile percentage of my time teaching Eliz-

abethan English in my classes instead of Bible. Many students did not understand (or they misunderstood) what they read in the King James Bible because of its archaic language. That encouraged me to participate in the editing of the new King James version.[10]

There are two things you should notice from this statement:

1. Dr. Price memorized the King James Bible "from early childhood."
2. He said that he was "investing a worthwhile percentage of [his] time teaching Elizabethan English in [his] classes instead of Bible."

If Dr. Price could memorize verses in the King James Bible as a child, shouldn't he expect his seminary students to at least be able to read and understand the English text remain unchanged?

And in response to his complaint of spending too much "time teaching Elizabethan English in [his] classes instead of Bible," we have to ask…

How hard is it to assign a list of vocabulary words to memorize?

We're talking seminary students. Smart kids—the kind that take Hebrew and Greek.

Evidently, the King James Bible was so difficult for them that Dr. Price had to build a brand spankin' new version of the Bible for them.

The fact is, **any** version of the Bible is loaded with many words some people don't use (or misuse) today. Anybody who wants to really understand God's word—in **any** version—has to learn a new vocabulary. They have to learn history and geography as well.

If it's too hard for his Hebrew and Greek students to learn a few English vocabulary words, then his students could never become carpenters. They'd have to memorize words like soffit, fascia, mullion, sash, ridge, sill, and gable.

---

[10] James D. Price, *King James Onlyism: A New Sect* (© James D. Price, 2006), preface.

It gets worse. What if they want to play football? Imagine the confusion:

- a "fair catch": How pretty is it?
- a "free kick": How much did it cost in the old days?
- a "Hail Mary": A Roman Catholic prayer in football? Who knew?
- a "nickelback": Change for your dollar?

Although the ©1982 NKJV is translated from the same Greek New Testament and virtually the same Hebrew Old Testament as the 1611 King James Bible, it is…

A new legal biblical document…

because it contains thousands of **different English words** (which are protected by copyright).

It would be one thing if all the ©1982 NKJV did was to simply "polish" the archaisms in the 1611 KJB. A number of publishers have done this, but their products have gone nowhere. Polishing is one thing, but "enhancing" the vocabulary is another.

What you may not know about the ©1982 NKJV

There are **material** translational differences between any edition of the 1611 King James Bible and the ©1982 NKJV. There has to be. You can't use different English words without changing the meaning in many passages. That doesn't mean either is necessarily a wrong translational choice, it just means they're different.

It's what keeps lawyers in business. If you've ever bought a house, financed a car, or been involved in a business agreement, you know how important the choice of words is; changing words can (and often does) mean **changing the deal**.

Have you ever gotten "revised" wording to your credit card agreement in the mail? Your bank is putting you on notice that they've changed the deal. Now you get to pay a higher rate of interest.

What's interesting about the ©1982 NKJV is the strange coincidence that some of the replacement words the committee chose turn out to be the same ones that were used in the Revised Version of 1881/1885, the

American Standard Version of 1901, and other modern versions like the NASB, NIV, and RSV.

We'll get to that in a minute.

But first...

The original language texts underlying the English translation are very much the same although not completely identical in the Old Testament.

The original 1611 King James Bible generally followed (although not entirely) the Hebrew OT text of the 1524–1525 Bomberg Edition of the *Ben Chayyim Masoretic Text,* whereas the ©1982 NKJV uses the *Biblia Hebraica Stuttgartensia* (BHS; 1967/1977).

The BHS is based upon a different manuscript (the Leningrad Manuscript B19a) than that of the *Ben Chayyim Masoretic Text*. It's been said that the differences between the two are microscopic.[11]

Nonetheless, the following differences in translation (not text) affect doctrine. For example, what's the Lord going to teach when he comes to...

The doctrine of...
"Man"

What constitutes a man? This rendering of the Hebrew word in Genesis 2 affects the cross-reference in Matthew 16:26.

Genesis 2:7

KJB: "... and man became a living **soul**."

NKJV "... and man became a living **being**."

NIV: "...and the man became a living **being**."

According to the King James Bible, you are a living **soul** and you are located in a body (or at least you used to be before the NIV and NKJV). Your soul has eyes, nose, and mouth. Your soul can see and talk.

---

[11] James D. Price, "A Response to D. A. Waite's Criticism of the New King James Version," September 1995, http://www.jamesdprice.com/newkingjamesversion.html.

Why can't the Lord choose the ©1982 New King James Version?

The biblical example is in Luke 16, the story of the rich man and Lazarus:

1. The rich man's **body** was buried:
   "…the rich man also died, and was buried" (Luke 16:22).

2. His spirit returned "unto God who gave it."
   "Then shall the dust return to the earth as it was: and the **spirit shall return** unto God who gave it (Ecclesiastes 12:7). If he set his heart upon man, *if* he gather unto himself **his spirit** and his breath; All flesh shall perish together, and man shall turn again unto dust (Job 34:14–15); Who knoweth the spirit of man that goeth upward, and the spirit of the beast that goeth downward to the earth? Ecclesiastes 3:21)

3. His **soul** was in hell:
   And in **hell he lift up his eyes**, being in torments, and seeth Abraham afar off, and Lazarus in his bosom (Luke 16:23).

Note how the King James Bible cross-references itself:

King James Bible 1611	
Genesis 2:7	And the Lord God formed man of the dust of the ground, and breathed into his nostrils the breath of life; **and man became a living soul.**
Matthew 16:26	For what is a man profited, if he shall gain the whole world, and **lose his own soul**? or what shall a man give **in exchange for his soul**?

Matthew cross-references with Genesis in the King James Bible but not in the New King James Version:

NKJV ©1982	
Genesis 2:7	And the Lord God formed man of the dust of the ground, and breathed into his nostrils the breath of life; and man became a **living being**.
Matthew 16:26	For what profit is it to a man if he gains the whole world, and loses his own **soul**? Or what will a man give in exchange for his **soul**?

Why didn't the **NKJV ©1982** translate **Matthew 16:26** this way…

For what profit is it to a man if he gains the whole world, and loses his own **being**? Or what will a man give in exchange for his **being**?

They didn't because everyone is already familiar with the saying as it appears in the 1611 KJB. The intended market for the ©1982 NKJV is evangelicals and fundamentalists who are concerned over "**SOULS**." (When has anyone gone to the mall to hand out tracts and called it "living being" winning?)

Certainly in this doctrinal cross-reference passage the 1611 King James Bible is a single unified Bible and the ©1982 NKJV isn't.

How does the Lord handle...

The doctrine of "Sin"?

What does the Bible say in Psalm 10:5 about the ways of the wicked?

NKJV (©1982)   His ways are always prospering...
King James Bible (1611)   His ways are always grievous...

In this case, the Lord is **forced** to choose between the King James Bible and the newer version. Are the ways of the wicked "**always prospering**" or are his ways "**always grievous**"?

Each Bible says and means two different things. The Lord can't have the same verses saying two different things without looking inconsistent. And that's exactly how he'd look if he decides to substitute the new translation for the one he's been using for the past 400 years.

Here's another example. Notice how this translation choice ultimately affects the **inerrancy of the Scriptures**:

Isaiah 9:3	
NKJV (©1982)	You have multiplied the nation *And* increased its joy...
King James Bible (1611)	Thou hast multiplied the nation, *and* **not increased** the joy...

The Lord can't recommend **both** of these Bibles because they say and mean the exact **opposite**. One reading is true; the other isn't. Only one can be correct, and the Lord **has** to choose **one**. He can't pick both.

Plus, if he picks the ©1982 NKJV reading, then he contradicts the reading he's been using for the past 400 years. That's not so good if you're looking for a God who's trustworthy.

This next example has…

The doctrine of "The seed of Abraham"

carried on **by a footnote**. Do you always read the footnotes?

The Lord Jesus Christ is the seed of Abraham in whom the whole world is blessed. First, here are the verses in the **1611 King James Bible**:

Genesis 13:15	Galatians 3:16
For all the land which thou seest, to thee will I give it, and to thy **seed** for ever.	Now to Abraham and his seed were the promises made. He saith not, And to seeds, **as of many**; but as of **one**, And to **thy seed, which is Christ.**

It's clear. Paul made a point that the OT reference was to a **singular** seed. Now look at what happens to the cross-reference in the ©**1982 NKJV**:

Genesis 13:15	Galatians 3:16
for all the land which you see I give to you and your **descendants** forever.	Now to Abraham and his **Seed** were the promises made. He does not say, "And to seeds," as of many, but as of **one**, "*And to your Seed*," who is Christ.

The cross-reference explanation of the Genesis 13 verse is Galatians 3:16. Abraham had many descendants. Some of whom were not even of Israel, such as Ishmael. But more importantly, Genesis 13:15 is not referring to **seeds** (plural) but to a singular **seed**, which is Jesus Christ as is made clear in Galatians 3:16.

The ©**1982 NKJV** loses the cross-reference twice (the same wording appears in Genesis 12:7) because it translates the text **correctly** as plural but uses the English word "descendants." They footnote the verse saying, "Literally *seed*, and so throughout the book."

That's nice, but…

Should doctrine be relegated to a footnote?

The English word as it appears in the 1611 KJB is "seed," which can be **both** singular AND plural. No footnote necessary. The doctrine of the seed of Abraham is carried in the ©1982 NKJV in a footnote and not in the text.

The NKJV translators and editors could have easily and properly used the word "seed." But they chose not to. Why is anybody's guess.

In the next case, the 1611 translators expanded on the name "Israel," giving the literal meaning in the text.

	Genesis 32:28
NKJV (©1982)	And He said, "Your name shall no longer be called Jacob, but Israel; for _____ you have struggled with God…."
King James Bible (1611)	And he said, Thy name shall be called no more Jacob, but Israel: for **as a prince** hast thou power with God…

The words "**as a prince**" are not included in the ©1982 NKJV. This is a translational choice. The ©1982 NKJV footnotes the verse saying, "Literally *Prince with God.*" Neither translation is wrong, but they're different.

And how does the Lord exegete Proverbs 18:8 when he decides to teach…

The doctrine of "Christian Ethics"?

What does the Bible really say about the words of a talebearer in Proverbs 18:8?

Why can't the Lord choose the ©1982 New King James Version?

Proverbs 18:8	
NKJV (©1982)	The words of a talebearer *are* like **tasty trifles**, And they go down into the inmost body.
King James Bible (1611)	The words of a talebearer are **as wounds**, and they go down into the innermost parts of the belly.

The ©1982 NKJV footnotes the verse saying, "A Jewish tradition reads *wounds*." But can there be a greater difference? What a shame that the Lord couldn't get it right the first time. By the way, the option of translating the Hebrew word as "tasty trifles" or the like wasn't unknown to the 1611 translators. Here's how it was translated by the Geneva Bible in 1560:

> The wordes of a tale bearer *are* as **flatterings**, and they goe downe into the bowels of the belly.

Whether "tasty trifles" or "flatterings" or the way Jews read the passage, the 1611 translators chose NOT to translate the word in such manner. And that's the way it's stood for the past 400 years.

And how does the Lord handle…

The doctrine of "visions"?

Proverbs 29:18	
NKJV (©1982)	Where *there is* no revelation, the people **cast off restraint**…
King James Bible (1611)	Where there is no vision, **the people perish**…

Both readings can't be correct. They may be the same in Hebrew but they sure aren't in English.

Here's another verse that is different and has nothing to do with putting old English into modern English. Surely the Lord would have advice for childrearing. So how does he teach…

The doctrine of "Biblical childrearing"?

Proverbs 19:18	
NKJV (©1982)	Chasten your son while there is hope, And **do not set your heart on his destruction.**
King James Bible (1611)	Chasten thy son while there is hope, and let not thy soul **spare for his crying.**

His teaching **depends** on **which** Bible he chooses. Setting "**your heart on his destruction**" can mean a lot of things. "**Spare for his crying**" means exactly that.

There are more cases like this, but you get the point.

Thomas Nelson and the Revised Standard Version

As you will see, some of the word choices used in the ©1982 NKJV match up with the Revised Standard Version of 1952. This is significant because the RSV was roundly criticized by fundamentalists and evangelicals alike back in the day because of its liberal bias and poor theology.

If the RSV was such a bomb, why use RSV phraseology in the ©1982 NKJV?

Dr. Laurence M. Vance said:

> The Revised Standard Version (RSV) was perhaps the most controversial version of the Bible ever translated. Its publication (the New Testament in 1946; the Old Testament in 1952) brought forth a multitude of books and pamphlets against it that attracted the attention of both the secular and religious press. Copies of the RSV were even burned.
>
> The RSV relegated Mark 16:9–20 and John 7:53–8:11 to footnotes, attacked the deity of Christ by changing the punctuation of Romans 9:5, dropped the word begotten from John 3:16, replaced the word *propitiation* throughout the New Testament, and, in what became the most controversial passage of all, changed the word *virgin* to

"young woman" in Isaiah 7:14. This is all in addition to the scores of omitted phrases and verses in the New Testament because of the corrupt Greek text that the RSV was translated from.[12]

Instead of ignoring the RSV and letting Mr. Market bury it like he did its predecessor, the Revised Version of 1881/1885, evangelical and fundamentalist leaders got into a tizzy. Instead of just preaching and teaching the book that had been so successful, the book their congregations actually believed, the "controversy over the RSV led to the translating of two other well-known versions, The New American Standard Bible (NASB) [and] the New International Version (NIV)."

Consider the legacy of the RSV:

NIV committee member Dr. Jack P. Lewis said:

> The RSV opened the era of the multiple translations flooding today's market, all competing with each other.[13]

Pretty interesting comment, isn't it? Note the words "**all competing with each other**." Does that sound like something the Lord is behind?

> The RSV is an authorized revision of the American Standard Version (ASV) of 1901. It was a production of the forerunner of what is now the National Council of Churches. The controversy stemming from the RSV helped reignite the King-James-Only Movement within the Independent Baptist and Pentecostal churches … Funding for the revision was assured in 1936 by a deal that was made with Thomas Nelson & Sons. The deal gave Thomas Nelson & Sons the exclusive rights to print the new version for ten years.[14]

By the way, in 2001, publisher Crossway Bibles released its own revision of the RSV called the English Standard Version (ESV). We'll examine how this happened in a later chapter.

---

[12] Laurence M. Vance, "The NRSV vs. the ESV," accessed December 2012, http://www.av1611.org/vance/nrsv_esv.html.

[13] Al Maxey, "A View of the Versions: The Revised Standard Version, a Critical Analysis," accessed December 2012, http://www.zianet.com/maxey/Ver3.htm.

[14] *Wikipedia*, s.v. "Revised Standard Version," last modified December 2, 2012, http://en.wikipedia.org/wiki/Revised_Standard_Version#Criticism_of_the_RSV.

Here are a few of the many places where the ©**1982 NKJV translators chose to follow the RSV vocabulary.**

Job 1:1

- KJV: There was a man ... whose name was Job; and that man was **PERFECT**...
- NKJV: There was a man ... whose name was Job; and that man was **BLAMELESS**...
- RSV: There was a man ... whose name was Job; and that man was **BLAMELESS**...

Job 3:7

- KJV: Lo, let that night be **SOLITARY**...
- NKJV: Oh, may that night be **BARREN**...
- RSV: Yea, let that night be **BARREN**...

Job 3:8

- KJV: Let them curse it that curse the day, who are ready to raise up **THEIR MOURNING**.
- NKJV: May those curse it who curse the day, Those who are ready to arouse **LEVIATHAN**.
- RSV: Let those curse it who curse the day, who are skilled to rouse up **LEVI'ATHAN**.

Job 13:8

- KJV: Will ye **ACCEPT HIS PERSON**? will ye contend for God?
- NKJV: Will you show **PARTIALITY** for Him? Will you contend for God?
- RSV: Will you show **PARTIALITY** toward him, will you plead the case for God?

Job 30:29

- KJV: I am a brother to **DRAGONS**, and a companion to **OWLS**.
- NKJV: I am a brother of **JACKALS**, And a companion of **OSTRICHES**.
- RSV: I am a brother of **JACKALS**, and a companion of **OSTRICHES**.

These are a few examples from just one book. It would make an interesting term paper if someone were to do a comprehensive comparison.

Sometimes the translational choices of the ©1982 NKJV match up exactly with the way other modern versions translate the text too. If the wording in modern versions is unacceptable to the Lord, then why should he accept it from the ©1982 NKJV?

There are plenty more examples where the choice of wording (which is a translator's prerogative) has nothing to do with changing thees and thous.

Reference	King James Bible	©1982 NKJV and Others
Acts 4:27	Thy **holy child**, Jesus	"**holy child**" changed to "**holy servant**" (NKJV, NASB, RSV)
Acts 8:9	**bewitched** the people	"**bewitched**" changed to "**astonished**" (NKJV, NASB)
Romans 1:25	**changed** the truth of God into a lie	"**changed**" changed to "**exchanged**" (NKJV, NASB, NIV)
Romans 4:25	Who was delivered **for** our offenses and was raised again for our justification	"**for**" changed to "**because of**" (NKJV, NASB)
2 Corinthians 10:5	Casting down **imaginations**	"**imaginations**" changed to "**arguments**" (NKJV, NIV, RSV)
Colossians 3:2	Set your **affection** on things above	"**affection**" changed to "**mind**" (NKJV, NASB, NIV, RSV)
1 Thessalonians 5:22	Abstain from all **appearance** of evil	"**appearance**" changed to "**form**" (NKJV, NASB, RSV)
2 Timothy 2:15	**Study** to shew thyself approved unto God	"**study**" changed to "**be diligent**" (NKJV, NASB)
Titus 3:10	A man that is an **heretick** ... reject	"**heretick**" changed to "**divisive man**" (NKJV, NIV)

The word meanings are clear in the 1611 King James Bible and they are clear in the ©1982 NKJV as well as the other versions. The words aren't the same and don't mean the same thing.

If we assume that the Lord was involved with the translation in the 1611 King James Bible, then we should also assume that he is pleased with the English words as they have appeared for the past 400 years.

There is no reason to assume he changed his mind in 1982 and decided to discard the wording he's presented billions of times in 400 years.

The ©1982 NKJV was successful mainly for three main reasons:

1. They grabbed the prefix "**NEW**" and attached it to their translation.

2. They jacked **the naming rights** of the 1611 King James Bible **for free**. They named their work after a proven winner. They piggybacked on a bestseller. A brilliant marketing move.

3. Sam Moore (the entrepreneur-owner of the publisher Thomas Nelson & Sons) also used **celebrity endorsements** to promote the product. Third-party endorsement with star power is a tried and true sales technique.

Who doesn't love Jerry Falwell?

Jack and Susan McElroy in front of DeMoss Learning Center at Liberty University

Falwell used the ©1982 NKJV as an appreciation gift for donation to the *Old Time Gospel Hour* back in the early '80s. As a premium it did well—but not so good as a substitute for the Book the Lord's been using for the past 400 years.

Should you use the ©1982 NKJV?

Why bother?

Even the editors who built the book aren't sold on it…

Their Bible has so much **authority** that the editors of the ©1982 NKJV actually encourage their readers to alter it as they see fit. You don't believe it? Here's what they said:

> It was the editors' conviction that the use of footnotes would encourage further inquiry by readers. They also recognized that it was easier for the average reader to delete something he or she felt was not properly a part of the text, than to insert a word or phrase which had been left out by the revisers.[15]

Look how their variant reading footnotes "encourage further inquiry" and make it "easier for the average reader to"…

- "Delete" the word "**yet**" from the text and present **Jesus a liar** like the NIV, NASB, ESV, and Holman Christian Standard (HCSB) do in John 7:8–10.
- "Delete" the phrase "**without a cause**," thereby presenting **Jesus a sinner** like the NIV does in Matthew 5:22 and Mark 3:5.
- "Delete" the **proof text for the Trinity** like the NIV, ESV, NASB, and HCSB do in 1 John 5:7–8.
- "Delete" **the proof text for the Incarnation explicitly stating that God became a man** like the NIV, ESV, and NASB do in 1 Timothy 3:16.

The revisers themselves aren't even sold on the Greek and Hebrew texts underlying the ©1982 NKJV. That's why they worded their comment as they did. And so they gave you footnotes you can use to…

- **Eliminate 16 entire verses like** the Greek text underlying the NIV, NASB, ESV, and HCSB does.

They're even broad-minded enough to provide a footnote so you can…

- Call **Jesus a "begotten God"** like the NASB does in John 1:18.

---

[15] *New King James Version,* Old Time Gospel Hour edition, 1235.

And never to be "out-scholared" by other versions, they provide a footnote so you can…

- Purposefully insert known errors into the text like the ESV does in Matthew 1:7, 8, 10. (so much for the "inerrancy of the Scriptures").

If they actually **believed** their text and wording was God's Holy words, then why encourage their readers to edit it by using the variant readings they present in their footnotes?

The truth is that the committee members, editors, and publisher of the NKJV as well as the men who promote it really believe that only *"The Original Bible"* is the real Bible. And only *"The Original Bible"* is inspired and inerrant. The New King James Version is just a shadow of the real thing. Look…

There's nothing wrong with footnotes.

The 1611 and subsequent editions of the King James Bible have marginal notes, footnotes, and even notations of variant readings. It's been noted that:

> Where a Hebrew or Greek word admits two meanings of a suitable kind, the one was to be expressed in the text, the other in the margin. The same to be done where a different reading was found in good copies.[16]

And Miles Smith, one of the 1611 translators, said:

> Now in such a case doth not a margin do well to admonish the Reader to seek further, and not to conclude or dogmatize upon this or that peremptorily? For as it is a fault of incredulity, to doubt of those things that are evident; so to determine of such things as the Spirit of God hath left (even in the judgment of the judicious) questionable, can be no less than presumption.[17]

---

[16] Price, "A Response to D. A. Waite's Criticism of the New King James," 8, citing *Report on the Making of the Version of 1611 Presented to the Synod of Dort,* November 16, 1611, http://www.jamesdprice.com/newkingjamesversion.html.

[17] Ibid., 11.

Miles was referring primarily to the translation of a word in English—not the substitution of a variant reading found in some manuscript, even though they did make note of some textual variants.

It's the motive that counts. The NKJV editors' motive, by their own admission, was to make it "easier for the average reader to delete something he or she felt was not properly a part of the text."

They provided a way for "he or she" to use the notes to **undo the text** that the Lord has been using for thousands of years. Do you think the Lord appreciates their motive?

But...

The editors said they were **convicted to do this**. Now each reader can create a Bible after their own heart. Who does this? Who **encourages** everyone to be a textual critic by making it easier for them to "**delete**" the holy words of God as they see fit? And these are the fellows who preach sermons on convictions versus preferences.

Now this is all really funny considering that it is coming out of the mouths of some fundamentalists.

In case you're new to the business, fundamentalists go out of their way to tell you exactly what's the right kind of music, what's the right kind of clothing, and what's the proper length of your hair.

But when it comes to the Bible...

You can do pretty much anything you want.

Sigh.

Here's another interesting comment. Liberty University's Elmer Towns said:

> It has been my privilege to serve on the Overview Committee for this translation. While I still preach only from the old King James Version, I heartily recommend the New King James Bible for study and clarification of archaic English terms.[18]

---

[18] Holypop, "What Does the Bible Say?"

Why would he preach "**only from the old King James Version**" when no one could understand its archaic English? Not very considerate is it? Evidently, the Old King James Version is good enough to preach out of but not good enough to study? Go figure.

The real question isn't whether or not the translators of the ©1982 NKJV did a good job at translation. They did.

The question is…

Did the Lord want it done in the first place?

Unless he wanted to:

1. **Dilute** his long-standing brand, and
2. **Compete with Himself,**

The answer has to be … **An emphatic** … **No.**

Before we get to the "which edition" question, we need to answer another oft-repeated question…

Chapter Nine

Where was the Bible before 1611?

Thy word is true from the beginning: and every one of thy righteous judgments endureth for ever. (Psalm 119:160)

Actually a better question for today is, "Where was the Bible after the invention of the printing press?"

Here's why…

The majority of the manuscripts in existence have variations in them. Textual critics call them…

Variant Readings

On the whole, all manuscripts are in general agreement; according to Dr. Maurice Robinson "… over 85% of the text found in all manuscripts is identical."[1]

If they weren't, you'd never have any cohesive Bible narrative. The problem lies in the fact that sometimes those manuscripts differ. And sometimes those differences are pronounced and affect doctrine (even though some of your teachers say it ain't so).

For example… Look at **John 1:18** as it appears in various manuscripts.

---

[1] Maurice A. Robinson, "The Case for the Byzantine Textform: A New Approach to 'Majority Text' Theory." Paper presented at the Southeastern Regional Evangelical Theological Society Meeting, Toccoa Falls, GA, March 8–9, 1991. (Available: Theological Research Exchange Network, www.tren.com).

Some read: "No man has seen God at any time; **the** only **begotten Son**…"
Others read: "No man has seen God at any time; **the** only **begotten God**…"
Still others read: "No man has seen God at any time; **an** only **one, God**…"

So we're faced with 3 possible options for John 1:18:[2]

1. the **only begotten Son**
2. the **only begotten God**
3. **an only one, God**

You can immediately see the problem.

In John 1:18, does God say Jesus is (1) the only **begotten son** of God, or is Jesus (2) the only **begotten God**, or is he (3) God himself?

Can you see now why our Christian leaders retreat to the safety of *"The Original Bible"*?

Let's take a look at another textual variant in **1 Timothy 3:16**:

Some manuscripts say: "**God** was manifested in the flesh…"
Others say: "**Who** was manifested in the flesh"
Another says: "**Which** was manifested in the flesh"

So we have three choices:

1. **God** was manifested in the flesh…
2. **Who** was manifested in the flesh
3. **Which** was manifested in the flesh

The passage is referring to Jesus Christ.

Door 1 makes a statement about Jesus being God.

Doors 2 and 3 don't.

Which of the three is authentic? That depends on **who** you ask. As soon as you introduce a choice into the text (a variant reading), objective truth becomes subjective in a hurry.

---

[2] Philip W. Comfort, *New Testament Text and Translation Commentary* (Carol Stream, IL: Tyndale House, 2008), 255.

There are thousands of these variations in the body of manuscript evidence. Some variations are worse than others, some are easy to spot as errors and some not. That's why, even today, there are so many Bibles that read differently. It's not just a translation issue—it's a textual issue.

Christian academics and thought leaders pick and choose which reading is original **in their opinion**. But they will always defer to *"The Original Bible"* as their final authority because it conveniently doesn't exist. No one can prove their opinion wrong. Of course, then we are never sure about what God said either.

Holding to *"The Original Bible"* theory is like experiencing a drug's side effect. The medicine may work, but it comes at a price.

What follows is a real good example of the experts not knowing what was in the so-called "Original Bible" and then insulting your intelligence with disinformation that rivals the propaganda you get from Homeland Security.

It is the footnote from Mark 16:9–20 as it appears in the ESV Study Bible.

First of all, notice that the scholars say they're "**puzzled.**"

This is no surprise since they have no final authority instructing them as to which are the words of men and which are the words of God.

> **Some** ancient manuscripts of Mark's Gospel contain these verses and others do not, **which presents a puzzle for scholars** who specialize in the history of such manuscripts. This longer ending is missing from various old and reliable Greek manuscripts (esp. Sinaiticus and Vaticanus), as well as numerous early Latin, Syriac, Armenian, and Georgian manuscripts. Early church fathers (e.g., Origen and Clement of Alexandria) did not appear to know of these verses. Eusebius and Jerome state that this section is missing in most manuscripts available at their time. And some manuscripts that contain vv. 9–20 indicate that older manuscripts lacked this section. On the other hand, some early and many later manuscripts (such as the manuscripts known as A, C, and D) contain vv. 9–20 and many church fathers (such as Irenaeus) evidently knew of these verses. As for the

verses themselves, they contain various Greek words and expressions uncommon to Mark, and there are stylistic differences as well. **Many think this shows to be a later edition.** In summary, vv. 9–20 should be read with caution… **And no point of doctrine is affected** by the absence or presence of vv. 9–20.)[3]

After reading their footnote, you'd think Mark 16:9–20 is a massive forgery.

So bad, in fact that the editors and publisher of the ESV felt compelled not only to double bracket the passage but also put a warning label on it:

"Read with Caution"

Like the robot on the popular 1960s TV program Lost in Space used to say … "Danger, Will Robinson!" Reading this passage might endanger your spiritual health!

They warn the reader:

"In summary, vv.9–12 should be read with caution."

Robot and Will Robinson from *Lost in Space* TV series

This is nothing more than old-fashioned fear mongering by the editors and publishers of the ESV.

But if the passage is so questionable…

Why don't they just eliminate it?

They can't. They're chicken. There are literally billions of King James Bibles out there, and every one of them has the verses. So the ESV editors double bracket these verses and create doubt as to their authenticity via the cleverly worded footnote.

They do all this to defend two defective manuscripts (Vaticanus and Sinaiticus), which don't even agree with each other in over 3,000 places in the Gospels alone (see chapter 2).

---

[3] Philip W. Comfort, *New Testament Text and Translation Commentary* (Carol Stream, IL: Tyndale House, 2008), 255.

Which fact the experts conveniently **ignore** when the readings don't fit what they think they should say. But that's a topic for another day.

Here's the truth they forgot to tell you in the footnote.

It's brought to our attention by Wilbur N. Pickering, Th.M., Ph.D., in his book *The Identity of the New Testament II*, Appendix G.[4]

Dr. Pickering reveals to us the fact that verses 9–16 are in every extant Greek MS (about 1,700) except three. Oh wait, they did say "**some**" ancient manuscripts contain the verses. They just conveniently left out that it's only three, and as you can see detailed in the footnote below, one of those is a forgery.

Now you'd never understand that from what they said, would you?

But here's what Dr. Pickering said:

> In the face of such massive evidence, why do the critics insist on rejecting this passage? Lamentably, most modern versions also cast doubt upon the authenticity of these verses in one way or another … As one who believes that the Bible is God's Word, I find it to be inconceivable that an official biography of Jesus Christ, commissioned by God and written subject to His quality control, should omit proofs of the resurrection, should exclude all post-resurrection appearances, should end with the clause "because they were afraid"! If the critics' assessment is correct … Mark's Gospel as it stands is mutilated (if it ends at v. 8), the original ending having disappeared without a trace…[5]

Then Pickering enumerates the evidence. Mark 16:9–16 is contained in:

---

[4] Wilber Pickering, *The Identity of the New Testament Text II*, 3rd ed. (Eugene, OR: Wipf and Stock, 2003). In the online version it is Appendix H.
[5] Ibid., 176.

- Every extant Greek manuscript—about 1,700 except three, and one of them (the infamous Sinaiticus manuscript) is a proven forgery at this point.[6]
- Every extant Greek Lectionary—about 2,000 of them.
- Every extant Latin manuscript—about 8,000 of them except one.
- Every extant Syriac manuscript except one.
- Every extant Coptic manuscript except one.

He asks: "Why do critics insist on rejecting this passage?"

The answer is because they are only presenting evidence to support their agenda. The critics (and editors of the most of the popular new translations) desperately want the verses gone because they don't appear in their two favorite "oldest and best" manuscripts.

He summarizes by saying:

> We have hard evidence for the "inclusion" from the II century (Irenaeus and the Diatessaron), and presumably the first half of that century. We have no such hard evidence for the "exclusion."[7]

---

[6] Ibid., 176, footnote 1: "Tischendorf, who discovered Codex Aleph, warned that the folded sheet containing the end of Mark and the beginning of Luke appeared to be written by a different hand and with different ink than the rest of the manuscript. However that may be, a careful scrutiny reveals the following: the end of Mark and beginning of Luke occur on page 3 (of the four); pages 1 and 4 contain an average of 17 lines of printed Greek text per column (there are four columns per page), just like the rest of the codex; page 2 contains an average of 15.5 lines of printed text per column (four columns); the first column of page 3 contains only twelve lines of printed text and in this way verse 8 occupies the top of the second column, the rest of which is blank (except for some designs); Luke begins at the top of column 3, which contains 16 lines of printed text while column 4 is back up to 17 lines. On page 2 the forger began to spread out the letters, displacing six lines of printed text; in the first column of page 3 he got desperate and displaced five lines of printed text, just in one column!

In this way he managed to get two lines of verse 8 over onto the second column, avoiding the telltale vacant column (as in Codex B). That second column would accommodate 15 more lines of printed text, which with the other eleven make 26. Verses 9-20 occupy 23.5 such lines, so there is plenty of room for them. It really does seem that there has been foul play, and there would have been no need for it unless the first hand did in fact display the disputed verses. In any event, Aleph as it stands is a forgery (in this place) and therefore may not legitimately be alleged as evidence against them."

[7] Ibid., 176.

The academic elites really know how to promote their own agenda, don't they? And by good words and fair speeches they intend to deceive the hearts of the simple. Now you know the truth.

In the grand scheme of things we really are dependent upon the Lord to provide his words to us in a printed book. That book has to be the 1611 King James Bible. Out of all the "Bibles" printed, it's the only one that:

- Looks like it's his,
- Acts like it's his,
- Sounds like it's his,
- Reads like it's his,

and most importantly…

Has the proven track record you'd expect if it belongs to him.

Keeping this in mind, let's quickly look at the history of Bible printing and of the King James Bible in particular.

The Gutenberg Bible was the first book printed with movable type. It was printed in Latin around the year 1450. It's been reprinted a number of times since then as a curiosity. Nobody uses it. Even when it was printed it was barely used.

Between 1450 and 1500, versions of the Bible in whole or in part appeared in German, Italian, French, Czech, Dutch, Hebrew, Greek, and English. William Caxton was an English merchant who established this new technology in England. In 1483 he printed *The Golden Legende,* which contained large amounts of Old and New Testament Scripture. Caxton says he translated the text into English from copies in French and Latin.[8]

Jack McElroy with a two-volume facsimile of the Gutenberg Bible

---

[8] Donald L. Brake, Sr., "World's Best-Selling Book," *Washington Times,* July 18, 2012, http://communities.washingtontimes.com/neighborhood/worlds-best-selling-book/2012/jul/18/bible-forbidden-book-banned-book.

None of these printed versions had any lasting effect on advancing biblical truth. It was only Reformation Bibles (printed after 1516) and specifically the Reformation Bible text that had life-changing effects on believers then and now.

Printing with moveable type was a quantum leap over handwritten manuscripts, replacing that old "technology" that had existed for thousands of years. Once typeset, God's word could be reproduced cheaply, in volume, and identically. That ability had never existed before.

If we assume the Lord gave us this new technology, then it's his responsibility to get his words into your hands in the form of a printed book.

The pressure was on the Lord to collect the appropriate and correct variant readings and put them into **one book**.

No Christian should have to worry about what God says. The Lord has to provide a book that does that. It's not like the Lord to leave us in a wilderness of competing readings or translations ("of making many books *there is* no end" [Ecclesiastes 12:12]) to determine what he says.

The only way for a Christian to "study" the Bible is to actually have one that he or she is sure contains all the words and only the words of the Lord.

So how does all this affect the King James Bible?

That's easy. What we observe is that from the printing of the first English New Testament in 1525 by William Tyndale right through the lineage of the English Bibles preceding the King James, we see the word of God being assembled until its final form as appeared in the 1611 First Edition of the Authorized Version, also known as the King James Bible.

There were a number of English Bibles printed before the King James. Coverdale's Bible was printed in 1535, Matthew's Bible in 1537, the Great Bible in 1539–1540, the Geneva Bible in 1560, and the Bishops' Bible in 1568.

The construction of the book was a process over a period of 86 years. Like translator Miles Smith said in his preface to the King James Bible:

> *Truly (good Christian Reader) we never thought from the beginning, that we should need to make a new Translation, nor yet to make of a bad one a good one ... but to make a good one better, or out of many good ones, **one principal good one**...*

And that's what they did. They left you with **one principal good one**. Unlike all the rest of the early printed Bibles, it's the only one the Lord Jesus Christ has been using and blessing nonstop for the past 400 years.

But some will object and say…

How can a 17th-century translation be "The" Bible?

How can the Lord pick only one Bible? And why should one language have priority over another?

Does this make any sense?

Sure it does.

As we have already seen, "The Bible" has to be one book—not two testaments in two different languages. Or worse, only exist as the mythical ***"Original Bible."***

Second, there has to be a standard—a "go-to" book you can trust—a book that contains all of God's words and only God's words.

In the Song of Solomon we are reintroduced to the biblical concept of Chiefest.

In Song of Solomon 5:10, the woman refers to her beloved as "the chiefest among ten thousand." The marginal note in the 1611 King James Bible says: "the chiefest. Heb. a standard bearer."

When it comes to Bibles produced after the invention of the printing press, the King James Bible is by any and all accounts "the chiefest among ten thousand." Not only of the previous translations but also of any pretender to the position of "chiefest" from any modern version.

Its 400-year, billions of copies history proves it to be the Lord's "standard bearer."

Consider also Daniel 6:3–4.

> Then this Daniel was preferred above the presidents and princes, because an excellent spirit *was* in him; and the king thought to set him over the whole realm. Then the presidents and princes sought to find occasion against Daniel concerning the kingdom; but they could find none occasion nor fault; forasmuch as he *was* faithful, neither was there any error or fault found in him. (Daniel 6:3–4)

Daniel was preferred above all because an excellent spirit was in him and forasmuch as he was faithful, neither was there any error or fault found in him.

Even so...

The King James Bible is preferred above all others because an excellent spirit is in it and forasmuch as it is faithful, neither is there any error or fault found in it.

But many have noted that there are slight differences in the printed editions of the KJB. And so they reason that This Book can't be "**The**" Bible.

So they ask the next question...

Chapter Ten

Which edition of the King James Bible is "The Bible"?

> The Lord gave the word: great was the company
> of those that published it. (Psalm 68:11)

That's a fair question and it's easy to answer, but it does take a little bit of background information and deductive reasoning.

Unfortunately, some fundamental and evangelical academics pose the question to get you to drop the issue. They think that spelling modernization as well as minute editorial and grammatical tweaks over the centuries disqualifies the King James Bible as the Lord's choice in spite of its obvious success and his blessing.

Was the success of the King James Bible due to luck? Was it mere chance that an estimated 5 billion copies have been produced over 400 years? If it's not his choice, then which one is?

There have been literally thousands of editions of the KJB, but the underlying original language text hasn't changed at all in 400 years. The English language presentation has been tweaked in some of those editions, but…

No matter which of the thousands of editions of the King James Bible you choose…

1. None **present Jesus a liar** like the NIV, NASB, ESV, and HCSB do in John 7:8–10 by eliminating the word "yet" from the narrative.

2. None **present Jesus as a sinner** like the NIV does by saying he got angry without a cause in Matthew 5:22 and Mark 3:5.

3. None say **Elhanan killed Goliath** (instead of David) like the NASB, ESV, and HCSB say in 2 Samuel 21:19.

4. None say **Jesus was "indignant"** (instead of compassionate) at the leper looking to get healed like the NIV says in Mark 1:41.

5. None call **Jesus a begotten God** (instead of begotten son) like the NASB does in John 1:18.

6. None contain **known errors purposefully inserted into the text** like the ESV does in Matthew 1:7, 8, and 10.

7. None **eliminate 16 entire verses** like the Greek text underlying the NIV, NASB, ESV, and HCSB do.

8. None **eliminate the proof text for the Trinity** like the NIV, ESV, NASB, and HCSB do in 1 John 5:7–8.

9. None **eliminate the proof text for the Incarnation explicitly stating that God became a man** like the NIV, ESV, and NASB do in 1 Timothy 3:16.

10. None have their **underlying original language source text revised** over time like the NASB and NIV.

11. None contradict themselves in Luke 4:44 like the NIV, ESV, and NASB do when they say the Lord was in Galilee when their own cross-reference says Judea. (Compare Luke 4:44, which says "Judea" with Matthew 4:23 and Mark 1:39, which say "Galilee." The King James is consistent, saying Galilee in all three verses.)

The Lord isn't ashamed of any edition of the King James Bible and has used them all.

Come to think of it, the Lord wouldn't be ashamed to bring **any** edition of the King James Bible to church with him. He has used and blessed them all over the past 400 years even with printing errors, spelling, grammar, orthographic differences, and translation tweaks.

He wouldn't even be ashamed to bring in a reprint of the 1611. Why? Because…

Which edition of the King James Bible is "The Bible"?

1. It's the standard issue all publishers wanted to compare their work to.
2. The Apocrypha provides valuable background information on the Old and New Testaments. The Apocrypha includes fourteen books: 1 Esdras, 2 Esdras, Tobit, Judith, The Rest of Esther, Wisdom of Solomon, Ecclesiasticus, Baruch, The Song of the Three Children, The Story of Susanna, Bel and the Dragon, The Prayer of Manasses, 1 Maccabees, and 2 Maccabees. Even if they're not inspired, those books would never have been originally included if they didn't have some value.
3. He could teach on the significance of the original spelling.[1]
4. He could teach on the variations in the translation (i.e., he/she and his/her).
5. He could teach on those translational and grammatical nuances that exist in later printings that evangelical and fundamentalist academics have been using for over 100 years to undermine the authority of the book.
6. He could teach on the question of English capitalization of the word Spirit/spirit.
7. He could teach on punctuation questions.

By the way, the famous 19th-century textual critic and noted scholar F.H.A. Scrivener, who was one of the translators of the English Revised Version (1885), edited an edition of the King James Bible called the Cambridge Paragraph Bible in 1873. In the preface, Scrivener referred to his Bible as "a critical edition of the Authorized Bible of 1611."

Everybody using a King James Bible today is using an edition of the Authorized Bible of 1611.[2]

But let's drill down and examine the question closely.

---

[1] Research into the significance of the original spelling of the first edition King James Bible and the creation of a concordance is being conducted by Pastor Howard Elseth and Mr. E. J. Blackstone at Holy Bible Ministries in Garrison, Texas.
[2] F.H.A. Scrivener, *The Authorized Version of the English Bible (1611): Its Subsequent Reprints and Modern Representatives.* Originally published in 1884, available from Wipf & Stock Publishers, Eugene, Oregon.

The facts are these:

1. There were printing errors in the first edition and some subsequent editions.

2. Spelling and grammar were modernized in various editions including the 1762 Cambridge Edition edited by Dr. Thomas Paris, as well as the Oxford University editions edited by Dr. Benjamin Blayney in 1769. According to scholar and author David Norton, the text was all but "fossilized" by 1769:

   > We must be absolutely clear what it really is: a text that all but fossilized in the 1760s. The modern KJB is a mutated version of a 17th-century text with partially modernized spelling, punctuation and presentation.[3]

3. The translation was tweaked in minor ways (on the whole to make it even more literal) up to 1638 by a couple of the original translators. Various publishers have produced editions reflecting a combination of these types of updates/tweaks over the centuries as well.

4. The first printing of 1611 was many times referred to as the model. It's been reproduced in three successive centuries. It was first reproduced word for word (in Roman type) in 1833 by Oxford University Press and reprinted in 2011. Cambridge University printed its own word-for-word reproduction in five volumes in 1908 and reprinted it in 2010. Hendrickson Publishers (1980s–present) and Thomas Nelson (1990–present) reprinted the 1833 Oxford. Zondervan printed a mass-market photographic reprint of the 1611 first edition in 2011 that was sold through Walmart. You can even get a 1611 on the Amazon Kindle.

5. There was never any revision of the underlying original language texts. The true revision took place in 1881/1885, which is why they appropriately titled it the **English Revised Version (ERV or RV)**.

---

[3] David Norton, *A Textual History of the King James Bible* (Cambridge, England: Cambridge University Press, 2005), 126.

Which edition of the King James Bible is "The Bible"?

Let's examine...

❶ Printing and typographical errors

The first and subsequent editions of the King James Bible had press errors. Some words were repeated, some left out, and some letters were printed upside down because of the painstaking process involved setting over three million letters—by hand with no electric lights.

Believe it or not, David Norton counted only 351 typographical errors (such as confusion of *u* and *n*, *e* and *t*, *c* and *t*) and listed them in Appendix 1 of *A Textual History of the King James Bible*. Printing errors were later corrected as we shall see. A press error is not a biblical error.

Most of these problems would not affect the sense of the text; but there is another kind of problem, "hidden errors" as Norton calls them, that would make a difference in the meaning. They are called "hidden" because they were likely to be invisible to the proofreader.

If you thought the Lord was going to miraculously do what hadn't been done before (i.e., come out with a flawlessly printed Bible), you'd be wrong. As a result, the Lord continued to touch up the King James Bible after the first edition rolled off the presses in 1611.

Much of this work was completed by 1638 by Dr. Samuel Ward and Dr. John Bois, two of the original group of translators that worked on the project up until that time.

Here is a list of some of the changes:

Production (printing) errors in the 1611 and corrections in later editions of the King James Bible

Reference	1611 edition	Current Pure Cambridge Edition	Year corrected
Exod 38:11	hoopes	hooks	1611, 2nd. ed.
Lev 26:40	the iniquity of their fathers	their iniquity, and the iniquity of their fathers	1616

165

Reference	1611 edition	Current Pure Cambridge Edition	Year corrected
1 Sam 18:1	he made an end of speaking	he had made an end of speaking	1629
2 Chr 13:6	his LORD	his lord	1629
Ezra 2:22	children	men	1638
Ezra 3:5	that willingly offered, offered a freewill offering	that willingly offered a freewill offering	1611, 2nd ed.
Psa 69:32	good	God	1617, 1629
Eccl 8:17	a man labour to seek it out, yea further	a man labour to seek it out, yet he shall not find it, yea further	1629
Isa 6:8	I said	said I	1629
Jer 49:1	God	Gad	1616, 1629
Ezek 6:8	that he may	that ye may	1613
Ezek 5:1	take the balances	take thee balances	1638
Ezek 24:7	poured it upon the ground	poured it not upon the ground	1613, 1629
Ezek 26:14	They	thou	1638
Ezek 36:2	had	hath	1630
Ezek 42:17	a measuring reed	the measuring reed	1638
Ezek 46:23	new	row of	1638
Ezek 11:24	brought me in vision	brought me in a vision	1769
Ezek 34:31	my flock of my pasture	my flock, the flock of my pasture	1629
Dan 1:12	let them give pulse	let them give us pulse	1769

Which edition of the King James Bible is "The Bible"?

Reference	1611 edition	Current Pure Cambridge Edition	Year corrected
Dan 6:13	the captivity of the children	the children of the captivity	1629
Zech 6:4	LORD	lord	1629
Acts 27:18	And being exceedingly tossed with a tempest the next day	And we being exceedingly tossed with a tempest, the next *day*	1638
1 Cor 7:32	belongeth	belong	1616/1629
1 Cor 15:6	And	After	1616/1629
2 Cor 11:32	kept the city with a garrison	kept the city of the Damascenes with a garrison	1629
2 Tim 4:13	bring with thee, but especially the parchments	bring with thee, and the books, but especially the parchments	1616, 1629
Heb 11:23	and they not afraid	and they were not afraid	1638
Rev 13:6	dwelt	dwell	1629

Correcting printing errors doesn't "revise" the text any more than a proofreader "revises" your term paper. Even though correcting printer's errors is not a "revision" of the text, some folks insist the KJB couldn't be the only true Bible even if it had one press error. Evidently, after 400 years and billions of copies later, the Lord must not be one of them.

❷ Spelling standardization

Spelling standardization (and slight orthography) is responsible for the overwhelming bulk of "changes" in

167

editions of the King James Bible, but it was the Lord's work in preparation for 20th-century computers.

In 1762 the Lord used Dr. F. S. Paris of the University of Cambridge and in 1769 Dr. Benjamin Blayney of Oxford to put some finishing touches on the work like enhancing the use of italics, correcting what printer errors remained, expanding marginal and introductory notes, and modernizing the spelling.

This was in preparation for exhaustive concordances of the 17th–20th centuries and finally computerized searches in the late 20th century. The 1762 Paris Edition was the first King James Bible with standardized spelling, based on Samuel Johnson's *Dictionary of the English Language,* which was published in 1755.

Now the Lord's children can word search the nearly 790,000 words of their King James Bibles in a split second.

This would have been impossible without standardized spelling (i.e., "seek" and "seeke" got standardized to "seek"; "son" and "sonne" to "son," etc.). The Lord was ahead of the curve by 200 years.

Speaking of spelling, here are examples of…

22 spelling changes in 6 verses of the 23rd Psalm

1611 Printing

1 [A **Psalme** of **Dauid**.] The Lord is my **shepheard**, I shall not want.

2 He maketh me to lie **downe** in **greene** pastures: he leadeth **mee** beside the still waters.

3 He restoreth my **soule**: he leadeth me in the **pathes** of **righteousnes**, for his names sake.

4 Yea though I **walke** through the valley of the **shadowe** of death, I will **feare** no **euill**: for thou **art** with me, thy rod and thy **staffe**, they comfort me.

5 Thou preparest a table before me, in the presence of mine enemies: thou anointest my head with **oyle**, my **cuppe** runneth **ouer**.

6 Surely **goodnes** and **mercie** shall **followe** me all the **daies** of my life: and I will dwell in the house of the Lord for **euer**.

You can see for yourself how many changes there are and what "sort" they are.

Spelling standardization is responsible for almost all of the tens of thousands of changes in editions of the King James Bibles. Standardizing spelling doesn't "revise" the text any more than spell check "revises" a term paper. Even though standardizing spelling is not a "revision," some folks insist the KJB can't be the only true Bible even if one word is spelled differently now than it was in 1611. Evidently, after 400 years and billions of copies later, the Lord isn't one of them.

Conforming the text to plain English rules of grammar

Along with spelling updates came a small number of modifications to conform the text to plain English rules of grammar like who vs. whom, which vs. who, that vs. which, than vs. then, word order, etc.; and punctuation like periods, commas, semicolons, colons, parentheses, apostrophes, italics, etc. The bulk of these changes were done in 1762 and 1769, and none of them affected or changed the original language text.

As a matter of fact, according to Dr. W. Edward Glenny, who contributed two chapters to the Anti-King James Only book, *One Bible Only? Examining Exclusive Claims for the King James Bible,* when commenting on these types of differences in manuscripts said they are "**insignificant matters**."

> About 98% are **insignificant matters** such as spelling, word order, differences in style, or confusion concerning synonyms.[4]

---

[4] Roy E. Beacham and Kevin T. Bauder, eds., *One Bible Only? Examining Exclusive Claims for the King James Bible* (Grand Rapids, MI: Kregel, 2001), 124.

OK, makes sense.

With this in mind, let's look at…

Some "insignificant matters" between the 1611 First Edition and later editions of the King James Bible

Passage	1611 First Edition	Changes made in subsequent editions
Genesis 15:18	that same day	the same day
Exodus 34:20	first borne	firstborn
Exodus 34:25	feast of Passover	feast of the passover
Leviticus 11:10	And all that haue not finnes nor scales in the seas	And all that have not fins and scales in the seas
Leviticus 15:33	which is unclean	that is unclean
Numbers 7:55	charger of	charger of the weight of
Numbers 9:13	from his people	from among his people
1 Chronicles 21:16	lift	lifted
Nehemiah 2:17	burnt	burned
Nehemiah 2:20	you	ye
Job 6:8	O	Oh
Job 27:5	my integrity	mine integrity
Job 31:21	lift	lifted
Psalm 73:25	besides	beside
Psalm 107:43	those things	these things
Psalm 116:16	thy handmaid	thine handmaid
Isaiah 28:4	seeth it	seeth
Isaiah 29:8	a hungry	an hungry
Isaiah 29:14	amongst	among
Jeremiah 15:7	sith	since (sith is an archaic word for since

Which edition of the King James Bible is "The Bible"?

Passage	1611 First Edition	Changes made in subsequent editions
Jeremiah 48:36	is perished	are perished
Matthew 9:34	casteth out the devils	casteth out devils
Matthew 13:6	had not root	had no root
Matthew 27:52	bodies of Saints	bodies of the saints
Luke 4:38	wives	wife's
Luke 8:5	the ways side	the way side
John 6:52	amongst	among
Acts 5:34	doctor of Law	doctor of the law
Acts 15:23	And wrote	And they wrote
Acts 18:5	pressed in spirit	pressed in the spirit
Acts 19:19	many also of them	many of them also
Acts 22:8	who thou	whom thou
Acts 26:22	Then	than
Romans 7:13	Was that then	Was then that
1 Corinthians 13:2	have no charity	have not charity
2 Corinthians 11:26	In journeying often	In journeyings often
2 Timothy 1:12	and I am persuaded	and am persuaded
James 5:4	which have reaped	who have reaped
1 Peter 2:2	new borne	newborn
1 John 4:3	You	ye
Revelation 22:2	of either side	on either side

Critics have been trying to "modernize" the King James Bible for over 150 years, but it's already been done. Notice that none of these modernizations alter the underlying original language text.

Conforming the text to English rules of grammar (orthography) doesn't "revise" it any more than a grammar check "revises" your email. Yet some folks insist the KJB can't be the only true Bible even if words like "who" in 1611 are standardized to "whom" today. After 400 years and billions of copies later, we have to assume that the Lord isn't one of them.

171

Any changes of spelling, diction, punctuation, italics, and capitalization (many early Greek manuscripts were written in ALL CAPS anyway) are all small brushstrokes that the master applied to his final masterpiece entitled **THE HOLY BIBLE**. The point is that the work is the Lord's, not men's. He is the author and publisher. It's his book.

③ Translational nuances in later printings are editorial choices, not printer's errors.

Here's an important point. The Lord allows his pure word to be presented in the English text in different ways. This leads some to conclude that either one or the other is "in error." Just because the English text may be presented slightly differently in different editions does not mean that either presentation is in error.

There were later editions, especially in 1629 and 1638 that tended to present the English translation in a more literal fashion to a more literal degree. Commentators confuse the degree of literalness with error, imperfection, and impurity.

Impurity is what happens when men's words are mixed with God's words. This mixture is a **textual** issue, not a **translation** issue.

Commentators confuse "pure" and "perfect" with identical or verbatim.

Moreover, some suppose that the Lord is under an obligation to preserve and present his words in English the way they demand.

They require that he express all nuances of the original languages exactly the same in all editions of the King James Bible. That is, they require that all printed editions be identical. The history of the text, however, shows some interesting deviations from their artificially imposed standard.

The Lord says his word is "pure" and "perfect."

- Thy word *is* very **pure**: therefore thy servant loveth it. (Psalm 119:140)

- Every word of God *is* **pure**: he *is* a shield unto them that put their trust in him. (Proverbs 30:5)

- The law of the LORD *is* **perfect**, converting the soul: the testimony of the LORD *is* sure, making wise the simple. (Psalm 19:7)

There is no requirement that all printings be identical.

Here's the thing. The first edition of the KJB is not always literal. Once you understand the translation technique used in the King James Bible, you'll be able to see the differences in various editions of the KJB in a different light.

Look at this example in **2 Chronicles 23:11**:

> Then they brought out the king's son, and put upon him the crown, and *gave him* the testimony, and made him king. And Jehoiada and his sons anointed him, and said, **God save the king.**

The Hebrew text literally says "Let the king live," whereas the translators presented the text idiomatically as "God save the king." "God save the king" is not wrong. It's just another way of saying the same thing in English.

The King James translators informed the reader by means of the marginal note what the literal Hebrew said. Here's how it appears in the 1611: "Hebr. Let the King liue."

Here's another one:

> Tribulation and anguish, upon every soul of man that doeth evil, of the Jew first, and also of the **Gentile**... (Romans 2:9)

Notice the word *Gentile*. It's *hellane* in the Greek text. The translators noted that in the margin: "Gr. Greek." The literal word for Gentile in Greek is *ethnos*, and five verses later the translators translated it that way:

> For when the **Gentiles** [*ethnos*], which have not the law, do by nature the things contained in the law, these, having not the law, are a law unto themselves... (Romans 2:14)

They translated two different Greek words, *hellane* and *ethnos*, with the same English word: Gentile. This is not an "error" in translation. It's a

173

choice in the way they presented the Greek text in English. In one case they **chose** not to be literal.

Some criticize the KJB for this, but all translators do the same thing to one degree or another. It's a method of translation that a critic may not like, but then most of them aren't Bible translators either.

A few times various editions display the pronouns he/she and his/her interchangeably. The underlying original language texts never changed, however, the English representation of that text exhibits a change from less literal to more literal in the various editions. Yet all still represent accurately the pure milk of the word.

For example:

Ruth 3:15

> ... And when she helde it, he measured sixe measures of barley, and laide it on her: and **he** went into the citie. (First printing, 1611.)

Here's the current reading, which started with the second printing in 1611:

> ... And when she held it, he measured six *measures* of barley, and laid *it* on her: and **she** went into the city. (Second printing, 1611.)

David Norton says, "Translators choose literalness over the demands of the context."

"He" is literal. The Hebrew text underlying the King James Bible reads "he" and so the first printing in 1611 has the literal "he." The second printing in 1611 is translated for context, i.e., "she" went into the city.

Interestingly, extant Hebrew manuscripts read both ways. The context has Ruth going into the city. A translator can translate for literalness or context.

The truth is that Boaz and Ruth both went into the city. Therefore, neither is wrong. The Lord preserved the truth with either option and in both options.

Here's another example:

Genesis 39:16

And she laid vp his garment by her, vntill **her** lord came home. (First Edition, 1611.)

And she laid up his garment by her, until **his** lord came home. (Current reading is literal, began in 1638.)

Neither is wrong. The context refers to Joseph and Potiphar's wife. Potiphar was "lord" of both of them. The Lord preserved the truth in either option.

By the way, here's how a couple of other translations handled the text:

New International Version (©2011)   … until **his** master came home.

New Living Translation (©2007)   … until **her** husband came home.

This scenario is repeated in other instances in various editions of the KJB. Sometimes a later edition will depart from the 1611 presentation and exhibit a more literal rendition of the text. In fact, that's the case in the majority of deviations from the 1611 printing.

If you could ever make the argument that the King James Bible has been "revised," tweaking the presentation of the English translation would be your best evidence. Making this charge is an excellent technique used to create doubt about veracity of the King James Bible, and critics use it constantly. However, as you've begun to see here and as you will see in the next couple of chapters, it turns out to be much ado about nothing.

University of North Carolina at Chapel Hill is a fully accredited university that trains students in the art of writing, so let's get their take on what it means to "revise" a document.

Revision literally means to "see again," to look at something from a fresh, critical perspective…

But I thought revision was just fixing the commas and spelling. Nope. That's called proofreading…

How about if I just reword things: look for better words, avoid repetition, etc.? Is that revision?

Well, that's a part of revision called editing. It's another important final step in polishing your work. But if you haven't thought through your ideas, then rephrasing them won't make any difference.[5]

Just because the Lord may not have preserved his words in the way some academics demand doesn't mean he didn't do it another way.

Still, you might ask...

But aren't these changes to the text?

Although the presentation of the English translation has been slightly modified, the underlying original language text remain unchanged.

The original committee that selected the textual readings and did the translation **disbanded** in 1610. Their work was completed. The original language texts didn't change after that because there was no one appointed to do it. All of the changes have to do with the **presentation** of the **texts** in English.

After a thorough examination of various editions of the King James Bible, here's what the Committee on Versions said to the Board of Managers of the American Bible Society in 1852:

---

[5] The Writing Center, University of North Carolina at Chapel Hill, "Revising Drafts," accessed December 2012, http://writingcenter.unc.edu/handouts/revising-drafts.

Which edition of the King James Bible is "The Bible"?

> AMERICAN BIBLE SOCIETY
> *Sharing God's Word with the World*
>
> The English Bible, as left by the translators [of 1611], has come down to us **unaltered in** respect to **its text** ... With the exception of typographical errors and changes required by the progress of orthography in the English language, **the text of our present Bibles remains unchanged, and without variation from the original copy as left by the translators.**[6]

You can buy an exact reproduction of the 1611 first printing (in Roman type for easy reading) from the Oxford University Press or from Hendrickson on Amazon.

Take it to a Bible study and see if you run into the same problems you do when multi-versions are used. You probably already know the confusion caused by the use of competing Bible versions in a Bible study.

The Bible versions don't say the same things and don't mean the same things, and everybody knows it. The emperor has no clothes and nobody says anything. The elephant's been in the living room since the **Revised Version** was published in 1885, but the damage done has accelerated in the last 40 years.

But what about new versions, aren't they derived from the same base as the King James?

Absolutely not.

They are built on very different New and slightly different Old Testament original language texts.

As a matter of fact, the producers of modern versions come right out and tell you that they **purposely** do not use the same materials used by

---

[6] American Bible Society. Committee on Versions, *Report on the History and Recent Collation of the English Version of the Bible. Presented by the Committee on Versions to the Board of Managers of the American Bible Society, and Adopted, May 1,1851.* Cornell University Library Digital Collections (Ithaca, NY: Cornell University Library, 1851), 7.

the King James translators because they believe they are inferior. (Not to mention, they'd be ridiculed by the scholarly community if they did.)

Even some of the translators who worked on the ©**1982 NKJV** didn't believe the text was the best as we saw in chapter 8.

Most modern scholars have been taught to disdain the materials that the **King James Bible** was built on. To them **the KJB** and the texts it was built on are unclean, defective, and adulterated with the words of men.

Sadly, we've already demonstrated the inferior quality of the texts used by modern Bible producers. Their Bibles are knockoffs. The reason they sell is because they look like the real thing, they're promoted heavily, and Christians aren't informed of the material differences.

One of the better techniques used to peddle modern versions is to convince unaware Christians that the King James Bible of today had its genesis in 1769, not in 1611.

Here's how this argument goes...

Chapter Eleven

What about the tens of thousands of differences between the 1769 edition (or any edition today) and the 1611 first edition?

> Ye blind guides, which strain at a gnat, and swallow a camel.
> (Matthew 23:24)

The last chapter showed some of the differences between various King James editions—differences appropriately labeled "insignificant matters" by a critic of King James Onlyism. Still, despite the fact that this argument is a nonstarter, you read all kinds of things like…

"The 1769 edition probably differs from the 1611 in 75,000 details."

Geisler and Nix's General *Introduction to the Bible* quotes Dr. Edgar Goodspeed as saying…

> but Blayney's edition has remained the standard form of the version ever since, unto this day. His edition probably differs from the 1611 in at least 75,000 details.[1]

University of Chicago theologian and Greek New Testament scholar Edgar Goodspeed (1871–1962), who published the "Goodspeed Bible" in 1935, could be right. Lots of well-meaning folks are handed that number and get nervous. They think "how could the King James Bible be the perfect word of God when there were over 75,000 changes?"

---

[1] Norman L. Geisler and William E. Nix, *A General Introduction to the Bible, Revised and Expanded* (Chicago: Moody Press, 1986), 117–118, citing Edgar J. Goodspeed, *The Complete Bible: An American Translation* (Chicago: University of Chicago, 1923).

Like Mark Twain said, "There are three kinds of lies: lies, d_ _ _ _ed lies, and statistics." The "75,000 details" is a boogie man statistic used to undercut the King James Bible and sway your opinion.

Meet a victim of scholarly propaganda.

You've already seen the nature of the changed "details." But now watch the effect of the propaganda apparatus at work on a man named Rick Beckman, who does "home improvement and repair in Marion, IN when [he's] not spending too much time on the internet."[2]

Rick's issue is mostly with the presentation differences in the various editions. The following quotes from his blog nicely summarize what we've all been taught about "revisions and editions of the King James Bible." It's a good case study because the comparisons he provides and the conclusions he draws are not new. They have been displayed and rehashed for years both on the web and in print.

This guy is looking for the truth. Unfortunately, he's been taught to misinterpret the evidence.

On March 24, 2007, Rick Beckman wrote:

> I have heard this enough in varying places that I wanted to post this just to help others not be duped by the statement: "The only changes made since the 1611 translation of the KJV until now have been changes of spelling or printing only."
>
> That statement is a lie, and people who love Jesus & the Bible should not make such a claim—even if they do have the best of intentions in doing so!
>
> So here is a list of significant changes (i.e., changes which affect meaning) made to the KJV text since 1611. The 1611 reading is first, followed by the 1769.[3]

---

[2] Rick Beckman, "KJV 1611 vs. KJV 1769" (blog), March 24, 2007, accessed December 2012, http://www.rickbeckman.org/kjv-1611-vs-kjv-1769.
[3] Ibid.

What about the tens of thousands of differences between the 1769 edition (or any edition today) and the 1611 first edition?

1	1 Corinthians 12:28	"helpes in gouernmets" vs. "helps, governments"
2	Joshua 3:11	"Arke of the Couenant, euen the Lord" vs. "ark of the covenant of the Lord"
3	2 Kings 11:10	"in the Temple" vs. "in the temple of the LORD"
4	Isaiah 49:13	"for God" vs. "for the LORD"
5	Jeremiah 31:14	"with goodnesse" vs. "with my goodness"
6	Jeremiah 51:30	"burnt their dwelling places" vs. "burned her dwelling places"
7	Ezekiel 6:8	"that he may" vs. "that ye may"
8	Ezekiel 24:5	"let him seethe" vs. "let them seethe"
9	Ezekiel 24:7	"powred it vpon the ground" vs. "poured it not upon the ground"
10	Ezekiel 48:8	"which they shall" vs. "which ye shall"
11	Daniel 3:15	"a fierie furnace" vs. "a burning fiery furnace"
12	Matthew 14:9	"the othes sake" vs. "the oath's sake"
13	1 Corinthians 15:6	"And that" vs. "After that"
14	1 John 5:12	"the Sonne, hath" vs. "the Son of God hath"

Wow. Looks pretty bad doesn't it? Maybe Geisler, Nix, and Goodspeed are right. The 1611 KJB is a mess with all those "revisions." But wait…

Here are the answers to Rick's concerns…

Let's look at his list again, except this time with the dates and nature of the modifications explained.

David Norton is a professor at Victoria University of Wellington and a renowned historian of the English Bible. He is author of the acclaimed *A History of the Bible as Literature* (2 vols.; Cambridge: Cambridge University Press, 1993) and its condensed volume, *A History of the English Bible as Literature* (Cambridge: Cambridge University Press, 2000). He is also the editor of the *New Cambridge Paragraph Bible* (Cambridge: Cambridge University Press, 2005.)

The following analysis is done with the historical backdrop and work as found in David Norton's 2005 book, *A Textual History of the King James Bible*.

1. **1 Corinthians 12:28**

   And God hath set some in the church, first apostles, secondarily prophets, thirdly teachers, after that miracles, then gifts of healings, **helps, governments**, diversities of tongues. (KJB today)

   And God hath set some in the Church, first Apostles, secondarily Prophets, thirdly Teachers, after that miracles, then gifts of healings, **helpes in gouernmets**, diuersities of tongues. (KJB 1611)

Here's how it was presented in earlier English Bibles...

   ...giftes of healyng, helpers, gouernours, diuersitie of tongues. **(Bishops' Bible)**

   ...giftes of healing, helpers, gouernours, diuersitie of tongues. **(Geneva Bible)**

   ...gyftes of healyng, helpers, gouerners, diuersitye of tonges. **(1540 Great Bible)**

   ...giftes of healinge, helpers, gouerners, dyuerse tunges. **(1535 Coverdale Bible)**

Norton says that "in" was the intent of the translators. Interestingly, the reversion of the preposition "in" so the text going forward matches the previous English translations was done under the auspices of two of the original KJB translators in 1629.

Norton says:

   Though this reading (in the 1611) is difficult to account for, it is not easily dismissed as a printer's error. MS 98 [Manuscript 98 is a copy of the only notes made by John Bois, a translator of the King James Bible] shows changes to *Bishop's Bible*, Bois's notes show the verse came under further notice.[4]

---

[2] David Norton, *A Textual History of the King James Bible* (Cambridge: Cambridge University Press, 2005), 334.

*What about the tens of thousands of differences between the
1769 edition (or any edition today) and the 1611 first edition?*

Norton keeps the 1611 reading in the *New Cambridge Paragraph Bible* because neither is wrong. Both readings represent optional ways of presenting the same Greek text.

2. **Joshua 3:11**

   Behold, the ark of the covenant **of** the Lord of all the earth passeth over before you into Jordan. (**KJB today**)

   Behold, the Arke of the Couenant, **euen** the Lord of all the earth, passeth ouer before you, into Iordan. (**KJB 1611**)

This change ("of" instead of "even") was made in 1629. Remember that this was done under the auspices of two of the original translators. Norton says: "1629's interpretation is followed by some (at least) modern translations, but 1611's reading remains possible."[5]

Norton keeps the 1611 reading because neither is wrong. They both represent optional ways of presenting the same Hebrew text.

3. **2 Kings 11:10**

   And to the captains over hundreds did the priest give king David's spears and shields, that *were* in the **temple of the** Lord. (**KJB today**)

   And to the captaines ouer hundreds, did the Priest giue king Dauids speares and shields, that were **in the Temple**. (**KJB 1611**)

The phrase "of the Lord" is literal and presented in 1638.

Norton notes: "This looks like an omission by the translators but may be deliberate."[6] That's because the 1611 translators were not always literal in their presentation of the text, as we discussed in chapter 10.

Note that in previous English Bibles the text appeared both ways:

---

[5] Ibid., 225.
[6] Ibid., 242.

... in the house of the LORDE   1535 Coverdale
... in the tēple _____ 1540 Great Bible
... in the temple _____ 1549 Matthew
... in the temple _____ 1568 Bishops'

Here's a parallel passage:

> Moreover Jehoiada the priest delivered to the captains of hundreds spears, and bucklers, and shields, that *had been* king David's, which *were* in the house of God. (2 Chronicles 23:9)

In other Scripture, we see the Temple referred to both ways: it's called "the temple of the Lord" in Luke 1:9 and "the temple" in Luke 1:31. The Lord historically presented the passage both ways. Neither rendering is wrong.

It's interesting to note that this parallel passage uses "God" instead of "Lord." We'll see more on this type of change coming up.

4. **Isaiah 49:13**

> Sing, O heavens; and be joyful, O earth; and break forth into singing, O mountains: **for the** Lord hath comforted his people, and will have mercy upon his afflicted. **(KJB today)**

> Sing, O heauen, and be ioyfull, O earth, and breake forth into singing, O mountaines: **for God** hath comforted his people, and will haue mercy vpon his afflicted. **(KJB 1611)**

The literal text reads Lord (Jehovah), not God (Elohim). However, notice how the previous English Bibles used God instead of Lord below.

Norton says that *God* "appears to be an error." If so, then correction was made in 1638 by two of the original translators. But a historical examination of the passage reveals:

> Heuenes, herie ye, ... **for the Lord** coumfortide... **(1380 Wycliffe)**

> Reioyse ye heauens ... **for God** wil cofōrte his people... **(1535 Coverdale)**

*What about the tens of thousands of differences between the
1769 edition (or any edition today) and the 1611 first edition?*

> Reioyse ye heauens ... **for God** wyll comforte hys people... **(1549 Matthew)**
>
> Reioyce, O heauens: ...: **for God** hath comforted... **(Geneva)**
>
> Reioyce ye heauens ... **for God** hath comforted his people... **(Bishops')**
>
> Sing, O heavens, ... For comforted hath **Jehovah** His people... **(Young's Literal Translation)**

Note that the Wycliffe Bible (1380) used the phrase "for the Lord." So this rendering was known.

This situation is much the same case as we find in **Genesis 6:5**:

> **And God** saw, that the wickednes of man was great in the earth, and that euery imagination of the thoughts of his heart was onely euill continually. **(KJB 1611)**
>
> **And GOD** saw that the wickedness of man was great in the earth, and that every imagination of the thoughts of his heart *was* only evil continually. **(Current Cambridge University printing)**

The issue here is the capitalization of God in the 1611 edition and GOD in the current printing by Cambridge University Press. Although this doesn't look like any big deal (and it isn't for most) it matters to some because of what the spelling reflects in the original Hebrew.

"God" in any edition of the King James usually represents the Hebrew word for God, "Elohim," and "GOD" (all caps) usually stands for "Jehovah." Sometimes Jehovah is represented as LORD (cap/small cap). Are you starting to see the problem?

So which is it?

- "and **Elohim** saw that the wickedness of man *was* great..." or
- "and **Jehovah** saw that the wickedness of man *was* great..."

It gets worse. Although the change was made in 1629 and many King James Bibles read **GOD**, many editions of the 1611 King James Bible still read **God**.[8]

2 Chronicles 28:11 poses the same issue:

> Now hear me therefore, and deliver the captives again, which ye have taken captive of your brethren: for the fierce **wrath of the** Lord *is* upon you. (Current Cambridge University printing)

> Now heare me therefore, and deliuer the captiues againe, which ye haue taken captiue of your brethren: for the fierce **wrath of God** is vpon you. (KJB 1611)

Like they say, things that are different can't be the same. Here we see that "God" is used for "the Lord" in some of the earlier English versions:

---

[8] **Reading GOD** are Canadian Bible Society—Collins' Clear Type Press; The British and Foreign Bible Society in Canada—Oxford; The British and Foreign Bible Society—Cambridge; International Bible Society-Permission-Cambridge; Oxford University Press--with Apocrypha; Trinitarian Bible Society—Interlinear Literal; Jehovah Crusade Bible Publishers, Inc; Zondervan Bible Publishers; World Publishing Company; Canadian Bible Society—Richardson, Bound & Wright, Limited; Queen's Printers; Canadian Bible Society—Oxford University Press; Cambridge University Press [posted by "Holy Bible," September 15, 2005, on AV 1611 God's Word bulletin board, Why KJV Only (topic), 8 places (thread), accessed December 2012, http://av1611godsword.yuku.com/topic/684/eight-places?page=2#.TyGwlvl17to; and 1715, 1768, 1769 Oxford], SRB Oxford, Oxford Classic, NPB Oxford; 1629, 1637, 1638 Cambridge, CSTE, DKJB; 1634, 1672, 1711, 1760, 1763, 1817 London (ibid., posted by "logos1560," November 26, 2010).

Reading God are Gideon's—National Publishing Company; Thomas Nelson Publishers; 1611 Edition Facsimile—Hendrickson Publishers; World Publishing Company; AMG Publishers—Eyre and Spottiswoode [Publishers] Limited; A.J. Holman Company [posted by "Holy Bible," September 15, 2005, on AV 1611 God's Word bulletin board, Why KJV Only (topic), 8 places (thread), accessed December 2012, http://av1611godsword.yuku.com/topic/684/eight-places?page=2#.TyGwlvl17to]; and1679, 1770, 1771, 1772, 1773, 1777, 1778, 1782, 1783, 1791, 1792, 1798, 1799, 1803, 1810, 1812, 1928 Oxford, 1952 PE, SSB Oxford; 1743, 1747, 1760, 1765, 1768, 1769, 1773, 1778, 1795, 1817, 1824, 2005 Cambridge; 1611, 1613, 1614, 1617, 1750, 1824 London; 1722, 1756, 1764, 1766, 1787, 1789, 1858 Edinburgh; 1782 Aitken; 1791 Collins; (1810, 1828 Boston; 1813 Carey; 1813 Johnson; 1816 Albany; Clarke; 1846 Portland; 1895, 1997 NPC; 1954 ABS; 1958 Hertel; 1968 Royal; 1973 REG; 1975 Open; 1978 GID; CSB; Nave's; RRB; LASB; FWP; 1984 AMG; 1976, 1987, 1989 TN; VB; EB; RSB; 2010 BRO; 1833 WEB (ibid., posted by "logos1560," November 26, 2010).

What about the tens of thousands of differences between the 1769 edition (or any edition today) and the 1611 first edition?

Wycliffe	for greet veniaunce of the Lord neiyith to you
Tyndale	the fierce wrath of God is vpon you
Coverdale	for the **wrath of þe LORDE** is fearce ouer you
Matthew	for **the great wrath of the Lorde** is vpon you
Great 1540	for els shall þe great wrath of God be vpō you
Geneva	for **the fierce wrath of the Lord** *is* toward you
Bishops'	the great wrath of God be vpon you
Bishops' 1602 (Bodleian Library)	wrath of God
1611 KJB	for **the fierce wrath of God** is vpon you
NKJV	for **the fierce wrath of the LORD** *is* upon you
Cambridge KJB	for **the fierce wrath of the LORD** *is* upon you
Hebrew	the fierce חָרוֹן wrath אַף of the LORD יְהוָה *is* upon you
Young's (YLT)	for the **heat of the anger of Jehovah** *is* upon you

If we assume that the Lord was overseeing his work in the King James Bible, then this difference in various editions should be easy to answer. And it is.

First, the 1611 translators may have chosen the nonliteral "God" in place of the literal "the LORD" in Isaiah 49:13, Genesis 6:5, and 2 Chronicles 28:11. As you can see, the English text was presented both ways in previous English Bibles.

Second, historical evidence shows that many times the Lord allows Jehovah ("LORD" in the English Bible) to be used interchangeably with Adonai in Hebrew ("Lord" in the English Bible).

Sometimes the Jews would read Adonai when Jehovah was written. They did this out of reverence to the name Jehovah.

Look at the scan of a Dead Sea Scroll (these manuscripts have been dated to various ranges between 408 BC to AD 318). Notice how Jehovah (LORD) is written over Adonai (Lord) and then reversed in the next line in this Isaiah scroll:

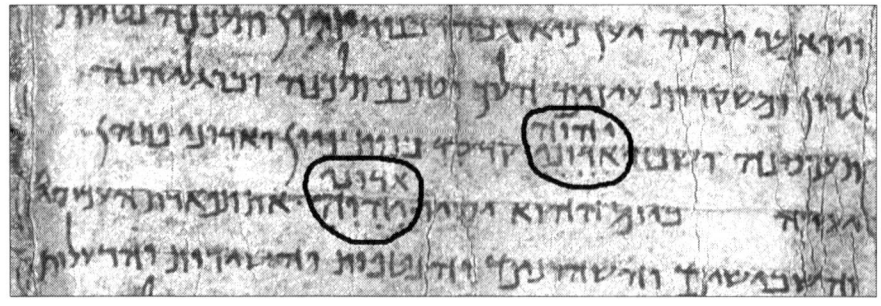

Dead Sea Scroll passage showing Isaiah 3:17–18.

The scanned passage is from Isaiah 3:17–18. Here's how it reads in the King James Bible:

> Therefore the Lord will smite with a scab the crown of the head of the daughters of Zion, and the Lord will discover their secret parts. In that day the **Lord** will take away the bravery of *their* tinkling ornaments *about their feet,* and *their* cauls, and their round tires like the moon…

Dr. Paul Wegner is an author and former professor at Moody Bible Institute and Phoenix Seminary. Here are his comments on the Dead Sea Scroll passage:

> In the third line dots appear below the MT [Masoretic Text] reading אדני ('dwny, "the Lord") and the alternate reading יהוה (yhwh, "Yahweh") appears above it. But in the fourth line the readings are reversed: dots appear below the word יהוה (yhwh) and the reading from the MT [Masoretic Text] appears above it.[9]

Notice how the Lord quotes himself in parallel passages, first in 2 Samuel:

> 2 Samuel 5:19 And David inquired of the Lord…
>
> 2 Samuel 5:20 David smote them there, and said, The Lord hath broken forth upon mine…
>
> 2 Samuel 5:23 And when David inquired of the Lord , he said,…
>
> 2 Samuel 5:24 for then shall the Lord go out before thee, to smite the host of the Philistines.
>
> 2 Samuel 5:25 And David did so, as the Lord had commanded him

And then in 1 Chronicles, where God is used instead of Lord:

1 Chronicles 14:10   And David inquired of **God**,

1 Chronicles 14:11   David smote them there. Then David said, **God** hath broken…

1 Chronicles 14:15   **God** is gone forth before thee to smite the host of the Philistines.

1 Chronicles 14:16   David therefore did as **God** commanded him…

These parallel passages prove that the Lord himself sometimes uses the word "God" interchangeably with "the Lord."

Here's another example: "The Lord" in the Old Testament is quoted as "God" in the New Testament…

And he believed in **the Lord**; and he counted it to him for righteousness. (Genesis 15:6)

Here's how Genesis 15:6 is quoted in the New Testament…

For what saith the scripture? Abraham **believed God**, and it was counted unto him for righteousness. (Romans 4:3)

Even as Abraham **believed God**, and it was accounted to him for righteousness. (Galatians 3:6)

Interesting isn't it? The Bible is a fascinating "book." And that's the point—The Bible is a unified book.

5. **Jeremiah 31:14**

And I will satiate the soul of the priests with fatness, and my people shall be satisfied **with my goodness**, saith the LORD. (KJB today)

And I will satiate the soule of the priests with fatnesse, and my people shall be satisfied **with goodnesse**, saith the Lord. (KJB 1611)

---

[9] Paul D. Wegner, *A Student's Guide to Textual Criticism of the Bible: Its History, Methods, and Results* (Downers Grove, IL: InterVarsity Press, 2006), 91.

Norton says: "1611 appears to be an error but may be deliberate."[10]

The more literal rendering "with **my** goodness" was made in 1629 by editors that included two of the original translators. Norton keeps the 1611 reading "with goodness" even though it is less literal. Neither is wrong. Both are true. Both are accurate renderings of the text. This is a stylistic update.

6. **Jeremiah 51:30**

> The mighty men of Babylon have forborn to fight, they have "remained in *their* holds: their might hath failed; they became as women: they have **burned her dwelling places**; her bars are broken. (KJB today)

> The mightie men of Babylon haue forborne to fight: they haue remained in their holdes: their might hath failed, they became as women: they haue **burnt their dwelling places**: her barres are broken. (KJB 1611)

This is a 1638 spelling ("burned" vs. "burnt") and stylistic update ("her dwelling places" vs. "their dwelling places"). Norton keeps the less literal 1611 rendering. Both are acceptable translations. Neither is in error, and both are accurate renderings of the text.

7. **Ezekiel 6:8**

> Yet will I leave a remnant, that **ye** may have *some* that shall escape the sword among the nations, when ye shall be scattered through the countries. (KJB today)

> Yet will I leaue a remnant, that **he** may haue some, that shall escape the sword among the nations, when ye shalbe scattered through the countreys. (KJB 1611)

This printing error was corrected in 1612.

---

[10] Norton, *Textual History of the King James Bible*, 285.

*What about the tens of thousands of differences between the
1769 edition (or any edition today) and the 1611 first edition?*

8. **Ezekiel 24:5**

   Take the choice of the flock, and burn also the bones under it, *and* make it boil well, and let **them** seethe the bones of it therein. (KJB today)

   Take the choice of the flocke, and burne also the bones vnder it, and make it boyle well, and let **him** seethe the bones of it therein. (KJB 1611)

This printing error was corrected in 1638.

9. **Ezekiel 24:7**

   For her blood is in the midst of her; she set it upon the top of a rock; she poured it **not** upon the ground, to cover it with dust; (KJB today)

   For her blood is in the middest of her: she set it vpon the toppe of a rocke, she powred it vpon the ground to couer it with dust: (KJB 1611)

This printing error was corrected in 1613.

10. **Ezekiel 48:8**

    And by the border of Judah, from the east side unto the west side, shall be the offering which **ye** shall offer of five and twenty thousand *reeds in* breadth, and *in* length as one of the *other* parts, from the east side unto the west side: and the sanctuary shall be in the midst of it. (KJB today)

    And by the border of Iudah, from the East side vnto the West side, shall be the offring which **they** shall offer of fiue and twentie thousand reedes in bredth, and in length as one of the other parts, from the East side vnto the West side, and the Sanctuarie shall be in the midst of it. (KJB 1611)

The more literal rendering was presented in 1638 again by two of the original translators. However, Norton retains the 1611 reading because:

> Though this seems to be an error, it is retained because the translators apparently chose to retain it from 1602 and G[eneva Bible] against, e.g., Great Bible ("ye shall set asyde").[11]

The point is that neither rendering is in error. Both are acceptable presentations of the text even though they are not identical.

11. Daniel 3:15

> Now if ye be ready that at what time ye hear the sound of the cornet, flute, harp, sackbut, psaltery, and dulcimer, and all kinds of musick, ye fall down and worship the image which I have made; *well*: but if ye worship not, ye shall be cast the same hour into the midst of a **burning** fiery furnace; and who is that God that shall deliver you out of my hands? (KJB today)

> Now if ye be ready that at what time yee heare the sound of the cornet, flute, harpe, sackbut, psalterie, and dulcimer, and all kindes of musicke, ye fall downe, and worship the image which I haue made, well: but if yee worship not, ye shall be cast the same houre into the midst of a fierie furnace, and who is that God that shall deliuer you out of my handes? (KJB 1611)

Norton keeps the less literal 1611 reading, opting to follow the Bodleian Library's 1602 annotated Bishops' Bible, which "suggests that the translators decided a second adjective was unnecessary."[12]

The more literal rendering was presented in 1638. Neither is wrong. Both are acceptable presentations of the text even though they are not identical.

12. Matthew 14:9

> And the king was sorry: nevertheless for the **oath's** sake, and them which sat with him at meat, he commanded *it* to be given *her*. (KJB today)

---

[11] Ibid., 293.
[12] Ibid., 294.

> And the king was sorie: neuerthelesse for the **othes** sake, and them which sate with him at meate, he commanded it to be giuen her: (KJB 1611)

This 1762 edit simply updates spelling and punctuation.

13. 1 Corinthians 15:6

> **After that**, he was seen of above five hundred brethren at once; of whom the greater part remain unto this present, but some are fallen asleep. (KJB today)

> **And that** hee was seene of aboue fiue hundred brethren at once: of whom the greater part remaine vnto this present, but some are fallen asleepe. (KJB 1611)

This printing error was corrected in 1616.

14. 1 John 5:12

> He that hath the Son hath life; *and* he that hath not the **Son of God** hath not life. (KJB today)

> Hee that hath the Sonne, hath life; and hee that hath not the **Sonne**, hath not life. (KJB 1611)

Norton says:

> Scrivener notes that "of God" continued to be omitted in a number of later editions (p. 193 n.). The omission may be deliberate though it is not literal and goes against the other versions; MS 98 shows that the translators' first thought was to keep the received reading. "Of God" is understood.[13]

Norton retains the 1611 reading assuming the translators decided not to render the phrase literally. The words "of God" appear in all the earlier English versions:

---

[13] Ibid., 353.

and he that hath not the sonne of god hath not lyfe. (1526 Tyndale)
He that hath not the sonne of God, hath not life. (1535 Coverdale)
& he that hath not the sonne of God, hath not lyfe. (1540 Great Bible)
and he that hath not the sonne of God, hath not lyfe. (1549 Matthew)
and he that hath not yt Sonne of God, hath not that life. (1560 Geneva)

The reading as it appears in earlier versions was reinstated in 1629, again by a team including two of the original translators. The Lord has had the verse appear both literally and nonliterally. Either way, it only appears with the words "of God" today in any edition.

Let's get back to Mr. Beckman's concerns. Rick goes on…

Additionally, even today there are two versions of the KJV in use: the Oxford and the Cambridge editions. Some of the differences in them affect the meaning of the text as well. For example, here are a couple Cambridge passages vs. their Oxford counterparts.

- Jeremiah 34:16   "whom ye had set" vs. "whom he had set" [see the discussion below]

- 2 Timothy 2:2   "heard from me" vs. "heard of me" [Someone led Rick astray on this one because both the Cambridge and Oxford printings say "heard **of** me."]

One cannot help to wonder about KJV-Onlyism in light of the above… Was the King James Version of 1611 perfect? If yes, why were there such substantial changes made to the text between then and 1769? By using a modern edition of the KJV, the Onlyists are admitting that the 1611 translation was flawed![14]

Rick continued to grapple with this subject the next day:

Again, my question to KJV-Onlyists is this: How do you determine what is perfect or not? If you had a 1611 KJV in your hands, would you be holding the perfect Word of God? Why or why not? At what point did the KJV become the perfect Word of God? Was it in 1612, 1613, 1616, 1629, 1638, or 1769? The KJV was edited a bit in each of those years. Is the 1769 edition perfect? Why? Which: the Oxford

---

[14] Beckman, "KJV 1611 vs. KJV 1769."

edition or the Cambridge edition? Why? What about the Modern King James Version or the Comfortable King James Version?

Was there a perfect Word of God in English in 1768? If so, why was it edited a year later?

Most importantly, I would like to ask this: if the 1769 edition of the English Bible is perfect, what was the perfect Bible a year before that? Clearly it couldn't have been the KJV 'cause it was still in need of editing.[15]

The literal translation choices made in 1611 and adjusted in later editions or the frequent spelling and grammar updates doesn't mean any edition was wrong or flawed. They are different ways of presenting the same original language text.

Rick is confusing pure and perfect with identical.

Printing errors notwithstanding, all those editions are the pure words of God. And all have been used by the Lord Jesus Christ.

And besides...

It's the King James "brand" that's important, not any particular edition.

> KJV-Onlyism is a divisive tradition full of more holes than a bowl of Cheerios. May the Lord open the eyes and ears of all those trapped by this stronghold, just as He did for me.[16]

Rick says the Lord opened his eyes and he's praying the Lord will do the same for you. Interestingly, Rick's eyes have been fully opened because in 2012 he presented his blog title as

> **Rick Beckman**
> Brazenly geek. Brazenly atheist. Brazenly me.[17]

---

[15] Rick Beckman, "More Changes Between the 1611 and the 1769 Editions of the KJV" (blog), March 25, 2007, accessed December 2012, http://rickbeckman.org/more-changes-between-the-1611-and-the-1769-editions-of-the-kjv.

[16] Ibid.

[17] Rick Beckman home page, accessed December 2012, http://www.rickbeckman.org.

And so Rick added to his list on March 25, 2007:

Here are some more changes between the 1611 and the 1769 editions of the KJV. You can see that the changes in some instances affect the meaning of the context quite significantly![18]

15	Deuteronomy 26:1	"which the Lord giueth" vs. "which the LORD thy God giveth"
16	Joshua 3:11	"tribe of Manasseh, by" vs. "tribe of the children of Manasseh by"
17	Ruth 3:15	"he went into the citie" vs. "she went into the city"
18	Psalm 69:32	"seeke good" vs. "seek God"
19	Jeremiah 49:1	"inherit God" vs. "inherit Gad"
20	Matthew 16:16	Thou art Christ" vs. "Thou art the Christ"
21	Mark 10:18	"There is no man good" vs. "*there* is none good" (note that now "there is" is marked as being added by the translators for clarity)
22	1 Corinthians 4:9	"approued to death" vs. "appointed to death"

Again, let's take a closer look at Rick's list:

15. **Deuteronomy 26:1**

> And it shall be, when thou *art* come in unto the land which the LORD **thy God** giveth thee *for* an inheritance, and possessest it, and dwellest therein; (KJB today)

> And it shall be when thou art come in vnto the land which the LORD giueth thee for an inheritance, and possessest it, and dwellest therein: (KJB 1611)

Norton explains that although it "appeared to be a printer's omission" in the 1611 KJB, the earlier Bodleian Bible "shows that it goes back to the translators."[19]

---
[18] Beckman, "More Changes Between the 1611 and the 1769 Editions of the KJV."
[19] Norton, *Textual History of the King James Bible*, 224.

What about the tens of thousands of differences between the
1769 edition (or any edition today) and the 1611 first edition?

The 1611 translators decided to drop the literal "Thy God." We know this because the 1602 Bishop's Bible they used as a printer's model had the words ~~Thy God~~ crossed out.

The more literal "LORD thy God" was used in 1629 by editors that included two of the original translators. Neither is wrong and both are acceptable presentations of the text even though they are not identical.

16. **Joshua 13:29**

> And Moses gave *inheritance* unto the half tribe of Manasseh: and *this* was the possession of the half tribe **of the children of** Manasseh by their families. (KJB today)

> And Moses gaue inheritance vnto the halfe **tribe of Manasseh**: and this was the possession of the halfe tribe of Manasseh, by their families. (KJB 1611)

Norton comments:

> Though 1638 is correct, the possibility remains that 1611 **chose** not to include G[eneva's] "the children of."[20]

The more literal rendering was made in 1638 by editors that included two of the original translators. Neither is wrong and both are acceptable presentations of the text even though they are not identical.

17. **Ruth 3:15**

> Also he said, Bring the vail that *thou hast* upon thee, and hold it. And when she held it, he measured six *measures* of barley, and laid *it* on her: and **she** went into the city. (KJB today)

> Also he said, Bring the vaile that thou hast vpon thee, and holde it. And when she helde it, he measured sixe measures of barley, and laide it on her: and **he** went into the citie. (KJB 1611)

---

[20] Ibid., 229.

Recall that this change was explained in chapter 10. "He" is literal. The Hebrew text underlying the King James Bible reads "he" and so the first printing in 1611 has the literal "he." The second printing in 1611 is translated for context. That is, "she," meaning Ruth, went into the city.

A translator can translate for literalness or context. The truth is that both Boaz and Ruth went into the city. Neither is wrong.

Jack McElroy with an original King James Bible known as The Great She Bible because of the reading in Ruth 3:15

18. **Psalm 69:32**

> The humble shall see *this, and* be glad: and your heart shall live that seek **God**. (KJB today)

> The humble shall see this, and be glad: and your heart shall liue that seeke **good**. (KJB 1611)

This printing error in the first edition was corrected in 1617.

19. **Jeremiah 49:1**

> Concerning the Ammonites, thus saith the LORD; Hath Israel no sons? hath he no heir? why *then* doth their king inherit *Gad*, and his people dwell in his cities? (KJB today)

> Concerning the Ammonites, thus sayth the LORD; hath Israel no sonnes? Hath he no heire? Why then doth their king inherit God, and his people dwell in his cities? (KJB 1611)

This printing error in the first edition was corrected in 1616.

20. **Matthew 16:16**

> And Simon Peter answered and said, Thou art **the** Christ, the Son of the living God. (KJB today)

> And Simon Peter answered, and said, Thou art Christ the sonne of the liuing God. (KJV 1611)

This is an orthographic/stylistic update that was done in 1762.

*What about the tens of thousands of differences between the
1769 edition (or any edition today) and the 1611 first edition?*

21. Mark 10:18

And Jesus said unto him, Why callest thou me good? *there is* **none** good but one, *that is,* God. (KJB today)

And Iesus said vnto him, Why callest thou me good? There is **no man** good, but one, that is God. (KJB 1611)

David Norton keeps the 1611 reading and says:

An unnecessary correction of 1611's English. S[crivener] notes: "a variation taken from Matt. 19:17. A like change might well be made in some other places, e.g. Matt. 11:27, [Mark?] 13:32. In John 10:28 "any," 29, "none" of 1638–1762 are rejected by 1769 and later Bibles for "any man," "no man" of 1611–30; "man" however being printed in italic type" (p. 187 n.)[21]

Even Strong's allows for either presentation of the text:

Strong's Greek Dictionary 3762. ουδεις **oudeis** ... from 3761 and 1520; not even one (man, woman or thing), i.e. none, nobody, nothing: —any (man), aught, man, neither any (thing), never (man), no (man), none (+ of these things), not (any, at all, -thing), nought.

The more literal "none" was chosen in 1638. The Lord preserved the truth with either option and in both options. Both renderings are the words of the Lord.

22. 1 Corinthians 4:9

For I think that God hath set forth us the apostles last, as it were **appointed** to death: for we are made a spectacle unto the world, and to angels, and to men. (KJB today)

For I thinke that God hath set forth vs the Apostles last, as it were **approued** to death. For wee are made a spectacle vnto the world, and to Angels, and to men. (KJB 1611)

This is an interesting choice in translation. Norton says:

---

[21] Ibid., 331.

Though "approved" is a hard reading (i.e. more difficult to understand), it fits with the positive sense of the Apostles in the passage. 1611 is a deliberate change, **and one knows from Bois's notes that this verse was the subject of close discussion.**[22]

All the earlier English Bibles used "appointed" and so the change was made in 1616 to return to the older reading…

> For I thinke that God hath set forth vs the last Apostles, as men **appointed** to death: for we are made a gasing stocke vnto the worlde, and to the Angels, and to men. (Geneva Bible)

> For me thynketh, that God hath set foorth vs, whiche are the last apostles, as it were men **appoynted** to death. For we are made a gasyng stocke vnto the worlde, and to the angels, and to men. (Bishops' Bible)

> Me thinketh that God hath set forth vs which are Apostles for the lowest of all as it were men **appoynted** to deeth. For we are a gasyngestocke vnto the worlde and to ye angels and to men. (Tyndale)

> Me thinketh that God hath sente forth vs, which are Apostles for the lowest, of al as it were men **appointed** to death. (1549 Matthew)

> For me thynketh, that God hath set forth vs (which are the last Apostles) as it were men **appoynted** to deeth. (1540 Great Bible)

We've addressed all the verses in Rick Beckman's lists, but Rick has one more for us…

> In addition to all of those variations, there is another interesting one at Jeremiah 34:16.[23]

The Jeremiah 34:16 passage is a well-known and oft-cited difference between the University of Oxford and University of Cambridge printings. But there are three others that Rick missed. We'll review them all in the next chapter, but let's take a quick peek.

---

[22] Ibid., 343.
[23] Beckman, "More Changes Between the 1611 and the 1769 Editions of the KJV."

What about the tens of thousands of differences between the
1769 edition (or any edition today) and the 1611 first edition?

The Cambridge printing reproduces the original 1611 text. The Oxford printing presents a slightly different presentation of the text...

	Reference	Cambridge	Oxford	1611
1	Joshua 19:2	**or**	**and**	And they had in their inheritance Beer-sheba, **or** Sheba, and Moladah,
2	2 Chronicles 33:19	**sin**	**sins**	His prayer also, and how God was intreated of him, and all his **sinne**, and his trespasse...
3	Jeremiah 34:16	**ye**	**he**	But yee turned and polluted my Name, and caused euery man his seruant, and euery man his handmaide, whome **yee** had set at libertie...
4	Nahum 3:16	**flieth**	**fleeth**	Thou hast multiplied thy merchants aboue the starres of heauen; ... & **flieth** away.

We'll answer these concerns in the next chapter. In the meantime, Rick concludes:

> If the KJV alone is our authority, how on earth would we ever figure it out? However, thankfully, the preserved manuscript evidence is our authority, not a translation from that preserved evidence. The Hebrew in that passage is plural, and so "you" (or, as the KJV would read, "ye") is the correct translation. But if all you have in your hands are two KJVs—one Oxford and one Cambridge—how could you ever come to any sort of conclusion? Even if you had the Hebrew text there, certain forms of radical KJV-Onlyism, such as that of Dr. Ruckman and his supporters, would prohibit using the

201

Hebrew text—especially if it would override what the KJV says (or, in this instance, what the preferred edition of the KJV says).

Thank the Lord that He has preserved His Word through a mass of manuscripts which allow us to know His Word thoroughly rather than a singular translation which limits our studies to the interpretations of fallible men (i.e., "God forbid" is an interpretation—the word "God" doesn't even appear in the Greek in those passages, but if you are forbidden to look at the Greek by an Onlyist doctrine, how would you ever know?).[24]

Rick may not realize it, but "**the preserved manuscript evidence**" has thousands of variant readings. Therein lies the problem. Which of the variants are authentic? You've already seen examples and learned they can vary widely (even saying the opposite). The variants not only affect doctrine but were introduced early on to do exactly that.

To say "**the preserved manuscript evidence is our authority**" naively assumes that the choices in variant readings are resolved. They aren't. No one can prove which of the variants that significantly affect the text of the New Testament are authentic because you'd have to have the originals to do that.

Critics have theories and can claim authenticity for any readings they want, but they can never prove their choice is 100% correct. Some ill-informed professors can profess anything they want. The textual critics who assembled the modern Greek New Testament actually grade themselves on their choices (A, B, C, etc.) just like in school. The point is—the Lord owns the score sheet.

Textual critics can cite manuscript evidence or internal and external evidence, but since there is **no judging authority** with the power to make the final determination, there can **never** be certainty as to the correctness of **any** of the variants. No one can **prove** any reading is "original" because there aren't any originals to compare to.

---

[24] Ibid.

What about the tens of thousands of differences between the 1769 edition (or any edition today) and the 1611 first edition?

According to Professor Maurice Robinson, over 85% of the Greek New Testament is the same for all texts. That includes Textus Receptus, Critical Text, and Majority Text.[25]

If any King James Bible today isn't the Bible--isn't the Book of the Lord,[26] isn't the Bible Jesus uses—then you're left with the fact that there can never be certainty as to the remaining 15% as long as there are differing scholarly opinions. That's what exists today. Of the 15%, no reading is 100% sure and nothing is certain because the scholars disagree among themselves. There are and will be only discussions of each man's preferences.

As a result, the controversy will continue as long as there are competing texts. Does it sound like the Lord to leave 15% of the text open to question?

Translation means nothing unless you first determine **what** words (that's the text) you translate. Then you can argue over how to translate them.

That's why there has to be "A Book" that the Lord provides. It should be easy to spot. And it is. And it's probably sitting on your bookshelf right now.

Next, let's take an even closer look at another red herring already alluded to in this chapter…

---

[25] Maurice A. Robinson, "The Case for the Byzantine Textform: A New Approach to 'Majority Text' Theory." Paper presented at the Southeastern Regional Evangelical Theological Society Meeting, Toccoa Falls, GA, March 8–9, 1991. (Available: Theological Research Exchange Network, www.tren.com).

[26] The King James translators called it "God's book" in the 1611 preface section entitled *The Translators to the Reader:* "Now what can be more available thereto, than to deliver God's book unto God's people in a tongue which they understand? Since of a hidden treasure, and of a fountain that is sealed, there is no profit…"

Chapter Twelve

What about the differences between King James Bibles printed by the Oxford and Cambridge University Presses?

> Thy testimonies are very sure: holiness becometh thine house,
> O LORD, for ever. (Psalm 93:5)

Rick Norris wrote a book that details different readings from different King James Bible publishers over the past 400 years.

He believes the differences in various editions invalidate the English text of the KJB as being the exclusive representative of the Lord's Bible.

He said…

> If the KJV is immutable, why do many variations exist within the various current editions of the KJV printed by different publishers?[1]

He's posed a fair question, and here's a short answer with four examples…

First of all, understand that the original language texts underlying the King James Bible haven't mutated (i.e., changed) in 400 years. How it's been presented in English has been tweaked as we have seen and will see in later chapters.

Every critic of the KJB knows the following places where Bibles printed by Oxford University Press and Cambridge University Press contain slightly different readings. These are the four big examples presented

---

[1] Rick Norris, "Rick Norris Responds to the 'Spelling Changes Onlyism' Argument Offered By Many in the 'King James Only' Camp," King James Only Resource Center, accessed January 2013, http://www.kjvonly.org/rick/norris_spelling.htm.

over and over again in online forums as a reason for you to ditch the King James Bible.

	Reference	1611 first edition	Cambridge	Oxford
1	Joshua 19:2	And they had in their inheritance Beer-sheba, **or** Sheba, and Moladah,	**or**	**and**
2	2 Chronicles 33:19	His prayer also, and how God was in-treated of him, and all his **sinne**, and his trespasse,…	**sin**	**sins**
3	Jeremiah 34:16	But yee turned and polluted my Name, and caused euery man his seruant, and euery man his hand-maide, whome **yee** had set at libertie at their pleasure,…	**ye**	**he**
4	Nahum 3:16	Thou hast multiplied thy merchants aboue the starres of heauen; the cankerworme spoileth & **flieth** away.	**flieth**	**fleeth**

The Cambridge printing matches the 1611 first edition. The Oxford varies. But is it "an error" to present those English words alternatively as representative of the original Hebrew words? Let's take a look…

1. **Joshua 19:2**

What's interesting here for the critics is how **Joshua 19:2–6** reads in the various printings and versions. Note that the Cambridge printing matches the NASB and the Oxford matches the ESV (the numerals are

What about the differences between King James Bibles printed by the Oxford and Cambridge University Presses?

inserted so you can easily count the number of cities):

Cambridge University Press
And they had in their inheritance (1) **Beersheba, or Sheba,** and (2) Moladah, And (3) Hazarshual, and (4) Balah, and (5) Azem, And (6) Eltolad, and (7) Bethul, and (8) Hormah, (9) And Ziklag, and (10) Bethmarcaboth, and (11) Hazarsusah, And (12) Bethlebaoth, and (13) Sharuhen; **thirteen cities** and their villages:
Oxford University Press
And they had in their inheritance (1) **Beersheba, and** (2) **Sheba**, and (3) Moladah, And (4) Hazarshual, and (5) Balah, and (6) Azem, And (7) Eltolad, and (8) Bethul, and (9) Hormah, And (10) Ziklag, and (11) Bethmarcaboth, and (12) Hazarsusah, And (13) Bethlebaoth, and (14) Sharuhen; **thirteen cities** and their villages:
New American Standard Bible (©1995)
So they had as their inheritance (1) **Beersheba or Sheba and** (2) Moladah, and (3) Hazar-shual and (4) Balah and (5) Ezem, and (6) Eltolad and (7) Bethul and (8) Hormah, and (9) Ziklag and (10) Beth-marcaboth and (11) Hazar-susah, and (12) Beth-lebaoth and (13) Sharuhen; **thirteen cities** with their villages;
English Standard Version (©2001)
And they had for their inheritance, (1) **Beersheba**, (2) **Sheba**, (3) Moladah, (4) Hazar-shual, (5) Balah, (6) Ezem, (7) Eltolad, (8) Bethul, (9) Hormah, (10) Ziklag, (11) Beth-marcaboth, (12) Hazar-susah, (13) Beth-lebaoth, and (14) Sharuhen—**thirteen cities** with their villages;

The Cambridge reads like the 1611 first edition. But is the Oxford "in error" if it agrees with **the ESV**? Note how the wording can affect the number of cities, leading one to believe there is an error in one of the Bibles.

Maybe Oxford University Press sees the expression "and Sheba" as a way of saying that Beersheba is known as "Sheba." Or as David L. Doughterty from learntheBible.org says:

> Beer-sheba is a "wilderness" (Genesis 21:14), and a "place" (vs. 31) containing a "well" (vss. 25&30). Abraham and Abimelech made a covenant "at" (not "in") that "place" so he called it Beer-

sheba (21:31), where he "planted a grove" (vs. 33), and he dwelt "at" (not "in") (22:19). **In all of these passages there is no reference to any CITY.**

Beer-sheba was the name of a place containing a well before any city was ever connected with the name. Isaac "pitched his tent there" (26:25). (You pitch a tent in a field, not in a city.) Isaac digged out the "well" that his father had digged, because the Philistines had filled it with earth (26:15), and called it by the same name that his father had used (26:18&32).

Note that there is still no mention of any CITY. Isaac swore a covenant there with Abimelech, as had Abraham (26:28&31). When his servants told him that they had found water in the "well" that they were digging, he gave it (the well, NOT a city) the name Sheba (the "place" now has two names); therefore the city is called Beer-sheba (26:33). Beer-sheba (**or** Sheba, since it has two names) is a place having a well outside of the city, but the city was called Beer-sheba after the name of the place that it was near to.

Also, note Joshua 17:8, land around a city is called by the same name as the city that it contained, and in this case the city belonged to Ephraim, but the land by the same name belonged to Manasseh. And in Genesis 13:18, Abram "dwelt in the plain of Mamre, which is in Hebron." Here a "plain" is said to be "in" a city. But it is "in" the land surrounding the city. This land is called the "suburbs," is used for growing crops and grazing cattle (Numbers 35:1–7), and is part of the city, though outside of it, and called by the same name. And wells were absolutely essential for watering of animals.

Note that two of these wells were striven for (26:20&21). (Even in the American west "water rights" were so essential that "range wars" were sometimes started over them.) To use "**and**" (in Joshua 19:2) indicates Simeon was given **the city** and the "**place**" and "**well**," **called Sheba**, outside of it. To use "**or**" indicates the common knowledge that the place was called by both names, and one of those names was also the name of the city.

What about the differences between King James Bibles printed by the Oxford and Cambridge University Presses?

Having "and" in the text does not increase the count of cities to fourteen, since "Sheba" is not the name of a city. Either one is equally correct.[2]

2. **2 Chronicles 33:19**

Sinne can be singular or plural. Hymn writer Robert Lowry understood that.

"What can wash away my sin? Nothing but the blood of Jesus."[3]

Whose sins are singular? Both are accurate renderings of the original Hebrew in English.

3. **Jeremiah 34.16**

Dr. Peter S. Ruckman explains this one:

> BOTH variants in the AV (Jer. 34:16) were correct grammatically, if one deals with the English text or the Hebrew text. They ("ye" in the Cambridge) were being addressed as a group (plural, Jer. 34:13; as in Deut. 29), but the address was aimed at individual men ("**he**" in the Oxford edition), within the group. Either word would have been absolutely correct according to that great critic of critics, the word of God (Heb. 4:12–13)...[4]

4. **Nahum 3:16**

> **flee:** verb
> 1. to run away, as from danger or pursuers; take flight. [**fleeth** away]
> 2. to move swiftly; fly; speed. [**flieth** away][5]

Both words carry the same meaning.

---

[2] David L. Doughterty, "Non Existent Revisions in the King James Bible," Accessed December 2012, http://www.learntheBible.org/non-existent-revisions-in-the-king-james-Bible.html. (emphasis mine)

[3] From Robert Lowry, *Nothing But the Blood,* 1876.

[4] Time for Truth, "The 'Whitewash' Conspiracy—Re: The King James Only Controversy by James White" (book review), citing Dr. Peter S. Ruckman, *Bible Believers Bulletin,* September 1995–March 1996 (see Sept. and Dec. 1995 issues), accessed January 2013, http://www.timefortruth.co.uk/content/pages/documents/1309647013.pdf, 183.

[5] *Dictionary.com,* s.v. "flee," http://dictionary.reference.com/browse/flee.

So, the differences in these readings turn out to be either the same word spelled differently or almost identical English language representatives of the same Greek or Hebrew words. That's why variations still exist between Oxford and Cambridge printings (i.e., **"fleeth"** vs. **"flieth,"** **"sins"** vs. **"sin,"** **"and"** vs. **"or,"** etc.)

Literally thousands of KJB editions have been printed, reset, and reprinted by hundreds of different print shops. Like the excellent systems engineer that he is, the Lord built redundancy into the King James brand. He provided more than one means to preserve his words in the various printings of the book.

> The Lord gave the word: great was the company of those that published *it*. (Psalm 68:11)

If you don't like the way the text has been presented in any edition of the King James Bible, you should dump the book. Find a better one.

Find the one that the Lord Jesus Christ cares more about. You don't need to have any brand loyalty if the brand is a stinker.

If you find a book that looks and acts more like it's the right book, pick it. Buy it. Believe that one. If the Lord couldn't figure out how to deliver his words into English and instead left that job up to "fallible man," as some say, then when it comes to the Bible the Lord is like a gymnast who performs a great routine but can't "stick" the landing.

If you don't like the presentation of "the original language words" made by different printings of the King James Bible enough to pick one printer, then you should...

- Reject the King James brand as "unreliable" and "unworthy" of presenting the original autographs in English and pick a different "unreliable" brand that you think, on your own authority, is close enough to the unobtainable originals.

- Continue to believe that the Lord wasn't concerned enough to deliver his words into one language properly and without error after the invention of the printing press.

What about the differences between King James Bibles printed by the Oxford and Cambridge University Presses?

If he didn't care or couldn't be bothered, why should you be guilt-tripped into reading a defective book? If it's a cocktail of men's words and God's words, let's face it, there are more important things to life. Let the experts sort out the details and have them call you when they're done.

We all do what's in our own best interest and so does the Lord (of course, what's in his best interest is also right). Assembling his words after the invention of the printing press into **one book**, in **one** language was **in his best interest** to do. That's because the Lord…

> …will have all men to be saved, and to come unto the knowledge of the truth. (1 Timothy 2:4)

Ancient Hebrew and Ancient Greek were great for the ancient Hebrews and Greeks but won't cut it for the folks on earth today, or 500 years ago for that matter. If men and women in the world today have to learn ancient languages in order to know the truth (which is more than just getting saved), then the Lord never finished his job.

He's the one who died for the world. Regular people need to get all his words without error in one book in a language current today. Why would he lock up the truth in dead languages?

Let's cut to the chase.

Kevin Bauder, former president of Central Theological Seminary of Minneapolis, Minnesota, said…

> The core issue in the King James only controversy is whether one must have the very words of God (*all* the words and *only* the words of the autographa) to have the word of God. The advocates of this theory are stymied by the fact that **no two manuscripts**, no two editions of the Masoretic text or Textus Receptus, and no two editions of the King James Version share all the same words.[6]

First of all, we're taught that the original autographs were in Hebrew and Greek not English so **the words of the autographa** aren't the same as the

---

[6] Roy E. Beacham and Kevin T. Bauder, eds., *One Bible Only? Examining Exclusive Claims for the King James Bible* (Grand Rapids, MI: Kregel, 2001), 164. (emphasis mine)

English words of the King James Bible anyway. He said you need "**all** the **words** and **only** the **words** of the *autographa*."

Applying this to the King James Bible, we find that once press errors have been eliminated you're left with the original autograph text represented by English words—even if those words differ slightly in various editions of the King James Bible. It's the **BRAND** that's the Lord's choice.

Bauder goes on to say...

> No two modifications of the King James Version contain exactly the same words, and the Bible nowhere tells us which edition, if any, does contain the exact words of the originals. These are not speculations; these are plain facts.[7]

So, "No two modifications of the King James Version contain exactly the same words," says Bauder. Big deal. As we have already seen, the words in any edition of the KJB are pure and perfect even if they're not identical.

Interestingly, Dr. W. Edward Glenny, who contributed two chapters to Dr. Bauder's book *One Bible Only? Examining Exclusive Claims for the King James Bible*, said some modifications in manuscripts are "insignificant."

Please keep in mind that what Dr. Glenny is saying concerns variations in manuscripts, not printed Bibles:

> About 98% are **insignificant matters** such as **spelling**, **word order**, **differences in style**, or **confusion concerning synonyms**.[8]

Who should you believe—
someone from Central Seminary or
someone from Central Seminary?

---

[7] Ibid., 155.
[8] Ibid., 124.

What about the differences between King James Bibles printed by the Oxford and Cambridge University Presses?

Both Dr. Glenny and Dr. Bauder have ThDs and PhDs. Both men have taught at Central Seminary.

Much of what Dr. Bauder is making a big deal over is what Dr. Glenny calls insignificant. Plus, it's irrelevant because these "modifications" found in editions of the King James Bible don't change the underlying original language text.

Maybe this whole thing depends on whether you're looking for the truth or looking to be "right." The fact that the translation is slightly different is insignificant.

If you decide to abandon the 400-year-old standard, you're left believing that **all** present Bible translations and Greek and Hebrew texts are adulterated with the words of men.

Plus, if you take Dr. Bauder's position, then in all honesty and in the interest of full disclosure, it's something you should make clear to the unbelievers you're witnessing to.

They'll find out soon enough anyway. Either you, someone at your church, or someone online will go out of their way to teach them to believe in the world's most politically correct Bible—*"The Original Bible"* that you can't get and that never existed.

It's ironic that Christians used to be known as "people of the book." Alas, that was when the King James Bible reigned supreme and before the 120-year-old dogma of Original Autograph Onlyism.

Before we leave this discussion, the commonly taught dogma of "**no two manuscripts ... share all the same words**" turns out **not** to be true. It's been repeated (without anybody checking) for over 100 years so it's not Dr. Bauder's fault. He's just repeating what he was taught.

In fact, there are…

107 identical Greek New Testament manuscripts.

Author and textual expert Dr. Wilbur N. Pickering, ThM and PhD, certifies in his report *In Defense of Family 35*:

…considering only the MSS that I myself have collated, we can say the following: I have in my possession copies of [107 identical manuscripts]:[9]

3 for Galatians	2 for James
2 for Ephesians	2 for 1 Peter
3 for Colossians	2 for 2 Peter
4 for 1 Thessalonians	2 for 1 John
7 for 2 Thessalonians	23 for 2 John
5 for Titus	23 for 3 John
14 for Philemon	15 for Jude

Dr. Pickering's manuscripts are of the same type that forms the base of the Greek New Testament underlying the King James Bible. The uniformity here is important. Remember that the two "oldest and best" manuscripts that are the foundation of all modern versions (except the NKJV) disagree between themselves in over 3,000 places in the Gospels alone.

A popular tactic used by those who oppose the primacy of the King James Bible is to subtly imply that there have been monumental changes to the English text over the past four centuries.

That's why they ask…

The trick question.

"Which revision of the King James Bible is inspired, the 1611 or the 1769 edition?" or in Dr. Bauder's case, "Which revision of the King James Bible contains all of God's words and only God's words?"

They pose this question to try and trick you into buying into their argument for rejecting the King James authority based on the "changes" that appeared in various editions.

---

[9] Wilbur N. Pickering, "In Defense of Family 35," accessed January 2013, http://www.walkinhiscommandments.com/Pickering/Miscellaneous/In%20Defense%20of%20Family%2035.pdf, 14, note 6.

What about the differences between King James Bibles printed by the Oxford and Cambridge University Presses?

There are revisions and revisions— don't buy the head fake.

When it comes to the King James Bible, there are two kinds of "revisions" you need to know about.

One is used to "game you" and the other is a legitimate revision of the underlying text that makes the Bible say and mean different things.

The Oxford English Dictionary *(OED)* is said to be the accepted authority on the evolution of the English language. According to Oxforddictionaries.com, the primary definition of *revise* is to "reconsider and alter (something) in the light of further evidence."[10]

A second meaning, one that critics of the King James Bible treat as though it means the primary definition above, is "to review; to re-examine; to look over with care for correction; as, to revise a writing; to revise a proof sheet."[11]

Chapters 10–12 in this book have detailed and answered the most difficult "revision" instances in all the editions of the King James Bible. Look around the Web and prove it for yourself. The instances you have just read are repeated over and over again in forums, blog posts, and articles.

When someone feeds you the "which revision" argument, keep this in mind:

If you held the copyright to the King James Bible and all you did was correct printing errors, update spelling and grammar, and make some very minor tweaks in the presentation of the English translation, could you in good conscience slap "revised edition" on the cover and charge an extra $20 when you didn't change the underlying text one bit?

And besides, there absolutely was...

A real "revision" of the King James Bible.

---

[10] *Oxford Dictionaries,* s.v. "revise," http://oxforddictionaries.com/definition/english/revise.
[11] *Webster's Dictionary* (1828), s.v. "revise," http://www.webster1828.com/websters1828/definition.aspx?word=Revise.

It was published in 1885 and was appropriately called The English **Revised** Version (ERV). They called it that because they took the King James Bible and "altered (it) in the light of further evidence." Just like the Oxford definition says.

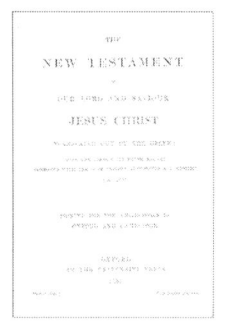

They substituted a different Greek New Testament newly created in 1881.

The Revised Version (or English Revised Version) of the Bible is a late 19th-century British revision of the King James Version of 1611. Here's what Cedarville University said about it:

New Testament Revised Version title page, 1881

> ... the English Revised Version, or Revised Version, ... was the first and **remains the only officially authorized revision** of the King James Bible.[12]

What's ironic is that the basic pitch for all new versions published in the past 130 years is that the Authorized Version needs to be "**updated**" and "**corrected**." The Lord did BOTH and everyone complains. Printer's errors were corrected and spelling and orthography were updated.

But that's not enough for the naysayers.

First of all, depending on whose material you read, "updating" may mean changing the word "baptize" to "immerse." It could mean updating the vocabulary. It could mean paraphrasing. It could mean substituting a different underlying Greek text. It could mean substituting a modified Hebrew text.

Correcting textual errors means substituting variant readings for the long-standing Received Text of the church. Correcting translational errors is nothing more than subjective substitution of one English word for another based on the subjective opinion of a lexicographer.

There are lots of ways men have proposed to "fix" the supposed errors in

---

[12] Cedarville University, "Biblical Heritage Gallery: The Revisions," accessed January 2013, http://www.cedarville.edu/cf/advancement/cbts/heritagegallery/exhibits/celebrating-the-Bible/. (emphasis mine)

[13] Logos Bible Software, "Overview: King James Version," accessed January 2013, http://www.logos.com/product/8586/preachers-essential-library. (See quote on next page).

the King James Bible. They've tried over 100 times, and yet according to **Logos**, publishers of the popular Bible study software:

> ...The King James Version of the Bible is still the most widely used text in the English language.[13]

All the smart guys teach us that it shouldn't be. They say it's an error-filled translation based on untrustworthy manuscripts. And yet after 400 years it is still the most widely used text in the English language.

What the experts missed is that the very things they proposed be done were done.

They claim they want to "update" the language. Although close examination of modern versions has proved that they did far more than change the thees and thous. They changed the text and translation drastically, as you have already seen.

Since the Lord is not given to change, it's not surprising that his book doesn't change. The original language text of the King James Bible was fixed when the translators finished their work in 1611.

There were no authorized textual changes made because the team that did the work was disbanded. Even so, that didn't mean the Lord was through with the presentation of the King James Bible.

The updates voices have clamored for over the past 200 years were primarily done in the 1762 Paris and 1769 Blayney editions of the King James Bible when spelling and orthography were "updated" in preparation for detailed concordances of the 18th–20th centuries and, conveniently for our own times, computer searches.

The Lord gave them what they cried for and they rejected it.

In the end, the Lord gave the voices what they wanted but not in the way they expected and neither was it in their perceived interests. The updates in spelling and orthography were way too mild for the critics. Scholars soon realize that the only thing that ensures that your name lives on after you die is what you publish. The saying is true: "publish or perish."

If your whole academic life revolves around the Bible, then the ultimate thing you can be involved in is biblical translation, modernization, revision, or alteration.

"Which **revision** of the King James Bible is **inspired**, the 1611 or the 1769 edition?" is a trick question. A better question is "Which edition of the King James Bible would the Lord use?" But that's a question textual critics never think to ask.

As we've already seen, the Lord wouldn't be ashamed of and has actually used and blessed **all the editions** of the King James Bible.

Why would someone even ask a trick question in the first place?

That's coming up next...

Chapter Thirteen

Why "Which Edition?" is (quite often) a trick question

> Behold, they say unto me, Where is the word of the Lord? let it come now. (Jeremiah 17:15)

Most folks who ask the "Which King James Bible" question aren't looking for a real answer. They're challenging your belief in a physical **BOOK** because they don't have a book they believe contains all of God's words and only God's words without error. The goal is to put you in bondage to an imaginary, nonexistent "book" and then get you to swear allegiance to it or risk having them call you a heretic.

If *you* don't have one pure book, *they* can be satisfied in believing in the adulterated one they own.

These folks say they believe in the Bible, but you find out on further questioning that "the book" they believe in doesn't exist and never did exist.

Dr. Bauder is no different in all this. For example, Bauder thinks King James onlyists have a dilemma:

> Confronted with these facts, King James only advocates are faced with one of two choices. Either they **may specify,** *a priori* and without biblical evidence, **a single manuscript** or edi-

Jack McElroy with an original two-volume 1633 Elizevir Greek New Testament containing the first appearance of phrase "Textus Receptus"

219

tion of the Bible in which **the exact words** are preserved, or they may begin to qualify their insistence upon exact preservation.[1]

The term "a priori" means "derived by reasoning from self-evident proposition," which is also known as deductive reasoning. Dr. Bauder says that King James only advocates must either, by deductive reasoning, choose "a single manuscript or edition of the Bible" that contains the exact, preserved words of God, or stop insisting that God did preserve his exact words.

While no knowledgeable King James only author has ever made the claim that "a single manuscript" contains the exact, preserved words, it is true that some folks who support the Textus Receptus do lay claim to a single printed edition as representing the original text.

Bauder is absolutely right that the King James only position is derived by **deductive** reasoning. Scholars have been using **inductive** reasoning to determine the original text of the Bible for hundreds of years and they're no closer now than they were then. Lots of scholars with lots of private agendas have lots of opinions.

There is no referee, judge, or Court of Appeals to determine which of the scholarly preferences among variant readings are correct. All that exists are their opinions and a roll of the dice.

Deductive reasoning versus inductive reasoning

Deductive reasoning is the process of reasoning from more general statements regarding what is known to reach a logically certain conclusion. It's also known as "top-down" logic.

In short, it's big picture. Deductive reasoning tells us that the Lord wouldn't leave us without a book. We believe he has provided us with a tangible Bible and that this Bible has all the correct "variant readings."

It's like he gives you a puzzle box cover so you know what it's supposed to look like. You trust that the box contains the right amount of puzzle pieces and that they all fit together perfectly.

---

[1] Roy E. Beacham and Kevin T. Bauder, eds., *One Bible Only? Examining Exclusive Claims for the King James Bible* (Grand Rapids, MI: Kregel, 2001), 154. (emphasis mine)

The King James Bible is the box. Its underlying text has just the right amount of pieces. No more, no less.

Inductive reasoning starts with specifics and constructs general propositions from the data. It's also known as "bottom-up" logic. Evolutionists use this type of logic all the time.

"Great Event of the Bible" by White Mountain Puzzles

They built "Nebraska man" out of one tooth that turned out to come from an extinct pig. Textual critics pour over thousands of variant readings in a vain attempt to reconstruct the text of *"The Original Bible."*

Dr. Bauder and most other academics use inductive reasoning as they continually examine the thousands of variant readings found in manuscripts all over the planet. Believe it or not, they're still finding manuscripts today.

Their biggest problem?

They have too many puzzle pieces and no box cover.

Academics and textual critics are ever learning and never able to come to the knowledge of the truth. They continually add to their buffet of choices.

They have a subjective Bible. None of them can be certain exactly what God says because every man gets to choose which variant reading he thinks is authentic.

You hear professors, pastors, teachers, and Bible study leaders constantly telling you what they think God says. All this does is leave you with a dyslexic God who can never find the right words to give you.

Bauder continues to describe the "dilemma" of a King James onlyist…

> Some of them choose the former alternative, usually naming a particular printed Greek or Hebrew text or else a particular edition of the King James Version that is supposed to contain all the words, and only the words, of the originals. The problem for them lies in trying to justify their choice. They cannot base their conclusion upon **any particular biblical promise**, for even if the Bible does contain a promise of its own preservation, it never specifies where the preserved words are to be found.[2]

Dr. Bauder says that some Christians have indeed testified that **they have in their possession** "a particular edition of the King James Version that is supposed to contain all the words, and only the words, of the originals."

They gave him what he asked for, they answered his "Which edition?" question, but he won't accept their answer. They told him that they believe a certain edition of their **King James Bible** contained "all the words, and only the words, of the originals." That's what they believe. Their proof doesn't satisfy him because it doesn't reach the arbitrary threshold he set. He's trying to win an argument—not determine the truth. It's hard to feed someone who's not hungry. The point is…

He was given a specific answer…

But he dismissed it because he had already predetermined that he needed a **specific promise** from "the Bible" that God would do what he demanded in the way he demanded it.

The specific answer to Bauder's question of "which printing of the King James Bible contains all the words, and only the words of the originals" is…

NONE.

Every edition of the King James Bible printed over the past 400 years has been in the English language. The words of the original autographs were in different languages.

We've already addressed this nonissue as to how those original language words are represented in the various editions of the King James Bible in chapters 10–12.

---
[2] Ibid., 155–156. (emphasis mine)

Why "Which Edition?" is (quite often) a trick question

But you're getting this question from a man who claims he will **ONLY** base his conclusions upon a "particular biblical promise." Sounds pretty convincing, and yet he believes lot of things without a promise…

- Does the inerrant and inspired *"Original Bible"* Dr. Bauder believes in **promise him** that it has **ONLY 66 books** in it? Surely Dr. Bauder believes there are **all the Books, and only the Books** in the Bible, yet he can't produce ANY evidence of a promise of God that supports this.

Dr. Gordon Fee is a textual critic and member of the NIV committee. His book on Bible translations is widely read and recommended. Fee recommends Roman Catholic scholarship. Ask a Jesuit scholar. He'll swear that there are **73 books** in the Bible. The Ethiopic Church has **81 books** in its Bible and the Greek Orthodox has **76**.

- Does the inerrant and inspired *"Original Bible"* Dr. Bauder believes in **promise him** that there are only **150 Psalms**? Surely Dr. Bauder believes **all the Psalms, and only the right number of Psalms** are in the Bible. But he has yet to produce ANY evidence of a promise of God that supports this.

Sure, that's how many Psalms are in the KJB, NKJB, NIV, ESV, NASB, and HCSB. But that would be news to Orthodox Greek, Slavonic, Georgian, Armenian, Apostolic Syriac, and Ethiopian churches because their Bibles have **151 Psalms**. How come Bauder doesn't have **Psalm 151** in his Bible? It's in a Dead Sea Scroll.[3] It's also in Codex Vaticanus and Codex Alexandrinus, two of the "oldest and best manuscripts."

- Does the inerrant and inspired *"Original Bible"* Dr. Bauder believes in **promise him** that Matthew wrote his *"autographa"* in Greek? *Papias* (AD 150–170), *Irenaeus* (AD 170), *Origen* (c. AD 210), *Eusebius* (c. AD 315), *Epiphanius* (AD 370), *Jerome* (AD 382), and others believe that it was originally composed in Hebrew.[4] Surely Dr. Bauder believes that

---

[3] *Wikipedia,* s.v. "Psalm 151," last modified December 28, 2012, http://en.wikipedia.org/wiki/Psalm_151. See footnote 4.

[4] As cited in James Scott Trimm, trans., "The Hebraic-Roots Version Scriptures," South Africa: Institute for Scripture Research, 2005, http://www.isr-messianic.org/downloads/hrv_intro.pdf, xxii, xxiii.

all Greek words, and only Greek words appeared in the New Testament of his *"Original Bible."*

If you were German and writing to Germans, would you use French? James wrote his letter to the 12 tribes. Who were the 12 tribes? Are they not Jews? If you are writing a letter to Jews, why would you write to them in Greek? Wouldn't you expect James, being a Jew, to write to other Jews in Hebrew?

- Does the inerrant and inspired *"Original Bible"* Dr. Bauder believes in **promise him** that Paul wrote a letter to the Hebrews in Greek? The Roman historian Eusebius of Caesarea "reports that the original letter had a Jewish audience and was written in Hebrew, and later translated into Greek, 'some say [by] the evangelist Luke, others… [by] Clement [of Rome]….'"[5] Surely Dr. Bauder believes that **all Greek words, and only the Greek words** Paul originally penned appeared in the Original Autograph Book of Hebrews.

- Did the inerrant and inspired *"Original Bible"* Dr. Bauder believes in **promise him** that Paul even wrote the book of Hebrews? The author is not identified in the text. The NIV, ESV, and NASB never identify Paul in the title. The King James Bible says "The Epistle of Paul the Apostle to the Hebrews." Plus it says "Written to the *Hebrews*, from Italy, by Timothie" at the end of the book.

The promises that God would preserve his word have been cited not only in this work but are all over the Web. Here are a few of the verses:

- Being born again, not of corruptible seed, but of incorruptible, by the word of God which **liveth and abideth forever**. (1 Peter 1:23)
- The words of the LORD *are* pure words: *as* silver tried in a furnace of earth, purified seven times. Thou shalt keep them, O LORD, thou shalt preserve them **from this generation forever**. (Psalm 12:6–7)
- The works of his hands are verity and judgment; all his commandments are sure. **They stand fast for ever and ever**, and are done in truth and uprightness. (Psalm 111:7–8)

---

[5] *Wikipedia*, s.v. "Authorship of the Epistle to the Hebrews," last modified December 15, 2012, http://en.wikipedia.org/wiki/Authorship_of_the_Epistle_to_the_Hebrews. See footnote 3.

- The grass withereth, the flower fadeth: but the word of our God **shall stand for ever.** (Isaiah 40:8)
- ...**the truth of the** LORD *endureth* **for ever**. Praise ye the LORD. (Psalm 117:2)
- Concerning thy testimonies, I have known of old that **thou hast founded them for ever.** (Psalm 119:152)
- Thy word is true from the beginning: and every one of thy righteous judgments **endureth for ever.** (Psalm 119:160)

Folks constantly argue about the meaning of these verses since they are translated differently in different versions—again casting doubt upon exactly what God said and by extension affecting doctrine.

Deductive reasoning tells us that God has to preserve his words even unto today, otherwise textual critics care more about his words than he does. After all, they spend their whole lives trying to determine which words are God's and which are not.

The scholarly teaching is to believe that it is up to men to find what God lost.

Are we to believe that God carefully inspired his words at the first, then lost interest in the project, setting them adrift over the sea of time awaiting modern scholars to find them and figure out which ones were authentic? That's what many scholars would have you believe.

Here's something else to ponder. Have you ever been able to answer the "Which Bible?" question to the satisfaction of the one posing the question?

Turns out there's a hidden agenda behind the "Which edition?" question…

Chapter Fourteen

The real reason for the fake question

Charity suffereth long, and is kind; charity envieth not; charity vaunteth not itself, is not puffed up… (1 Corinthians 13:4)

Asking the "Which edition?" question is an excellent control technique meant to suppress discussion. Ridicule works too. Both are used frequently at most Christian colleges, Bible institutes, and seminaries to pressure students into uncritical acceptance of the politically correct position offered by modern scholarship of *Original Bible* Onlyism.

Teachers will say "it's a reliable translation" and at the same time go out of their way to point out their "pet" list of errors and teach you that the KJB text is defective.

But some students see the duplicity and hypocrisy in that, challenging teachers and pastors: "How can you recommend the King James Bible as 'reliable' when it's so different from other versions? After all, it's got 16 entire verses extra. That's a pretty big difference, isn't it?"

No wonder *Original Bible* onlyists get flack. It happens in churches all the time. Unfortunately, the discussion turns contentious because of the fundamental belief in the authority of "the Scriptures" and because the truthfulness of God is at stake.

Some believers didn't grow up in Christian homes nor did they go to a Christian college. It's not their parent's religion; it's their own. They left off their sins and trusted in Christ based on the words of **a book** not based on a backpack full of uncertain words and phrases.

These folks jettisoned sex, drugs, and rock 'n roll for something far more lasting and valuable; they grabbed onto someone who could really fill the void.

They were looking for the truth and were happy to judge their ill-spent lives and meager experiences by the words written in **a book**. They staked their eternal destinies on those words and now they've committed their lives and fortunes to the Savior who wrote it.

It's widely taught that the King James Bible (or any Bible) is adulterated with men's words. It's taught that all Bibles in any language contain errors in text and translation.

But really, it's not the educators' fault. They too have been taught that no Bible is infallible and inerrant.

Christian educators are all too happy to present sophist arguments to back up their claims. They think they do God service by fighting against anyone who believes that God is capable of and indeed has produced **one Book** that contains all of his words and only his words today.

They were taught and so teach that you should replace a real Bible with an imaginary one made out of the Original Manuscripts—*"The Original Bible."*

Some ex-heathens have seen that game before. They know bait and switch when they see it. And they are not going to be duped again if they can help it.

They've got a lot riding on "the Bible." That book better be true and it better be certain because it's supposed to represent a God who tells the truth.

When they hear someone in authority saying that the book is adulterated and error-filled, they do their own research and question authority.

Most of the time "authority" doesn't like to be questioned. That's when the games begin. The problem is, we're not talking about relationships, sports, politics, money, or even religion, we're talking about truth. People who have been lied to their whole lives about "what is truth" are passionate in the pursuit of "the truth."

They never would have gotten saved if they weren't.

The "Which Edition?" question is the last line of defense in the attempt to stop you from electing one book as **The Book**.

We're taught that none of the books are **The Book**.

If you believe **the King James Bible is The Book**, you're smirked at and told it can't be because of typos, standardized spelling, orthography, and translational tweaks. Sure the text remained the same for 400 years, but that's not good enough to make the cut.

So in its place we're offered…

A promised election.

We're taught that all books are allowed to be candidates for the position of The Book and all books are allowed to have supporters. And you think you'll get to vote for your preferred candidate.

But…

There's **not** going to be an election. It's too controversial. Elections have losers. And nobody wants to see their candidate lose.

Think of the disappointment on the faces of pastors, teachers, and believers in The New Living Translation, the NIV, ESV, NASB, HCSB, or NKJV if their book turned out to be a loser. If there ever were an election, too many people would be offended.

And above all, no one is allowed to ask the pregnant question: "Which Bible would the Lord Jesus Christ vote for?" Alas…

He doesn't get to vote.

What's worse is that he can't even pick a candidate. No indeed, the experts have already decreed **which** candidate he **must** vote for.

More than that, they have already voted for him.

Their choice for him?

He must approve all candidates…

At least those candidates **each expert** deems viable in **his** own eyes. But even that doesn't matter since those candidates can't win. Here's why…

The election is rigged.

The "winner" was chosen by professional Christians about 130 years ago. It's *"The Original Bible"* made up of the "Original Autographs" you've heard tell about.

It's the only Bible that's inspired and inerrant. More importantly, it's the **only** copy of real "Scripture" in existence. It's the **only** "Scripture" that is "given by inspiration" of God.

Introducing…
"The Imaginary Bible."

A good name for *"The Original Bible"* is *"The Imaginary Bible"* since the "Original Autographs" **were never gathered into A BOOK in the first place**. And that's the only "Bible" the experts think is authentic.

How odd.

Intellectual dishonesty.

Most fundamental and evangelical academics believe that the words of God are found in the multiplicity of extant manuscripts scattered throughout the world today. Too bad the Lord never saw fit to assemble them into a printed book we can believe in.

But they will swear on a stack of errant "Bibles" containing a cocktail of God's words mixed with men's words that the "real" Bible is *"The Original Bible."*

There's more evidence for Bigfoot than for "a Bible" of the Original Autographs.

To even imply that such a thing ever existed in the first place is intellectually dishonest. God gave Moses the Ten Commandments written on two tables of stone. That was the original autograph of the Ten Commandments. Any copy Moses made of it was, by the experts' definition, not inspired and not inerrant. Even if Moses himself made it, it's still a copy of what God made, and they teach that copies aren't inspired, as we'll soon see.

Even if you argue that Moses made an inspired copy of the tables of stone, that all occurred about 1450 BC. The mythological *"Original Bible"* couldn't have been "assembled" into one book until after AD 90 when the apostle John finished writing the book of Revelation. That's a span of 1,500 years.

Do you suppose the Jews, at odds with this new sect they called heretical, could be persuaded to turn over their Old Testament "Original Autographs" to Christians so that they could be assembled with the New Testament portion to make up the first edition of the *"Original Bible"*?

What a priceless artifact. Who wouldn't pay to see it?

Of course, on further questioning, the experts will argue that they are only looking for the original text of that imaginary book and not the literal book itself. Yet they constantly refer to that text as "the Bible"—a book. And they actually have the chutzpah to say that this imaginary assemblage is the "plenary, inerrant, infallible word of God."

The whole concept is absurd on its face. The *"Original Bible"* is as rare as the horse of a different color you've heard tell about. And you'll only find this horse in the Land of Oz.

Since textual critics say that copies aren't inspired, we need to take a closer look at biblical inspiration…

Chapter Fifteen

Inspiration of Scripture—
What it is and what it isn't

> But *there is* a spirit in man: and the inspiration of the Almighty giveth them understanding. (Job 32:8)

According to the Bible, *inspiration* not only applies to the original autographs but it's also an ongoing ministry of the Holy Spirit whereby he gives men (including you) *understanding* of the words of God.

Understanding is the fruit of the *inspiration* given by the Holy Ghost.

We'll get to this shortly, but first…

With all the talk about the inerrant, inspired original autographs that were "breathed out by God" and that are supposed to be our final authority you'd think that influential Christian leaders, the "professional Christians" teaching us, really understood what *inspiration* is.

Alas, this turns out not to be the case.

Here's what some of the more renowned experts[1] have said:

Louis Gaussen (1790–1863) authored such classics as *The Divine Inspiration of the Bible: The Inspiration of the Holy Scriptures; Theopneustia: The Plenary Inspiration of the Holy Scriptures Deduced from Internal Evidence, and the Testimonies of Nature, History and Science;* and *The Canon*

---

[1] The synopsis that follows is from William P. Grady, *Given by Inspiration: A Multifaceted Study on the A.V. 1611 with Contemporary Analysis* (Swartz Creek, MI: Grady Publications, 2010), 62.

of the Holy Scriptures from the Double Point of View of Science and of Faith. Gaussen said:

> Were we asked that, then, how this work of divine *inspiration* has been accomplished in the men of God, we should reply, that we do not know.

Lewis Sperry Chafer (1871–1952), an American theologian, founded and served as the first president of Dallas Theological Seminary and was influential in the founding of modern Christian dispensationalism. Chafer said:

> The doctrine of *inspiration*, because it is supernatural, presents some problems to human *understanding*.

Henry C. Theissen (1883–1947) was former president of The Master's College in Santa Clarita, California, and author of *Lectures in Systematic Theology.* Theissen said:

> Accepting [his preceding explanation] is the best definition of *inspiration*, we observed that we do not know the mode of *inspiration*.

Harold Lindsell (1914–1998), longtime editor of *Christianity Today,* conservative evangelical scholar, teacher, and author of more than 20 books, staunchly advocated literal interpretation of the Bible. Lindsell said:

> Of course there is a mystery connected with a product that is the result of the confluence of the human and the divine.

Benjamin Warfield (1851–1921) was professor of theology at Princeton Seminary. Some conservative Presbyterians consider him to be the last of the great Princeton theologians before the split in 1929 that formed Westminster Seminary and the Orthodox Presbyterian Church. When writing about *inspiration* and 2 Timothy 3:16, Warfield said:

Inspiration of Scripture—What it is and what it isn't

In a word, what is declared by this fundamental passage is simply that the Scriptures are a Divine product, without any indication of how God has operated in producing them.[2]

Let's see…

What Scripture says about scripture.

The word "scripture(s)" is used in the Scriptures 53 times, and it refers to copies you can read. Never once is it referring to the originals.

Go ahead, do a word search. Read the context and check it out for yourself.

Then read 2 Timothy 3:16. This verse is constantly quoted to prove that the Lord inspired the original autographs. He did, but the context in 2 Timothy has nothing to do with any originals. It has to do with the Scripture making Timothy wise (verse 15) and how the Scripture will be profitable to him (verse 16).

Read it. **But** make sure you read verse 15 first. Paul is referring to Scriptures that Timothy was reading. **None** of which was an original autograph.

> And that **from a child thou hast known the holy scriptures**, which are able to make thee wise unto salvation through faith which is in Christ Jesus. **All scripture is given by** *inspiration* **of God**, and is profitable for doctrine, for reproof, for correction, for instruction in righteousness… (2 Timothy 3:15–16)

Timothy's mom and grandmother had "the holy scriptures" in their possession. They had copies—not originals.

If Paul is referring to the original autographs in verse 16, then he is shifting gears and introducing something that is outside of the context. A careful reading shows that Paul isn't introducing new information about how God "inspired" Moses to rewrite the Ten Commandments on two tables of stone or how he "inspired" Jeremiah to write a warning to the

---

[2] Benjamin Warfield, "Inspiration," from *The International Standard Bible Encyclopedia*, edited by James Orr, vol. 3 (Chicago: Howard-Severance, 1915), 1473–1483. (Available: http://www.Bible-researcher.com/warfield3.html).

king of Judah on a piece of parchment that the king ends up cutting up with a knife and pitching into the fire.

The whole context is dealing with how the Scriptures that Timothy's family owned were going to help him.

While we're at it, here's something you'll never get taught in seminary…

Inspiration of the originals doesn't do anybody any good…

Unless they're (a) still "inspired" today, and (b) you have access to them. And it doesn't matter which language the original autographs **were** written in unless you have the translation of those words in your own language **today**.

And yet the experts constantly tell us that our language (or any language for that matter) isn't equivalent to Hebrew or Greek. They teach that it's literally impossible to transfer the words from one language to another without losing some meaning in the process.

Their whole teaching is self-serving propaganda.

Businessmen translate catalogs, brochures, and websites all the time. Business agreements and treaties are translated and signed, binding corporations and nations as well as putting trillions of dollars at risk.

Christian biblical experts don't give God any credit. They think he hasn't been able to figure out how to transfer his inspired, living, and life-giving words from one language into another without error.

Like Hamlet said: "Aye! there's the rub"…

Inerrancy—without error.

None of the experts want to defend any Bible (i.e., book) in particular because they have been taught that there are textual and/or translational errors in **all** of them. And there's nothing worse for a professional than to have egg on his face. So they'll avoid embarrasement at almost any cost.

That's why there are no NIV, ESV, NASB, HCSB Onlyists. They are afraid to commit to the Bible version they use. They need to be careful defending these versions because they never know when the copyright owner will pull the rug out from under them and change the text via a new and improved update.

The safe position is that only the autographs were without error. It's not only safe, it's politically correct. The designers of most institutional and church "statements of faith" are pretty clever. They always refer to *"The Bible"* generically—as a commodity—never as a Bible by brand name.

When someone points out discrepancies in versions or a supposed contradiction in *"The Bible,"* the experts can just say "Well, it is correct in the original autographs!"

It makes their life a lot easier. No one can argue against what no longer exists.

What they don't get is that it also means…

The Lord has failed to deliver his words to his people.

Sometimes very smart guys can miss some very important things.

Consider this…

2 Timothy 3:16, the verse they always quote to support the idea that *"**the Original Bible**"* is inspired, doesn't even **say** what they teach—in any of the popular Bible versions.

	2 Timothy 3:16
New International Version (©1984)	All Scripture is God-breathed…
English Standard Version (©2001)	All Scripture is breathed out by God…
New American Standard Bible (©1995)	All Scripture is inspired by God
Holman Christian Standard Bible (©2003)	All Scripture is inspired by God
New Living Translation (©2007)	All Scripture is inspired by God
The New Revised Standard (©1989)	All scripture is inspired by God
New King James Bible (©1982)	All Scripture *is* given by *inspiration* of God
King James Bible (1611)	All scripture *is* given by *inspiration* of God

Note, the operative word "IS"—present tense—which means the Scripture "IS" presently either "God-breathed" or "inspired" according to all the versions.

The King James and New King James say the Scripture is **"given by"** *inspiration*. Sounds like *inspiration* is a method or process, doesn't it?

We've all been taught that no English Bible (or one in any other language or translation) can claim the title of "inspired and inerrant" because **only the original autographs are "inspired and inerrant."**

Come to find out, this definition of *"inspiration"* is really only 130 years old as you will soon see. But before we get to that…

If you ask, "Where **are** the original autographs that **are** inspired?" you get the answer, "They're lost."

If that's the case, isn't proper English to say that the original autographs **"were"** inspired since they don't exist anymore?

Most fundamentalists and evangelicals claim to adhere to the doctrine

Inspiration of Scripture—What it is and what it isn't

in the multiplicity of readings found in whatever manuscript evidence is out there.

The problem with this view is that it means God didn't see fit to assemble those words into a book you can hold in your hands.

Isn't that swell? The real question is, **who** gets to pick **which** readings out of that pile are authentic? And then **who** gets to be the judge of the picks?

There are literally thousands of variant readings (not to mention permutations among adjacent variants). Nobody can even pick the winners of the 32 NFL games "on any given Sunday" let alone which variant readings are original to any degree of certainty.

This leads to various levels of mischief. The choices can be arbitrary and capricious (given to sudden and unaccountable changes of mood or behavior).

Even the fellows who built the Greek New Testament behind virtually all modern versions self-graded their choices of variant readings from A–D.

According to the preface of *UBS4*, the grading is as follows:

- [A] Indicates the text is certain;
- [B] Indicates the text is almost certain;
- [C] Indicates the text is difficult to determine;
- [D] Indicates the text is very difficult to determine.[3]

UBS4 is the latest revision of this Greek text published by the United Bible Societies as *The Greek New Testament* (4th ed., 1993).

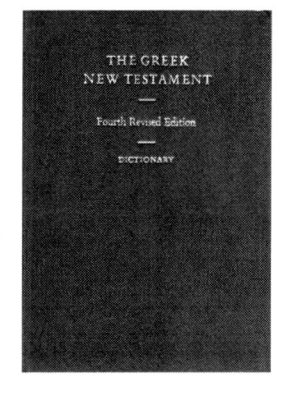

Wouldn't you have liked to self-grade all your work in school?

We're constantly taught that "*inspiration*" only refers to God "breathing out" or "theopneustos" the originals. And yet…

---

[3] Peter Ballard, "The Bible Is Reliable Despite Textual Errors," last updated July 19, 2008, accessed January 2013, http://www.peterballard.org/catalog.html.

With all the "breathing out" the Lord did...

You have to ask:

- Did God "breathe out" the written record made by King Cyrus of Babylon as it appears in Ezra 6:3–5? The record was written in Chaldee—not Hebrew or Aramaic, despite the fact that we are taught that the Bible was written in Hebrew, Aramaic, and Greek.

- Did God "breathe out" 15 verses through the Persian king Artaxerxes when his letter to Ezra appears in Ezra 7:12–26? It was Artaxerxes' letter. He wrote it and he was not exactly a "holy man of God," was he?

- Did God breathe through an unsaved Greek poet quoted by Paul?

  > For in him we live, and move, and have our being; as certain also of **your own poets have said**, For we are also his offspring. (Acts 17:28)

- Did he breathe through Bathsheba (assuming King Lemuel refers to Solomon)?

  > The words of king Lemuel, the prophecy that his mother taught him. (Proverbs 31:1)

So much for "holy men of God" speaking by the Holy Ghost.

- Solomon "spake three thousand proverbs" (1 Kings 4:32). There are only 915 verses in Proverbs so even at two proverbs/verse, at least 1,000 are lost. Yet there were certain of them "which the men of Hezekiah king of Judah copied out" (Proverbs 25:1) and show up in your copy of the Book of Proverbs.

Did the Lord "inspire" those men to copy out only the inspired proverbs? They "copied" them out. Those are the ones you have.

We are taught by the experts that "*inspiration*" doesn't extend to "copies."

And what about 1 Samuel 24:13?

> As saith the proverb of the ancients, Wickedness proceedeth from the wicked: but mine hand shall not be upon thee. (1 Samuel 24:13)

Who exactly are "the ancients"? Did the Lord inspire them? Did their words become inspired when David repeated them to Saul or did they become "inspired" when someone wrote them down? If they became inspired when written down, then what were they before that? Uninspired?

This whole "*inspiration*" thing is a lot deeper than anyone lets on. People argue all the time over questions like:

- Are the words inspired or the men?
- Is it only Greek and Hebrew words that are/were inspired or other languages as well?

Trying to satisfactorily answer those rhetorical questions is like getting stuck in a tar pit. You can hardly win.

But the good news is…

The Bible has the answer.

The word "*inspiration*" only shows up twice in the King James Bible.

Once, in the verse everybody quotes:

> All scripture *is* given by *inspiration* of God, and *is* profitable for doctrine, for reproof, for correction, for instruction in righteousness… (2 Timothy 3:16)

And a second time in the verse hardly anybody quotes:

> But *there is* a spirit in man: and the *inspiration* of the Almighty **giveth them *understanding*.** (Job 32:8)

Comparing the two helps you understand how the Bible defines the word. It's just that hardly anybody does it.

Here is the essence of the comparison:

Job 32:8   **Understanding**   is given to men by *inspiration* of the Almighty.

2 Timothy 3:16   All ***scripture***   is given by *inspiration* of the Almighty.

Maybe the Lord "*inspired*" Cyrus by giving him "*understanding*" of the great God of the Jews and the need to rebuild his Temple in Jerusalem.

Maybe the Lord "*inspired*" Artaxerxes by giving him "*understanding*" of the times. Then Artaxerxes wrote his letter as recorded in Ezra 7:12–26 and the Lord included it in his Bible.

Maybe the Lord "*inspired*" Bathsheba by giving her "*understanding*" of "the prophecy."

How about 1 Corinthians 7:12? Paul says:

> But to the rest speak I, not the Lord: If any brother hath a wife that believeth not, and she be pleased to dwell with him, let him not put her away.

Paul makes it clear his comments are his own and not the Lord's per se. Yet those words **are** Scripture. Maybe the Lord "*inspired*" Paul by giving him "*understanding*" of how a believing brother ought to deal with an unbelieving wife.

Paul writes the letter and the Lord includes it in his Bible. The words are truly Paul's (just like he says) yet the Lord gave him *understanding* to know them by *inspiration*.

Who really knows the details of the mechanism?

But here's the interpretation of 2 Timothy 3:16 as it applies to you…

Inspiration is a method by which the Holy Ghost imparts understanding to men. The *inspiration* of the Almighty gives you *understanding* of the Scripture. It's a ministry of the Holy Ghost.

The context of 2 Timothy 3:16 is present tense. Not past. It's all about you, right now—just like it was all about Timothy when he got Paul's letter.

Just like the Lord gave the Scriptures to Timothy by *inspiration*, he has given you a Book, so you too can become wise unto salvation and understand doctrine, reproof, correction, and righteousness.

It's the Lord who gives *understanding* to your heart. Like he said to Job…

Inspiration of Scripture—What it is and what it isn't

> Who hath put wisdom in the inward parts? or who hath given **un-derstanding** to the heart? (Job 38:36)

And like Job 32:8 says, the *inspiration* of the Almighty giveth *understanding*.

You can give someone the physical Scriptures by handing them a Bible, but only the Lord *by inspiration* gives *understanding* of those words to the heart of a man. And those words are able to make that person wise unto salvation.

Psalm 119:130 says: The entrance of **thy words** giveth light; it **giveth understanding** unto the simple.

Look at how the cross-references explain the connection between *understanding* and *inspiration*:

> All scripture *is* given by *inspiration* of God, and *is* profitable for doctrine, for reproof, for correction, for instruction in righteousness:... (2 Timothy 3:16)

1. **Doctrine**

   > Whom shall he [the Lord] teach knowledge? and whom shall he make to **understand doctrine**? *them that are* weaned from the milk, *and* drawn from the breasts. (Isaiah 28:9)

2. **Reproof**

   > He that refuseth instruction despiseth his own soul: but he that heareth **reproof getteth** *understanding*. (Proverbs 15:32)

3. **Correction**

   > My son, despise not the chastening of the Lord; neither be weary of his **correction**: For whom the Lord loveth he **correcteth**; even as a father the son *in whom* he delighteth. Happy *is* the man *that* findeth wisdom, and the man *that* **getteth** *understanding*. (Proverbs 3:11–13)

4. **Instruction in righteousness**

> For **the LORD giveth** wisdom: out of his mouth *cometh* knowledge and *understanding* ... **Then shalt thou** *understand* righteousness, and judgment, and equity; *yea,* every good path. (Proverbs 2:6, 9)

> O ye simple, understand wisdom: and, ye fools, be ye of an *understanding* heart ... All the words of my mouth *are* in righteousness; *there is* nothing froward or perverse in them. (Proverbs 8:5–8)

Every time you *understand* the meaning of Scripture, it is only by *inspiration* of the Almighty that you are *given* that *understanding*. It is a continual process.

At the end of the day, the only way to identify which words are God's and which aren't is by finding **THE BOOK** that contains them. Otherwise, you join the scholarly community in the fog of competing readings, never being certain which readings are real and which are fake.

You need a "variant readings" identification Application.

There's an App for that.

The Lord provided an "App" so you can tell the wheat from the chaff. That App is the King James Bible.

Now that you have the Bible definition for inspiration, let's see what the definition used to be, what it is now, and when things changed...

Chapter Sixteen

Inspiration—What it was and what they say it is now

>My son, fear thou the Lord and the king:
>*and* meddle not with them that are given to change: (Proverbs 24:21)

First of all, here's what the word "*inspiration*" meant to John Wesley (1703–1791), founder of the Methodist church:

> The Spirit of God not only once inspired those who wrote it, but **continually inspires**, supernaturally assists, those that read it with earnest prayer. Hence it is so profitable for doctrine, for instruction of the ignorant, for the reproof or conviction of them that are in error or sin, for the correction or amendment of whatever is amiss, and for instructing or training up the children of God in all righteousness.[1]

Wesley said that the Spirit of God "continually inspires" believers. You'll note that his view of inspiration matches the Bible definition we saw in the last chapter.

Here's what the word "*inspiration*" meant in the early 19th century.

Inspiration as defined in Webster's 1828 Dictionary…

---

[1] Brandon Staggs, "Inspired Translation of Copies Required for Bible Study," The King James Bible Page, citing John Wesley commentary on 2 Timothy 3:16, accessed January 2013, http://av1611.com/kjbp/articles/staggs-inspired-translation.html. (emphasis mine)www.peterballard.org/catalog.html.

n. [L. *inspiro.*]

1. The act of drawing air into the lungs; the inhaling of air; a branch of respiration, and opposed to expiration.

2. The act of breathing into any thing.

3. The infusion of ideas into the mind by the Holy Spirit; the conveying into the minds of men, ideas, notices or monitions by extraordinary or supernatural influence; or the communication of the divine will to the understanding by suggestions or impressions on the mind, which leave no room to doubt the reality of their supernatural origin.

All Scripture is given by inspiration of God. 2 Tim.3.16[2]

Noah Webster explained many of his definitions with quotes from the King James Bible. It's said of Webster that he "taught millions to read but not one to sin."

You'll notice there is no reference to original autographs here. This definition is consistent with the scriptural definition we saw in the last chapter—especially Job 32:8.

The reason Webster quoted 2 Timothy 3:16 and didn't mention the "original autographs" is because...

The theory that only the original autographs were inspired didn't exist yet.

That theory would be developed later in the 19th century. The whole idea of *"the Original Bible"* you learned about at the beginning of this book is an invention of late 19th and 20th century fundamentalists and evangelicals.

So here we are in the 21st century and we're being fed whole new definitions for the words *scripture* and *inspiration* that tie them **exclusively** to the original autographs only.

Read on to learn how the experts define *inspiration* now...

Inspiration—What it was and what they say it is now

In October 1978, 200 prominent evangelicals got together and came up with a statement of faith called *The Chicago Statement on Biblical Inerrancy*.[3] The Chicago Statement was signed by a who's who of Protestantism. They meant well. But all that's meant well doesn't always end well.

> The "Chicago Statement on Biblical Inerrancy" was produced at an international Summit Conference of evangelical leaders, held at the Hyatt Regency O'Hare in Chicago in the fall of 1978. This congress was sponsored by the International Council on Biblical Inerrancy.
>
> The Chicago Statement was signed by nearly 300 noted evangelical scholars, including James Boice, Norman L. Geisler, John Gerstner, Carl F. H. Henry, Kenneth Kantzer, Harold Lindsell, John Warwick Montgomery, Roger Nicole, J. I. Packer, Robert Preus, Earl Radmacher, Francis Schaeffer, R. C. Sproul, and John Wenham.[4]

Lots of churches, Christian colleges, and universities ascribe to the Chicago Statement or something close to it. Read these excerpts carefully. The folks who wrote it chose the words carefully. They mean what they say.

Article VI[5]

We affirm that the whole of Scripture and all its parts, down to the very words of the original, **were given** by divine inspiration.

Note: the Scriptures "**were given**…" (past tense).

Article VII

We affirm that inspiration was the work in which God by His Spirit, through human writers, gave us His Word.

---

[2] *Webster's Dictionary* (1828), s.v. "inspiration," http://www.webster1828.com/definition.aspx?word=Inspiration.
[3] International Council on Biblical Inerrancy, "The Chicago Statement on Biblical Inerrancy," 1978, accessed January 2013, http://www.reformed.org/documents/index.html?mainframe=http://www.reformed.org/documents/icbi.html.
[4] Bible Research, "Chicago Statement on Biblical Inerrancy with Exposition," accessed January 2013, http://www.Bible-researcher.com/chicago1.html.
[5] The Articles quoted throughout this chapter are from International Council on Biblical Inerrancy, "Chicago Statement on Biblical Inerrancy." (emphasis mine)

Note: "inspiration **was**" (past tense), and yet Bible versions say "is" inspired or "given by" inspiration (present tense).

Article VIII

We affirm that God in His Work of inspiration utilized the distinctive personalities and literary styles of the writers whom He had chosen and prepared.

Note: "God ... **utilized** ... personalities..." (past tense). Inspiration is limited to the original writings of men.

Article IX

We affirm that inspiration, though not conferring omniscience, guaranteed true and trustworthy utterance on all matters of which the Biblical authors were moved to speak and write.

Note: "inspiration ... **guaranteed** ... the Biblical authors..." (past tense).

Article X

WE AFFIRM that *inspiration*, strictly speaking, applies **only to the autographic text of Scripture**, which in the providence of God can be ascertained from available manuscripts **with great accuracy**. We further affirm that **copies and translations of Scripture** are **the Word of God** to the extent that they faithfully represent the original.

A careful reading of Article X introduces us to…

The dirty little secret of Biblicism—evangelical style…

Their statement introduces a whole new entity in the realm of Bible-centered Christianity called…

"The Word of God"

Note: "copies and translations of Scripture" become something called *"the Word of God"*—spelled with a capital "W." *"The Word of God"* is absolutely not a book. It is a theoretical representation of *"The Original Bible"* they are still searching for.

Inspiration—What it was and what they say it is now

"The Word of God" can be anything they want it to be. It is what they say it is. It is purposely undefined. It is—by design—not tied to any real tangible document.

It is referencing an imaginary document that has **no defined number** of letters, words, or verses—in Hebrew, Greek, English, or any other language. Even the absolute identity of the words (in any language) that constitute the text does not exist.

And the beauty is that no one can challenge them because *"The Word of God"* doesn't exist.

"The Word of God" is made up of words supposedly "**ascertained … with great accuracy**." But because you don't have the originals to compare to, you have to take the Chicago Statement framers' opinion that some experts have ascertained the autographic text "with great accuracy."

First of all, how accurate is "great" accuracy?

And how convenient that they don't have "**the autographic text**." How are you supposed to compare words that you've got to words that you haven't got?

"When I use a word," Humpty Dumpty said, in rather a scornful tone, "it means just what I choose it to mean—neither more nor less."

For example:

In **2 Samuel 15:7 the ESV says**: "…at the end of **four years** …" and yet the NASB says: "…at the end of **forty years**…"

The magic about this thing called *"The Word of God"* is that it can be both 4 years and 40 years!

No longer do you have to wonder what God said. He talks out of both sides of his mouth.

For example: The NKJV has **18 more verses** than the ESV. But both are called *"The Word of God."*

Now you may think that "Autographic Text" and "Original Autographs" are different, but they aren't.

249

How can you tell? Because they say that the "Autographic Text" is "inerrant and inspired." As you will soon see, the "Autographic Text" is taken to mean the "original manuscripts" by everyone in the business.

And according to their definition, **only** what was originally written fits that description. The original writings, which constitute the "autographic text," **were** inerrant and inspired.

And the evangelical experts teach that...

There's a difference between the Bible (a book you can hold in your hands) and "the *Scriptures*."

According to Chicago Statement Article X, "copies and translations" in themselves are not *Scriptures*.

Only the "autographic text" is *Scriptures*. If copies and translations were *Scriptures*, they'd be "inspired."

The evangelicals at Wheaton College were careful readers of the statement and incorporated it into their profession of faith:

> WE BELIEVE that God has revealed Himself and His truth in the created order, **in the Scriptures**, and supremely in Jesus Christ; and that the Scriptures of the Old and New Testaments are verbally inspired by God and **inerrant in the original writing**, so that they are fully trustworthy and of supreme and final authority in all they say.[6]

Notice that they don't mention the word **Bible** once. These folks are sharp cookies. Wheaton believes in scriptures that were verbally inspired and inerrant. And yet those very scriptures **are** fully trustworthy and **are** their **final authority** except for one thing—**they don't have them.**

And look at this statement of faith by Denver Theological Seminary. Notice how they do not reference any book called Bible but start off by commenting on *"The Word of God"*...

---

[6] Wheaton College, "Statement of Faith and Educational Purpose," accessed January 2013, http://www.wheaton.edu/About-Wheaton/Statement-of-Faith-and-Educational-Purpose. (emphasis mine)

Inspiration—What it was and what they say it is now

THE WORD OF GOD—We believe the Scriptures of the Old and New Testaments are the inspired Word of God, **inerrant in the original writings**, complete as the revelation of God's will for salvation, and the supreme and final authority in all matters to which they speak.[7]

Denver's "Scriptures" are "complete," "supreme," and their "**final authority**." It's sad that they don't actually have them.

As an aside…

Don't forget what you saw in chapter 3. Despite what the framers of the Chicago Statement BELIEVE, the experts who produced the Greek New Testament, which they say represents "the original writings," tell us that they absolutely are NOT inerrant.

They openly admit that Matthew 1:7–8 and 10; Mark 1:2; Luke 4:44; and John 7:8, 10 (as they appear in the Greek New Testament that underlies the ESV, ©1984 NIV, ©2011 NIV, NASB, HCSB, and over 100 others) were erroneous in "the original writings" and were later fixed by orthodox Christians in an effort to help God out.

In the future, any version of the Bible whose New Testament is based on the same Greek New Testament text will likewise be erroneous.

Zenith Televisions used to have a slogan that said: "The quality goes in before the name goes on."

For new Bible versions based on the same critical text, the slogan should read: "the errors are put in before the name goes on."

Getting back to the story…

Unfortunately the following institutions must not have gotten the memo because

Dan Schumann next to corporate sign outside of World Headquarters of Zenith Electronics Corporation, Glenview, IL

---

[7] Denver Seminary, "Our Statement of Faith," accessed January 2013, http://www.denverseminary.edu/about-us/what-we-believe/. (emphasis mine)

they claim they actually believe in some imaginary book they refer to as *"the Bible."*

Statements of Faith about the Bible	
Dallas Theological Seminary	"We believe that the whole Bible in the originals **is** therefore without error."[8]
Trinity International University	"We believe ... the Bible **is** without error in the original writings..."[9]
Gordon-Conwell	"The ... books of the Bible as originally written **were** inspired of God, hence free from error."[10]
Talbot School of Theology	"...the Bible **is** without errors of any kind in its original manuscripts."[11]
Moody Bible Institute	"The Bible **is** without error in all it affirms in the original autographs..."[12]
The Master's Seminary	"We teach that the Bible **is** ... absolutely inerrant in the original documents, infallible, and God breathed"[13]
Bethel University	"We believe that the Bible **is** the Word of God, fully inspired and without error in the original manuscripts..."[14]

---

[8] Dallas Theological Seminary, "DTS Doctrinal Statement," accessed January 2013, http://www.dts.edu/about/doctrinalstatement.
[9] Trinity International University, "Statement of Faith," accessed January 2013, http://www.tiu.edu/about/statement-of-faith.dot.
[10] Gordon-Conwell Theological Seminary, "Statement of Faith," accessed January 2013, http://www.gordonconwell.edu/about/Statement-of-Faith.cfm.
[11] Talbot School of Theology, Biola University, "Biblical Inerrancy," accessed January 2013, http://www.talbot.edu/about/biblical-inerrancy/.
[12] Moody Bible Institute, "Doctrinal Statement," accessed January 2013, http://www.moodyministries.net/crp_MainPage.aspx?id=334.
[13] The Master's Seminary, "Statement of Faith—The Holy Scriptures," accessed January 2013, http://www.tms.edu/AboutSOFTheHolyScriptures.aspx.
[14] Bethel University, "Affirmation of Faith," accessed January 2013, http://www.bethel.edu/about/faith.

Inspiration—What it was and what they say it is now

Statements of Faith about the Bible *(continued)*	
Bob Jones University	"We believe in the verbal, plenary *inspiration* of the Bible in the original manuscripts…"[15]
Central Baptist Theological Seminary of Minneapolis	"We believe that the Bible … **is** without error in the original manuscripts."[16]
Pensacola Christian College	"We believe that the Bible **is** the verbally inspired and infallible, authoritative Word of God and that God gave the words of Scripture by *inspiration* without error in the original autographs."[17]
Detroit Baptist Theological Seminary	"'We believe in the verbal, plenary inspiration of **the Bible**, the sixty-six books of the Old and New Testament canon, which, **being inerrant in the original manuscripts**, is the final authority on all matters of faith and practice and any other subject on which it touches.' … Though preachers do not normally tell their congregations that their particular translation of the Bible has errors in it, neither should they tell them that their translation of the Bible has *no* errors in it. No such guarantee is possible."[18]

---

[15] Bob Jones University, "Statement about Bible Translations," accessed January 2013, http://www.bju.edu/communities/ministries-schools/position-statements/translation.php.

[16] Central Baptist Theological Seminary of Virginia Beach, "Biblical Foundations Statement," accessed January 2013, http://www.baptistseminary.edu/about/doctrine.html.

[17] Pensacola Christian College, "Articles of Faith," accessed January 2013, http://www.pcci.edu/GeneralInfo/ArticlesofFaith.html.

[18] William W. Combs, "Errors in the King James Version?" Detroit Baptist Seminary Journal 4 (Fall 1999): 151–152. (Available: http://www.dbts.edu/journals/1999/Combs.PDF.) Combs, who was academic dean and professor of New Testament at Detroit Baptist Theological Seminary, quotes the DBTS doctrinal statement regarding the Bible in this article.

At least you get the straight skinny from Gordon-Conwell: "the Bible" **was** inspired and **used to be** without error.

Enter the fundamentalists

Central Baptist Theological Seminary of Minneapolis goes on to say: "We believe that the Bible is the sole authority for faith and practice."[19] How can a "Bible" that doesn't exist (and never existed) be anybody's "sole authority for faith and practice"?

Bob Jones University, Pensacola Christian College, Central Seminary, Detroit Baptist Theological Seminary, and a host of others have doubled down on the *"Word of God"* accommodation and have created a whole new kind of animal known as *"The Bible."*

When they say *"The Bible,"* they are never referring to a specific book but to the same imaginary document that has no defined number of letters, words, or verses—in Hebrew, Greek, English, or any other language.

And they have a dirty little secret too…

The fundamentalists have gone beyond the evangelicals. What the evangelicals call the *"Word of God,"* the fundamentalists actually call *"The Bible."*

It's the same dirty little secret for both, actually. They are both referring to *"The Original Bible"* mentioned in the introduction. They promote a nonexistent book.

For example:

The NKJV has **18 more verses** than the ESV. But both versions are referred to as *"The Bible"* by fundamentalists. Both are "trustworthy, conservative" translations. But why stop there?

The NASB includes Matthew 12:47 and the ESV doesn't. Yet they're both *"The Bible."* And they're both reliable.

---

[19] Central Baptist Theological Seminary, "Doctrinal Statement," accessed January 2013, http://www.centralseminary.edu/about-central/foundational-documents/doctrinal-statement.

Inspiration—What it was and what they say it is now

The Holman Christian Standard Bible (HCSB) does not contain 2 Corinthians 13:14, yet the NIV, NASB, and ESV do. What's up with that?

Did God "inspire" 2 Corinthians 13:14 or not? Was it in the *"Word of God"* (the original Bible of the evangelicals) and *"The Bible"* (the original Bible of the fundamentalists) but **not** in *"The Original Bible"*?

It's no wonder "Bible-believing" Christianity is in such a mess—their leaders don't have a book.

Anyway, *"The Bible"* of the fundamentalists is truly a wonder—especially because it's so versatile. It says whatever they say it says. It includes whatever they say it includes. And they can change it at will.

It's an embarrassment to the name of Christ to even suggest that the only place you can really discover what the Lord actually said is found in *"The Original Bible"* made up of these nonexistent pieces of paper.

Any critical thinking man knows it's just a cowardly and unbelieving way to avoid dealing with Bible discrepancies and tough questions about your beliefs. And if this isn't bad enough…

Think about a new convert.

He or she will eventually be confused because new converts are instructed to believe in **the Bible.**

Eventually, they're going to learn the truth. **The Bible** they thought was the one they were given as a gift at conversion doesn't really exist. The real Bible is *"The Original Bible."* The imaginary one made up of the original manuscripts. The literal Bible they were given is a generic version of the real McCoy. Unfortunately, theirs is not inspired or inerrant. And worse, it is a mix of men's words and God's words.

Like James said: "My brethren, these things ought not so to be" (3:10). It's just not right.

Our religion has **no other foundation** than the words of a book. And it better not be a fictional book like *"The Original Bible"* or its counterparts, *"The Word of God"* and *"The Bible."*

Your teacher will object and say, "No, there **is** Scripture today!" but according to The Chicago Statement and the popular dogma there are only copies and translations of Scripture, which by their definition are NOT Scripture.

And yet...

Scripture can be **read**:

- "Jesus saith unto them, Did ye never **read** in **the scriptures**..." (Matthew 21:42). The Jews **had** Scriptures long after the originals were gone.

Scripture can be **searched**:

- The Lord Jesus Christ said "Search the scriptures..." (John 5:39). The Lord said that the Jews **had** Scriptures even though they didn't have any original autographs.

- The Bereans "... **searched the scriptures** daily, whether those things were so" (Acts 17:11). The Bereans **had** Scriptures even though they didn't have any original autographs.

- Scripture was in the Ethiopian eunuch's possession: "The place of **the scripture** which he **read** was this..." (Acts 8:32). He surely didn't have an Original Autograph.

Scripture was in Timothy's possession:

- "from a child ... hast **known the holy scriptures**" (2 Timothy 3:15). Timothy didn't have any original autographs.

Scripture gives hope:

- "for whatsoever things were written aforetime were written for our learning, that we through patience and comfort of **the scriptures** might have **hope**" (Romans 15:4). What a dumb thing for Paul to tell the Romans (who didn't have any original autographs) or you if you don't have (present tense) the Scriptures.

Oh, by the way, here's a mistake the Lord made. Remember in Luke 4 when the Lord stood up to read from Isaiah in the synagogue on the Sabbath in his hometown of Nazareth?

> And he began to say unto them, This day is **this scripture** fulfilled in your ears. (Luke 4:21)

The poor Lord, he actually thought he was reading "scripture."

Obviously, he must not have realized that the **copy** he was reading from (the "original" if available at all would have been in the Temple at Jerusalem) wasn't **scripture** at all and wasn't inspired because only the original autographs are "scripture."

Too bad, you would have thought the Lord would have chosen his words more carefully like the evangelical politicians who prepared the Chicago Statement on Inerrancy.

So the folks from the Chicago meeting go on to say…

> *WE DENY* that any **essential** element of the Christian faith is affected by **the absence of the autographs**. We further deny that **this absence** renders the assertion of Biblical inerrancy invalid or irrelevant.

Fascinating. They tell you twice that the "**autographs**" (a.k.a. "the scripture") are **absent**.

But don't worry, all **essential** elements of the Christian faith are **not** affected.

Wouldn't you like to know what the **unessential elements** of the Christian faith are? Nobody's asking that one.

And you're branded a wise guy if you ask: "Isn't there any book I can get that has God's inspired, inerrant words in it?"

And the follow-up: "Where can I get a copy of it in my own language?"

Your teacher will be uncomfortable with your questions. He can't answer honestly. That's because he's holding the conflicting idea of a real Bible and an imaginary Bible in his mind simultaneously. He can't answer your questions without first resolving the conflict in his own mind.

It's called "**cognitive dissonance**," which is the discomfort one feels by holding two conflicting ideas simultaneously.

How did this dreadful state of affairs come to pass?

That's coming up next…

Chapter Seventeen

Who changed the definition of *inspiration,* and when did they change it?

> … but he honoureth them that fear the L<small>ORD</small>.
> *He that* sweareth to *his own* hurt, and changeth not. (Psalm 15:4)

The switch took place when some real smart Christian scholars couldn't defend the book they held in their hands.

Tying the definition of *inspiration* to the dogma of Original Autograph Onlyism began in the late 19th century. So the Chicago Statement that you read about in the last chapter had its genesis about 130 years ago.

But let's start back even further than that.

In 1516 Desiderius Erasmus produced what became the standard "Greek New Testament text" that (with minor variations) would be passed on to succeeding generations. It became known as the Textus Receptus, or Received Text, and is the underlying Greek New Testament text of the King James Bible and New King James Version.

Along the way, men who had access to numbers of different manuscripts realized that the manuscripts were not always "dead on" copies of each other.

There were variations in wording. The dilemma for these scholars was which words were authentic, which words were honest mistakes in copying, and more importantly, which words were corruptions added or subtracted to the text by men with an agenda.

But average Christians believed "the Bible" they possessed was without error, or inerrant. That's because they believed God wrote it.

All that would change, especially in 1707 when English theologian John Mill (1645–1707) produced a Greek New Testament that gave…

Title page to John Mill's Greek New Testament, 1707

the readings of 100 Greek manuscripts as well as those of several church fathers and versions. This apparatus revealed 30,000 variants among the witnesses [various manuscripts], causing Roman Catholic scholars to decry the Textus Receptus as a "paper pope" which was contradicted by the MSS of the New Testament. Some Protestants, too, attacked Mill's work because they saw it as a threat to the Reformation principle of sola scriptura.[1]

The Protestants who attacked Mill's work did so because they were scared. They knew that if the integrity of the Scripture could be called into question, their whole movement would be viewed as illegitimate—which is exactly how the Church of Rome viewed it.

In other words, the Protestants' final authority (i.e. the Bible) was a corrupted document.

Echoing the mantra of today, Protestant scholar Johann Albrecht Bengel (1687–1752) examined Mill's work on the variant readings and "concluded that no Protestant doctrine was jeopardized by any of the variants."[2]

Bengel probably got this view from an earlier textual critic named Richard Bentley (1662–1742), who said:

> The real text of the sacred writers does not now (since the originals have been so long lost) lie in any MS. or edition, but is dispersed in them all. Tis competently exact indeed in the worst MS. now extant;

---

[1] Center for the Study of New Testament Manuscripts, "John Mill—*Novum Testamentum*," accessed January 2013, http://www.csntm.org/printedbook/viewbook/JohnMillNovumTestamentum1707.

[2] Ibid.

nor is one article of faith or moral precept either perverted or lost ... Make your 30,000 [variations] as many more, if numbers of copies can ever reach that sum: all the better to a knowing and a serious reader, who is thereby more richly furnished to select what he sees genuine.[3]

Richard Bently

Here you see the first steps in moving away from the authority of **a book** to the authority of a scholar. Note that only "a knowing and a serious reader" gets to "select what he sees genuine." After all these years, the "knowing and serious" readers are still looking for *The Original Bible*.

Bengel just repeated the **opinion** that no doctrine was jeopardized by the variants.

This same untrue opinion is repeated *ad nauseam* today. If it were true, you'd never have a Bible version "controversy" in the first place.

Dr. Bart Ehrman is the James A. Gray Distinguished Professor of Religious Studies at the University of North Carolina, Chapel Hill, and is a leading authority on the New Testament and the history of early Christianity. He is the author of more than twenty books, including four *New York Times* bestsellers.

Dr. Ehrman reveals that:

> [t]he scribes who copied the texts changed them ... **intentionally**.

Moreover he asks:

> [were] ... the surviving texts ... ever modified in light of the doctrinal controversies of the second and third centuries? **Yes, there is abundant evidence [they were]**...[4]

---

[3] Bible Research, "The Apparatus of a Critical Text," citing Richard Bentley, *Remarks upon a Late Discourse of Free Thinking, in a Letter to F.H., D.D., by Phileleutherus Lipsiensis* (London, 1713), Part I, Section 32, accessed January 2013, http://www.bible-researcher.com/tisch02.html.

[4] Bart D. Ehrman, *Lost Christianities: The Battles for Scripture and the Faiths We Never Knew* (New York: Oxford University Press, 2005), 219–221.

Here's the thing. Doctrines are based on words. Changing words can easily change doctrine as you have already seen in this book.

Now all this really didn't affect the Christian on the street because on the whole he was unaware of the textual variants that appeared in the apparatus of Mill's Greek New Testament.

It was easy for informed evangelical leaders to simply pass off the variations as minor and unimportant if they were even questioned by the flock. And this is what went on for decades.

Fast-forward to the 19th century.

The challenge of variant readings was about to become more formidable…

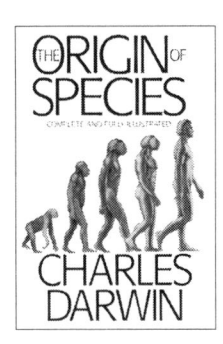

The mid-19th century saw the publication of a work that would pave the way for the unbelief, wickedness, and democide[5] of the 20th century.

In 1859 Charles Darwin published *On the Origin of Species*. The new religion of Evolution featured its own definition of man—nothing more than an evolved beast. Evolution's religious ceremony is natural selection. Man's hope for life is reduced to survival of the fittest.

Pile onto this the work of the German school of Theological Rationalism and things start to go south in a hurry.

Theological Rationalism rejected, among other things, the divine authority of the traditional canon of Scripture and the inspiration of the text. In short, their rationalistic view was that the Bible was a very human book.

The authority of the Bible was now being attacked on multiple fronts.

The theory of evolution caught Christian leaders off guard. It was hard enough for the leadership to answer the supposed "scientific" basis for it.

---

[5] "Democide is a term revived and redefined by the political scientist R. J. Rummel as 'the murder of any person or people by a government, including genocide, politicide and mass murder.' Rummel created the term as an extended concept to include forms of government murder that are not covered by the term *genocide*, and it has become accepted among other scholars." (*Wikipedia*, s.v. "democide," last modified January 13, 2013, http://en.wikipedia.org/wiki/Democide).

Who changed the definition of *inspiration*, and when did they change it?

But when it came to defending the inspiration of Scripture, the scholars at the time couldn't deal with the nagging problem of variant readings. They weren't sure in their own minds which readings were authentic and which readings were not.

This is still the case today with many scholars because (a) there are even more variant readings in existence, and (b) most still don't believe that God has provided them with a book that contains all the correct readings.

It is with this backdrop that 19th-century Christian leaders invented a new theory that only the original autographs were inspired and therefore inerrant.

It appears that three men originated and popularized this theory: James H. Brookes, B.B. Warfield, and A.A. Hodge. We'll look at each in turn.

The genesis of fundamentalism and the dawn of Original Autograph Onlyism

Author Timothy Demy introduces us to James H. Brookes, who helped shape the key doctrines of fundamentalism:

> In the years between the end of the Civil War in 1865 and the dawning of the Twentieth century, Premillennialism—and especially dispensationalism—grew significantly in American religious thought and culture. Much of this early growth came as a result of the preaching, teaching, and publications of Presbyterian minister James Hall Brookes (1830–1897).
>
> ... Brookes became a nationally recognized proponent of dispensational premillennialism and the pre-trib rapture. Brookes was one of the first to prominently teach the pre-trib rapture in this country and most likely should be viewed as the father of Christ's "any moment" return in America.[6]

It was Brookes who introduced C.I. Scofield, author of the famous Scofield Study Bible, to the teachings of dispensational premillennialism.

---

[6] Timothy Demy, "James Hall Brookes," Pre-Trib Research Center, accessed January 2013, http://www.pre-trib.org/data/pdf/Demy-JamesHallBookes.pdf.

Brookes was one of the founders and president of an annual conference that eventually became known as the Niagara Bible Conference.

> The Niagara Bible Conference (officially called the "Believers' Meeting for Bible Study") was held annually from 1876 to 1897, with the exception of 1884...
>
> Most of the leading dispensationalists of the late 19th and early 20th century attended the conference regularly, including William Eugene Blackstone, Charles Erdman, James H. Brookes, William Moorehead, Adoniram Judson Gordon, Amzi Dixon, C.I. Scofield, and James Hudson Taylor (who founded the China Inland Mission).
>
> In 1878, the Believers' Meeting for Bible Study produced the document that came to be known as the "Niagara Creed." This 14-point statement of faith was one of the first to explicitly proclaim faith in the premillennial return of Jesus Christ to earth.[7]

The Niagara Creed laid the foundation for a movement that would later be called fundamentalism.[8]

> The Niagara Creed does not explicitly affirm dispensationalism, but it refers to several key dispensationalist beliefs, including the reality of the millennium, the restoration of Israel, and the distinction be-

---

[7] *Wikipedia*, s.v. "Niagara Bible Conference," last modified February 1, 2013, http://en.wikipedia.org/wiki/Niagara_Bible_Conference.

[8] "On the broader front, the dispensational organizers of the Niagara Bible Conference were joined by non-dispensationalists like B.B. Warfield and J. Gresham Machen in their fight against modernism. In 1910, the fourteen-point Niagara Creed was distilled into 'five fundamentals' by the General Assembly of the Presbyterian Church. These five fundamentals were as follows:
1. The inerrancy of Scripture
2. The virgin birth and deity of Jesus Christ
3. The substitutionary atonement through God's grace and human faith
4. The bodily resurrection of Jesus Christ
5. The authenticity of Christ's miracles (or later, by some dispensationalists, the imminent return of Jesus Christ)
...Those who embraced the five fundamentals (and were thus associated with The Fundamentals pamphlets) came to be known as "fundamentalists." Nathan Busenitz, "Our Fundamentalist Future," Looking at Truth (blog), October 5, 2006, http://lookingattruth.blogspot.com/2008/08/our-fundamentalist-future-nathan.html.

tween the judgment of the saved and the damned.[9]

In point 1 of the 14-point creed, Brookes stated…

> We believe "that all Scripture is given by **inspiration** of God," by which we understand the whole of the book called the Bible; nor do we take the statement in the sense in which it is sometimes foolishly said that works of human genius are inspired, but in the sense that the Holy Ghost gave the very words of the sacred writings to holy men of old; and that His Divine inspiration is not in different degrees, but extends equally and fully to all parts of these writings, historical, poetical, doctrinal, and prophetical and to the smallest word, and inflection of a word, **provided such word is found in the original manuscripts**: 2 Tim. 3:16, 17; 2 Pet. 1:21; 1 Cor. 2:13; Mark 12:26, 36; 13:11; Acts 1:16; 2:4.[10]

Queen's Royal Hotel, Niagara-on-the-Lake, Ontario, location of the Niagara Bible Conference since 1883

Brookes obviously is aware of the variant reading of the manuscript evidence, so he limits "inspiration" exclusively to the "original manuscripts." This phrase signified a monumental change in how Christians would view the Bible for years to come, reaching even into our day.

The variant readings dilemma was also a thorn in the side of two famous Princeton Seminary professors.

Here's their story…

B.B. Warfield (1851–1921) was professor of theology at Princeton Seminary from 1887 to 1921.

---

[9] *Wikipedia*, s.v. "Niagara Bible Conference."
[10] Point 1 of the Niagara Creed cited by Will Kinney, "The Infallibility of Scripture: Are You a Bible Believer or a Bible Agnostic?" accessed January 2013, http://brandplucked.webs.com/biblebelieveragnostic.htm. (emphasis mine)

Disciple magazine, an outreach of Advancing the Ministries of the Gospel (AMG) International, said Warfield was:

> "perhaps the most accomplished scholar of the evangelical church." New editions of his works have been "excellent sellers" even to this day.[11]

B.B. Warfield

He is still a hero to both fundamentalists and evangelicals. His passion was to refute the liberal element within Presbyterianism and within Christianity at large. His heart was in the right place.

He contended with German Rationalists, who exalted human reason and ruled out revelation as a source of knowledge for man. To them, the Bible was a mere human book.

Warfield sought to defend his position of a verbally inspired Bible, but even he doubted the text he held in his hands. That's because of the textual uncertainty caused by the variant readings. This uncertainty still exists today unless you have determined which Book really is the Bible.

Warfield was embarrassed by equally smart biblical agnostic scholars because he couldn't prove which variant was original. Mind you, he wasn't trying to defend the English Bible. Perish the thought. He couldn't even defend the Greek and Hebrew texts from which any version is translated.

The higher critics didn't believe in the Book. They didn't believe in inspiration, inerrancy, or anything you couldn't rationally explain: like the resurrection of the dead, for instance; or feeding 5,000 men with five loaves and two fishes; or that a woman was created from the rib of a man. They couldn't answer questions like where did Cain get his wife? Or how many angels can dance on the head of a pin? Oh, wait; just kidding. That was the smart-aleck remark in the middle ages. But you get the point.

---

[11] Bernard R. DeRemer, "Church Builders: B.B. Warfield, Scholar," *Disciple Magazine*, vol. 3, no. 20 (October 24, 2011): 9, citing John D. Woodbridge, ed., *Great Leaders in the Christian Church* (Chicago: Moody, 1989). (Available: http://www.disciplemagazine.com/www/articles/155.628.)

Who changed the definition of *inspiration*, and when did they change it?

A.A. Hodge (1823–1886) succeeded his father, influential Presbyterian theologian Charles Hodge, as principal of Princeton Seminary from 1878 to 1886.

In an effort to protect the doctrine of biblical *inspiration* and *inerrancy*, B.B. Warfield and A.A. Hodge moved the locus of *inspiration* and *inerrancy* from the Bible (meaning a real printed book) to the nonexistent originals. In so doing they redefined the words *inspiration* and *scripture*.

Using this theory, modern-day fundamentalists and evangelicals have redefined the Bible—that is, a printed book—into two fictitious creations called *"The Word of God"* and *"The Bible."*

The point is that Warfield and Hodge popularized the theory that…

"Only the original autographs were inspired and inerrant."

In 1881 Benjamin Warfield and A.A. Hodge wrote an article for *The Presbyterian Review*:

> We do not assert that the common text, **but only that the original autographic text was inspired.** No error can be asserted, therefore, which cannot be proved to have been aboriginal in the text.[12]

Ernest R. Sandeen (1931–1982), James Wallace Professor of History and co-director of the Living Historical Museum at Macalester College in St. Paul, Minnesota, said:

> Princeton in this article took its stand upon the absolute inerrancy of the Bible and, in a sense, seemed to risk the whole of the Christian faith upon one proved error.[13]

The academics weren't going to lose the debate and let all of Christendom down. So they invented new definitions for *inspiration* and

---

[12] Archibald Hodge and Benjamin Warfield, "Inspiration," *Presbyterian Review* 6 (April 1881), 225–260. (Available: http://www.bible-researcher.com/warfield4.html.) (emphasis mine)

[13] Ernest R. Sandeen, *The Roots of Fundamentalism: British and American Millenarianism, 1800–1930* (Chicago: University of Chicago Press, 2008), 126. ©1970 by The University of Chicago. All rights reserved. Published 1970. Paperback edition 2008. Used by permission.

267

inerrancy. From now on these doctrines would only be tied to the original manuscripts.

Sandeen ties Brookes, Hodge, and Warfield together in the conspiracy:

> That Brookes's Niagara Creed affirmed the inspiration of the "original autographs" in the same year that that phrase became a part of the apologetic of the Princeton theologians demonstrates remarkable similarity of views if not direct influence.[14]

Sandeen traces the "refinement" of the Princeton doctrine:

> Verbal and inerrant inspiration was claimed not for the Bible as we now find it, but for the books of the Bible as they came from the hands of the authors—the original autographs. This emphasis upon the original manuscripts is another example of the way in which the Princeton doctrine of the Scriptures was refined and tightened in the face of growing critical opposition. A.A. Hodge said nothing of the original autographs in the first (1860) edition of his *Outlines of Theology*, but saw fit to introduce it into the 1879 edition. The collaborative article of A.A. Hodge and B.B. Warfield in the *Princeton Review* (1881) elevated the concept to an especially prominent place in the Princeton doctrine of inspiration. That this concept of the original autographs had been recently added to their apologetic was never mentioned by Warfield and Hodge.[15]

The fact that "this concept of the original autographs had been **recently** added to their apologetic" is still virtually unknown. Warfield and Hodge kept their mouths shut about this new theory and just pretended that it was long-standing Christian doctrine. They had to. That's the only way they could get the brethren to accept it. And the brethren have believed it unto this day.

---

[14] Ernest R. Sandeen, *The Roots of Fundamentalism: British and American Millenarianism, 1800–1930* (Chicago: University of Chicago Press, 2008), 168. ©1970 by The University of Chicago. All rights reserved. Published 1970. Paperback edition 2008. Used by permission.

[15] Ernest R. Sandeen, *The Roots of Fundamentalism: British and American Millenarianism, 1800–1930* (Chicago: University of Chicago Press, 2008), 127–128. ©1970 by The University of Chicago. All rights reserved. Published 1970. Paperback edition 2008. Used by permission.

> This new emphasis was introduced just at the time that the number of biblical errors or discrepancies turned up by the critics was growing too large to be ignored … Hodge and Warfield retreated … The Princeton claim to an inerrant Bible was maintained only by resource to lost and completely useless original autographs. Once again the completely scholastic, theoretical nature of the Princeton mind is illustrated. And once again Princeton is caught propagating a dogma which is flatly contradicted by the Westminster Confession. In that creed the Scriptures are declared to be authentic not only at the mount of their description but now: …"**being immediately inspired by God, and, by His singular care and providence, kept pure in all ages**, are therefore authentical." … There is a second and even more important sense in which the **original autograph theory** marked a retreat for the Princeton apologetic. Warfield in particular phrased his defense of the inerrancy of the original autographs in such a way that no further discussion was possible.[16]

Note that Sandeen calls Warfield's apologetic "**the original autograph theory**." And that's exactly what it is—a theory. It's a clever argument invented because the thought leaders of the day didn't know what do with the textual variations they found in Greek manuscripts.

But you'd never know that today. Warfield's theory that **only** the original autographs are/were inspired and inerrant is repeated as fact in most Christian schools, colleges, and universities.

Instead of just accepting The Book that the Lord had so exalted as the determiner of the variants, they decided to lean on their own understanding.

The result is blind faith in a book that never existed in the first place— **"The Original Bible."**

It's just like the theory of evolution taught in secular schools. If you don't believe that theory, you're ridiculed or even branded a heretic. It would

---

[16] Ernest R. Sandeen, *The Roots of Fundamentalism: British and American Millenarianism, 1800-1930* (Chicago: University of Chicago Press, 2008), 128–129. ©1970 by The University of Chicago. All rights reserved. Published 1970. Paperback edition 2008. Used by permission.

be helpful if teachers would do more research on their own instead of just repeating what they were taught.

Because sometimes…

Questioning authority is the right thing to do.

Sandeen goes on…

> Since in order to prove the Bible in error became necessary to find the original manuscripts … inerrancy could never be denied … the Princeton professors' insistence that they were doing nothing new, while creating a unique apologetic which flew in the face of the standards they were claiming to protect, cannot be judged as a historically honest or laudable program.[17]

And to top it all off…

Not all Presbyterians were on the same page.

Not all Presbyterians were in agreement with this new inerrancy doctrine coming out of Princeton Theological Seminary. The minutes from the Presbyterian General Assembly for 1893 reveal that 80 ministers and elders protested the suspension of Charles Augustus Briggs from the ministry on the grounds that his condemnation had been possible only because the Presbyterian clergy and elders had accepted the Princeton doctrine of inerrancy as the equivalent of a confessional standard.

Among other things, Briggs said that errors may have existed in the original text of the Holy Scripture, which is exactly what the experts whose text is behind the NIV, ESV, NASB, NLT, HCSB, and a host of others say today.

Anyway, 80 of Briggs' fellow clergy and elders proceeded to file a lengthy protest. Here are some of the highlights:

> The undersigned enter respectful and earnest protest against the action of this Assembly, which declares the inerrancy of the origi-

---

[17] Ernest R. Sandeen, *The Roots of Fundamentalism: British and American Millenarianism, 1800–1930* (Chicago: University of Chicago Press, 2008), 130. ©1970 by The University of Chicago. All rights reserved. Published 1970. Paperback edition 2008. Used by permission.

nal autographs of Scripture to be the faith of the church. We protest against this action.

1. Because it is insisting upon a certain theory of inspiration, when our Standards have hitherto only emphasized the fact of inspiration. So far as the original manuscript came from God, undoubtedly it was without error. But we have no means of determining how far God controlled the penmen in transcribing from documents in matters purely circumstantial…

4. Because it is setting up an imaginary Bible as a test of orthodoxy. If an inerrant original Bible is vital to faith, we cannot escape the conclusion that an inerrant present Bible is vital to faith.

5. Because it is disparaging the Bible we have, and endangering its authority under the pressure of a prevalent hostile criticism. It seems like flying for shelter to an original autograph, when the Bible we have in our hands today is our impregnable defense.

Believing these present Scriptures to be "The very Word of God" and "immediately inspired by God," "kept pure in all ages" and "our only infallible rule of faith and practice," notwithstanding some apparent discrepancies in matters purely circumstantial, we earnestly protest against the imposing of this new interpretation of our Standards upon the Church, to bind men's consciences by enforced subscription to its terms.[18]

The 80 ministers objected because Warfield and Hodge had invented a new doctrine. The fact that Briggs was a heretic and may have deserved the title is beside the point. You can't find a man guilty of not believing a "Bible doctrine" you just made up.

Warfield's influence on contemporary evangelicalism can also be seen in the Chicago Statement on Biblical Inerrancy.

---

[18] Ernest R. Sandeen, *The Roots of Fundamentalism: British and American Millenarianism, 1800-1930* (Chicago: University of Chicago Press, 2008), 170–171. ©1970 by The University of Chicago. All rights reserved. Published 1970. Paperback edition 2008. Used by permission.

The point is that inspiration and inerrancy of the **original manuscripts only** is a late 19th-century theory repeated as Bible doctrine today.

The beauty of the Niagara Creed, Warfield, Hodge, and the Chicago Statement is that when anyone finds a supposed error in the Bible, you get to say: "Yeah, but that's not what it says in the original autographs!" Which you conveniently don't have.

So you win the argument.

But not so fast.

Look at what you give up...

The Bible **doctrine** of **Preservation** is jettisoned by this novel theory. Too bad Warfield didn't just believe the words of the Lord Jesus Christ...

- Heaven and earth shall pass away, but **my words shall not pass away**. (Matthew 24:35)

- Heaven and earth shall pass away: but **my words shall not pass away**. (Mark 13:31)

- Heaven and earth shall pass away: **but my words shall not pass away**. (Luke 21:33)

- ... **and his truth endureth to all generations**. (Psalm 100:5)

- ... **thy word is truth**. (John 17:17)

Warfield thought your Savior couldn't deliver on his promises and dropped the ball in the end zone. Conservative scholars will protest and claim that the true words are out there somewhere. And someday they're going to finally determine which ones they are.

In short, they're working on it. As well-meaning as these folks may be, they'll still be looking for *"The Original Bible"* until the Lord returns.

Here's the point...

In John 6:63 the Lord says...

> ... the **words** that I speak unto you, *they* are spirit, and *they* **are life**.

Who changed the definition of *inspiration*, and when did they change it?

And 1 Peter 1:23 says:

> Being born again, not of corruptible seed, but of incorruptible, by the word of God, **which liveth** and abideth for ever.

The Lord spoke those John 6 words in Hebrew. And Peter may have originally written his epistle in Hebrew. Hence, every one of the Lord's words (whether spoken by him or Peter) "are life" and "liveth." It doesn't matter what language they're written in. They are alive.

The Lord's words transcend any and all language barriers.

His life-containing, life-giving, and living words **aren't restricted** to any language (i.e., Paleo Hebrew, Ancient Greek, Syriac, Chaldean, etc.) or any time period (i.e., when first written or now). Which means that **all** "versions" of the Bible, even the so-called corrupt ones, contain **to some degree or another** the living words of God.

But the Lord has to provide **one book** that is the determiner or standard for what should be included in the corpus of Scripture.

All you have to do is find which book contains all of his words and only his words and is the standard to which all others can be compared. It's 2013…

He has given you a book.

It's too bad some folks just don't recognize its value.

Which makes us ask…

Chapter Eighteen

Did the Lord preserve error instead of truth in the extant biblical manuscripts?

> For the LORD is good; his mercy is everlasting;
> and his truth endureth to all generations. (Psalm 100:5)

Some conservative Christian apologists say the Lord preserved error.

Although it sounds pretty strange, that's what some of the very intelligent brethren think.

Think of all the **numbering discrepancies** in Scripture. They are fertile ground for unbelief. The discrepancies are there **by design**. The Lord puts them there to test your faith and make you dig for the truth.

These discrepancies are constantly pointed out by Christian apologists in an effort to prove the King James Bible and indeed all Hebrew manuscripts are corrupted with copyist, translation, and printing errors.

For example, Dr. Norman L. Geisler unashamedly tells you there are errors in all books masquerading as "the Bible." That's why his Bible of choice is *"The Original Bible,"* which nobody's ever seen let alone read. No one can search it and prove it wrong because it doesn't exist.

Here's one numbering discrepancy that stumped Dr. Geisler:

> **1 Kings 4:26**—how can this first say Solomon had 40,000 stalls when 2 Chronicles 9:25 says he had only 4,000 stalls?

Problem: in recording the prosperity of Solomon, this passage states that he had 40,000 stalls of horses for his chariots. However 2 Chronicles 9:25 affirms that Solomon had only 4,000 stalls for horses. Which one is right?

Solution: this is undoubtedly a copyist error. The ratio of 4,000 horses to 1,400 chariots, as found in the second Chronicles passage, is much more reasonable than a ratio of 40,000 to 1,400 found in the first Kings text. In the Hebrew language, the visual difference between the two numbers is very slight ... The manuscripts from which the scribe worked may have been smudged or damaged and have given the appearance of being 40,000 rather than 4,000.[1]

If it's a "copyist error," then your God wasn't adroit enough to handle the preservation of his own words and deliver them to you error-free.

But be assured, the Lord God of heaven and earth doesn't do mistakes; especially when it comes to his words. Maybe Dr. Geisler is seeing errors that aren't there...

Why does Dr. Geisler have difficulty believing the words of the King James Bible?

Here's why Dr. Geisler is stymied by the versions and the extant Hebrew manuscripts. First, take a look at the words as written in the various Bibles...

---

[1] Norman L. Geisler and Thomas Howe, *The Big Book of Bible Difficulties: Clear and Concise Answers from Genesis to Revelation* (Wheaton, IL: Victor Books, 1992), 181.

Who changed the definition of *inspiration*, and when did they change it?

1 Kings 4:26		2 Chronicles 9:25	
4,000 stalls and 12,000 horses	40,000 stalls, and 12,000 horsemen	4,000 stalls and 12,000 horses	4,000 stalls and 12,000 horsemen
NIV (©1984)	ESV (©2001)	NIV (©1984)	NASB (©1995)
Solomon had four thousand stalls **for** chariot horses, and twelve thousand horses.	Solomon also had 40,000 stalls of horses **for** his chariots, and 12,000 horsemen.	Solomon had four thousand stalls **for** horses and chariots, and **twelve thousand horses**, which he kept in the chariot cities and also with him in Jerusalem.	And Solomon had 4,000 stalls **for** horses and chariots, and **12,000 horsemen**, whom he stationed in the chariot cities and with the king in Jerusalem.
NLT (©2007)	NASB (©1995)	NLT (©2007)	NASB (©1995)
Solomon had 4,000 stalls **for** his chariot horses, and he had 12,000 horses.	Solomon had 40,000 stalls of horses **for** his chariots, and 12,000 horsemen.	Solomon had 4,000 stalls **for** his horses and chariots, and he had **12,000 horses**. He stationed some of them in the chariot cities, and some near him in Jerusalem.	Now Solomon had 4,000 stalls **for** horses and chariots and **12,000 horsemen**, and he stationed them in the chariot cities and with the king in Jerusalem.

Here's the solution:

The King Kames Bible uses two different words, "of" and "for." All the others use just the word "of." The riddle can't be solved unless you believe the reading as it appears in the right Bible.

277

1 Kings 4:26	2 Chronicles 9:25
forty thousand stalls **of** horses	**four** thousand stalls **for** horses
And Solomon had **forty thousand** stalls of horses for his chariots, and twelve thousand horsemen.	And Solomon had **four** thousand stalls for horses and chariots, and twelve thousand horsemen; whom he bestowed in the chariot cities, and with the king at Jerusalem.

Analysis:

1. He had 4,000 literal stalls for horses.

2. He had forty thousand stalls of horses, that is, 40,000 stalls (worth) of horses is a unit of measurement. He had 40,000 horses.

3. There wasn't a stall for each horse. There was 1 stall per 10 horses. Each horse doesn't need to have its own stall. Not all your cars have to be garaged.

4. Notice that even using the NIV we come to the same conclusion.

Bible	Horsemen	Horses	Stalls	Stalls/Horse
KJB	12,000	40,000	4,000	1 stall/10 horses
NIV	??	12,000	4,000	1 stall/3 horses

See the similar wording here:

> I have compared thee, O my love, **to a company of horses** in Pharaoh's chariots. (Song of Solomon 1:9)

Dr. Geisler says the **King James Bible** "died of old age" and yet this Lazarus Bible gives him the answer to the supposed conundrum. All he had to do was be a careful reader of the text and believe what he read.

Here's another "Bible difficulty." Sadly, the experts quit on you.

They intimate that the Lord **preserved error** and then the modern version manufacturers changed the original words of the Bible to cover it up.

How sad. Take a look at this…

Who changed the definition of *inspiration*, and when did they change it?

	2 Kings 8:26	**2 Chronicles 22:2**
NIV (©1984)	Ahaziah was **twenty-two** [22] **years** old when he became king, and he reigned in Jerusalem one year…	Ahaziah was **twenty-two** [22] **years** old when he became king, and he reigned in Jerusalem one year…
ESV (©2001)	haziah was **twenty-two** [22] **years** old when he began to reign, and he reigned one year in Jerusalem…	Ahaziah was **twenty-two** [22] **years** old when he began to reign, and he reigned one year in Jerusalem…
NASB (©1995)	Ahaziah was **twenty-two** [22] **years** old when he became king, and he reigned one year in Jerusalem…	Ahaziah was **twenty-two** [22] **years** old when he became king, and he reigned one year in Jerusalem…
King James Bible	**Two and twenty** [22] **years** old *was* Ahaziah when he began to reign;…	**Forty and two** [42] **years** old *was* Ahaziah when he began to reign, and he reigned one year in Jerusalem…

Dr. Geisler says…

> **Problem:** According to the statement in 2 Kings 8:26, Ahaziah was 22 years old when he began to reign in Judah. However, in 2 Chronicles 22:2 (KJV) we find the claim that Ahaziah was age 42 when he took the throne in Judah. Which is correct?
>
> **Solution:** this is clearly a copyist error, and there is sufficient evidence to demonstrate that Ahaziah was 22 years old when he began to reign in Judah. In 2 Kings 8:17 we find that Joram, father of Ahaziah and son of Ahab, was 32 years old when he became king. Joram died at age 40, eight years after becoming King. Consequently, his son Ahaziah could not have been 42 when he took the throne after

his father's death, otherwise he would've been older than his father.[2]

1. Everybody knows 22 years old and 42 years old **are the readings in Hebrew**. The NIV Study Bible footnote admits that the original Hebrew reading is 42 years old. "The Hebrew reading of '42' would make Ahaziah older than his father…"[3]
2. Everybody knows that Ahaziah was 22 years old when he began to reign in Judah. That is clear in 2 Kings 8:17.
3. Famous Christian apologist Dr. Geisler says "copyists" made the error. If that's the case, then God "preserved" that error for us today. You would've thought the Lord could do better than that.
4. Famous Christian apologist Gleason Archer repeats a tired old chestnut: "Yet we may be sure that the original manuscript of each book of the Bible, being directly inspired by God, was free from all error. It is also true that no well attested variation in the manuscript copies that have come down to us alter any doctrine of the Bible."[4]

Notice that old narrative about how we may be sure that the original manuscripts were "free from all error" but nothing we have today is. We saw in the last chapter that this probably began with Richard Bentley in the 18th century. Again, the Lord failed to deliver. He evidently inspired his words but dropped the ball when it came to preserving the words of the text.

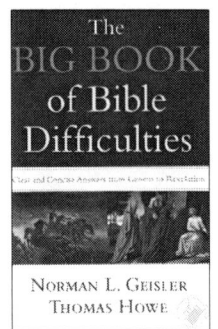

Clearly, apologists Geisler and Archer think the true reading got corrupted and naturally the King James Bible repeats the error.

Oh, by the way, the oft-repeated story of how no doctrine is altered is again reiterated by Dr. Archer. He must not have read chapter 3, "Doctrinal Problems in the King James Version," in NIV committee member Dr. Jack P. Lewis' book.[5] Evidently, Dr. Lewis is charging the King James

---
[2] Ibid., 194.
[3] *The NIV Study Bible, 10th Anniversary Edition* (Grand Rapids, MI: Zondervan, 1995), 640.
[4] Gleason L. Archer, *New International Encyclopedia of Bible Difficulties: Based on the NIV and the NASB* (Grand Rapids, MI: Zondervan, 1992), 194.

Who changed the definition of *inspiration*, and when did they change it?

Bible WITH doctrinal error. You don't even have to read his book. This chapter title says it all.

As you have seen, this "no doctrine affected" mantra is disingenuous at best. Isn't it funny how it's the most prestigious, bestselling Bible that's got problems?

The solution adopted by the NIV, ESV, and NASB is simply to change the text. They changed the number from 42 (which is what it says in the original Hebrew) to 22, which is what they want it to say. In short, they didn't **translate** the text; they had the audacity to **change** the text.

Don't you wonder how the Lord feels about this kind of tampering? Would you have the guts to do it?

Here's the Bible-believing answer from Richard Wurmbrand (1909–2001). He was a Romanian pastor of Jewish descent who was imprisoned and tortured for his beliefs. He wrote more than 18 books, the most widely known is *Tortured for Christ*.

> It is said twice in **2 Chronicles 21** that King Jehoram died at the age of forty. Then how could his son Ahaziah have been forty-two when he succeeded him to the throne? (**2 Chronicles 22:2**) In 2 Kings 8:26 this same story is told again. But according to this author King Ahaziah was twenty-two years of age when he began to reign.
>
> **Which is true?**

In this case, there is a good explanation for the apparent contradiction. In the Hebrew Bible the literal translation of 2 Chronicles 22:2 reads, "Forty-two years of old Ahaziah in the kingdom."

Many commentators feel that the forty-two refers to the age of the godless reign of the house of Omri in Israel. Ahaziah's father was Jehoram, who had taken to wife the daughter of King Ahab in Israel and therefore introduced the godless idolatry of Ahab to Judah. The

---

[5] Jack P. Lewis, *The English Bible from KJV to NIV: A History and Evaluation with Indexes* (Grand Rapids, MI: Baker, 1982), 35–68.

short reign of the house of Omri was forty-two years: Omri six, Ahab twenty-two, Ahaziah two, and Joram, the last one, twelve years. This totals forty-two years. Ahaziah was really twenty-two years old but became king in the forty-second year of the house of Omri.[6]

Why is it that a Bible-believing pastor gets the answer and famous Christian apologetics experts don't?

> At that time Jesus answered and said, I thank thee, O Father, Lord of heaven and earth, because thou hast hid these things from the wise and prudent, and hast revealed them unto babes. (Matthew 11:25)

Here's more detail from Brother Jonathan Crosby of the Church of Greenville:[7]

"What Do Bible Believers Do?"

1. They study the Bible instead of fawning over Mel Gibson's "The Passion of the Christ," and they rightly divide the word of truth (II Tim 2:15).
2. They find that Ahaziah, his son Joash, and his son Amaziah, were cut out of the lineage of the kings of Judah leading to Jesus Christ (Matt 1:8), which points out another "contradiction" that scholars choke on.

Kings	Chronicles	Matthew 1:8
Jehoshaphat	Jehoshaphat	Jehoshaphat
Jehoram	Jehoram	Joram = Jehoram
Ahaziah	Ahaziah	
Joash	Joash	
Amaziah	Amaziah	
Azariah = Uzziah	Azariah = Uzziah	Ozias = Uzziah

---

[6] Richard Wurmbrand, *Answer to Half a Million Letters* (Faridabad, India: Dr. P.P. Job, 2nd ed., 1988), 142–143.
[7] Jonathan Crosby, "Why Does the Bible Contradict Itself? A Case Study of Ahaziah's Age," accessed January 2013, http://www.letgodbetrue.com/bible/scripture/ahaziah-contradiction.php. I would like to thank Brother Crosby for graciously allowing me to quote extensively from his material.

3. They realize God did not consider Ahaziah a proper king of Judah, but an imposter from Ahab's line, for the Lord eliminated him and the next two generations from Matthew's genealogy of Jesus Christ (Matt 1:8).
4. God hated Omri and Ahab and the wicked affinity that began with Jehoshaphat (II Chron 18:1). Because there were good things in Jehoshaphat, God punished the profane grandson and his sons (II Chron 19:1–3).

How Was Ahaziah 42?

Ahaziah, a king of Judah, was 42 years old in the kingdom of Omri and Ahab, wicked kings of Israel, his maternal family, though only 22 years old biologically.

King of Israel	Reigned	References
Omri	11	1 Kings 16:15 cf. 1 Kings 16:29
Ahab	20	1 Kings 22:41 cf. 1 Kings 22:51
Ahaziah	1	1 Kings 22:51 cf. 2 Kings 3:1
Jehoram	10	2 Kings 3:1 cf. 2 Kings 9:29
Total	42	

Taken from inspired history.

Event	After Creation
Omri of Israel began to reign	3189
Ahaziah of Judah began to reign	3231
Total	42

Edwards, Anstey, and the Jewish chronologers.

King of Israel	Reigned	References
Omri	11	1 Kings 16:23
Ahab	20	1 Kings 16:29
Ahaziah	1	1 Kings 22:51
Jehoram	10	2 Kings 3:1
Total	42	

Lightfoot, Poole, Ben Gershon

Was It a Contradiction?

1. No! It was how God told Bible believers He counted Ahaziah among the wicked kings of Israel, and not among the kings of Judah, so they would know why Jehu killed him when cutting off the house of Ahab (II Chron 22:7).

2. No! It was how God told Bible believers He counted Ahaziah among the wicked kings of Israel, and not among the kings of Judah, so they would know why He removed Ahaziah, his son, and his grandson from the lineage of Jesus Christ (Matt 1:8).

3. No! It was to test whether men believe God and his word or the "research" of textual critics, commentators, and seminary professors. As Jesus gloriously thanked His Father, God has hid such things from the wise and prudent and revealed them unto babes (Matt 11:25–26).

4. No! It was how God showed any Bible with "22" in 2 Chronicles 22:2 is not His word. He exposed the liars that worship the "originals" but change them whenever they wish! And He exposed any preacher or commentator by their submission or rebellion to 2 Timothy 2:15.

Does the Bible Count Years from other Political Events?

1. Yes! Did Baasha, king of Israel, fight against Asa, king of Judah, 10 years after he was already dead?

    "So Baasha slept with his fathers, and was buried in Tirzah: and Elah his son reigned in his stead ... **In the twenty and sixth year of Asa** king of Judah began Elah the son of Baasha to reign over Israel in Tirzah, two years." 1 Kings 16:6–8

*"In the **six and thirtieth year of the reign of Asa** Baasha king of Israel came up against Judah, and built Ramah, to the intent that he might let none go out or come in to Asa king of Judah." 2 Chronicles 16:1*

2. Asa's reign is counted from the divided kingdom, when Rehoboam lost ten tribes to Jeroboam. Baasha came up against Asa in the 36th year of the kingdom of Judah.

Rehoboam	17
Abijam	3
Asa	16
Total	36

Does the Bible Count Years from other Political Events?

1. Yes! Jehoiachin was a notable king of Judah taken captive to Babylon (Matt 1:11–12). To identify this great epoch, his reign is measured from Nebuchadnezzar.

    "Jehoiachin was eighteen years old when he began to reign, and he reigned in Jerusalem three months. And his mother's name was Nehushta, the daughter of Elnathan of Jerusalem." 2 Kings 24:8

    "Jehoiachin was eight years old when he began to reign, and he reigned three months and ten days in Jerusalem: and he did that which was evil in the sight of the LORD." 2 Chronicles 36:9

2. Jehoiachin was taken captive in Nebuchadnezzar's eighth year (2 Kgs 24:12), an important epoch in Israel's history. Jehoiachin's person and reign were quite inferior in importance to Nebuchadnezzar and his reign.

3. Furthermore, it was the eighth year since the first raid on Jerusalem, when Nebuchadnezzar put down Jehoiachin's father, Jehoiakim. It was common to date events from captivities like this (Ezek 1:2; 8:1; 20:1).

Conclusion

1. You may trust every word in your Bible, if you are using the King James Version.

2. As Jesus and Paul argued from single words, you may have the same confidence in the King James Version (Matt 22:32,43; John 8:58; 10:35; Gal 3:16; 4:9; Heb 8:13; 12:27).

3. What looks like a contradiction in the KJV is a trap set by God to confuse and shame men who would rather question and criticize God's word than believe and study it. Enjoy solving it without a PhD or ThD!

4. Paul gave a ministerial secret to Timothy about studying the Bible in 2 Timothy 2:15. It must be divided in many places to avoid failure and shame, which we just put into practice studying Ahaziah.

5. Modern versions even alter this verse to lose Paul's wise advice, because "handling" is not "dividing."

6. A little time spent in God's word will make you wiser than your enemies, your teachers, and the ancients (Ps 119:98–100). Believe it!"

Brother Crosby has just walked you through steps that Bible "experts" can't seem to grasp. Somehow there's just no substitute for…

Actually believing and studying the right Bible.

At the end of the day, you have to trust that the Lord is big enough to figure out how to get his words into your language. You should **expect the Lord** to get **all** his **words** into **a book** and do it **without any copyist's errors**. And that he did.

One book must contain the **whole** truth and **nothing** but the truth. That one book has to have a **fixed text**. Otherwise, God's holy words stating

Too Little   Just Right   Too Much

"**Ye shall not add** unto the **word** which I command you, **neither shall ye diminish** *ought* from it" (Deuteronomy 4:2) is nothing more than an empty suggestion of an impotent god.

If the Lord can't deliver **that book** to you in the 21st-century right before the lights are about to go out, then you should go shopping for a new God.

Because if he didn't care enough to place **100%** (not 99.1% or 99.5% or 110%) of his words in **a book** that his own children can **read**, then maybe he didn't care enough to inspire them in the first place.

And if that's the case, then maybe the Bible is nothing more than what the textual critics like to think it is—just another book.

But wait … It's absolutely **not** another book made by men. It's a masterpiece produced by the Lord himself. He is the author. He is the publisher. He is the marketer. And he holds all men accountable for the words written in his book.

It's not politically correct to believe that **one** Bible is the final authority for Christians.

Yet, no one has proven any error in the King James Bible and no one can disprove that the readings found in the King James Bible are original. That's because there are no originals to compare to. And there never will be.

Do any of the other Bible versions contain **all** the words of God **without error**?

None—according to anyone who promotes and uses them. That's why you don't see any influential Christian leaders who profess to be…

NIV ONLYISTS, ESV ONLYISTS, or NASB ONLYISTS...

or any other version Onlyists, and you **never** will. They **all** believe that their Bibles **have** errors in text and translation and they're not ashamed to admit it. This is why they make the "Which Bible?" issue one of **preference** and not of **conviction**.

Since they still aren't completely sure which **words** are **original** and which are **imposters**, the only thing that's really important to them is **the message** and **not the words**.

That's why there is a Bible version called *The Message*.

Just because the academic elite can't see the Lord's hand in the provision of his words to mankind doesn't mean you have to follow them…

Chapter Nineteen

How to spot a standard Bible

The law of the Lord is perfect, converting the soul:
the testimony of the Lord is sure, making wise the simple.
(Psalm 19:7)

Businessmen, engineers, scientists, and other professionals always work with "standards." They can't make things or do business without them. There are 12 inches in 1 foot, not 11¾" or 12¼", but exactly 12". Every profession has its own set of standards.

There **has** to be a standard Bible. The academic elites and their marketers know this. But let's start back even further than that.

They are well aware of the textual variants in the extant manuscripts, which stops them from having a finished, real, tangible Bible. That's why they believe in *"The Original Bible."* They're just not too sure what to put in it.

For example, consider the following "standard" Bibles in light of a few verses:

2 Corinthians 13:14

- ☐ The Holman Christian Standard Bible (HCSB) **does not contain** it.
- ✓ The New American *Standard* Bible (NASB) and the English *Standard* Version (ESV) **do contain** it.

Matthew 12:47

- ☐ The English *Standard* Bible (ESV) **does not contain** it.

- ✓ The Holman Christian *Standard* Bible (HCSB) and the New American *Standard* (NASB) **do contain** it.

And that's not all…

How about James 1:7?

- ☐ The New Revised *Standard* Version (NRSV) **does not contain** it.

- ✓ The Holman Christian *Standard* Bible (HCSB), the New American *Standard* Bible (NASB), and the English *Standard* Version (ESV) **do contain** it.

We're not done yet…

Matthew 21:44, Luke 24:12, and Luke 24:40

- ☐ The Revised *Standard* Version (RSV) **does not contain** these verses.

- ✓ The Holman Christian *Standard* Bible (HCSB), the New American *Standard* Bible (NASB), and the English *Standard* Version (ESV) **do contain** them.

And here's something you're not going to learn at your "standard" Christian college or university…

Almost all modern versions are nothing more than personal versions of **"The Original Bible"** the experts are still searching for. They are "personal versions" because they reflect the editors' choices as to which variant readings are authentic and which are not. Plus, they provide plenty of footnotes and encourage you to choose how "the Bible" should read.

You have just seen some examples of how one publisher includes some verses and the others don't. That's child's play.

The **real experts** (not apologists like Dr. Geisler or Gleason Archer) are the textual scholars who built the base Greek text from which the modern versions are translated. They believe…

There are at least 31 and possibly as many as 39 complete verses that shouldn't be in the Bible.

On pages 306–311 of *The Text of the New Testament,* textual scholars and authors Kurt and Barbara Aland, who were the "go-to" folks in New Testament textual criticism, cited examples of verses no longer considered authentic by modern scholarship.

Naturally, if the verses appear in any Bible version and are **not** authentic, that absolutely affects the doctrine of Biblical Inerrancy because they are falsely identified as God's words.

The following 31 complete verses are **no longer considered authentic** by the experts. So they must be impure forgeries. There are more, but these are good examples:

- Matthew 5:44, 6:13, 16:2b–3, 17:21, 18:11, 20:16, 20:22–23, 23:14, 25:13, 27:35
- Mark 7:16, 9:44, 9:46, 11:26, 15:28
- Luke 4:4, 9:54–56, 17:36, 23:17, 24:42
- John 5:3b–4
- Acts 8:37, 15:34, 24:6b–8, 28:16, 28:29

As we have seen, the editors and committee folks who produced the modern versions are in agreement about some of these.

But what about the rest?

The following seven Gospel verses are still left in the text but placed in brackets to show their doubtful authenticity, so they are (by modern textual criticism standards) probably impure forgeries as well:

- Mark 10:7, 10:21, 10:24, 14:68; Luke 8:43, 22:43–44

The experts are all in competition with each other. They all claim that it's their mandate to update the *"Word of God"* or *"The Bible"* into a language you can understand, and yet they can't even agree on which verses they should translate, let alone how they should be translated.

It would actually be funny, but God's integrity is at stake.

The experts have produced **competing** *standards* that are an insult to the Lord and an embarrassment to the name of the Lord Jesus Christ.

Have you met all the wannabe "standard" Bibles?

- Published in 1901, the **American Standard Version (ASV)** is nobody's standard. It's dead.

- Published in 1952, the **Revised Standard Bible (RSV)** is a revision of the 1901 ASV and is nobody's standard. A second edition came out in 1971. They even published a Roman Catholic edition in 1966. They're all dead.

- Published in 1971, the **New American Standard Bible (NASB)** got overhauled in 1995 and it's on life support today. Did the *"The Original Bible"* get updated? Since 1971, the NASB has come out with five different editions (1972, 1973, 1975, 1977, and the major update of 1995). Each of these editions differs from the other in both the English translation and the underlying Greek New Testament text.[1]

The ©1995 NASB now has almost 7,000 fewer words than did the previous 1977 edition.[2] It was in 9th place (out of 10) for "Bible Translations—Based on Dollar Sales" in August 2011 according to the Christian Booksellers Association (CBA). It didn't even make the top 10 in unit sales. It even got beat out by *The Message*.[3] How embarrassing.

- Published in 1990, the **New Revised Standard Bible (NRSV)** is a revision of the 1952 RSV. This "standard" didn't even make the CBA top 10 in either category. It's a nonstandard.

- Published in 2001, the **English Standard Bible (ESV)** is nothing more than another power-washed revision of the 1952 Revised Standard Version.

---

[1] Will Kinney, "The Ever Changing NASBs," accessed January 2013, http://brandplucked.webs.com/everchangingnasbs.htm.
[2] Laurence M. Vance, *Double Jeopardy: The New American Standard Update* (Pensacola, FL: Vance Publications, 1998).
[3] Christian Booksellers Association, "CBA Best Sellers," accessed January 2013, http://www.cbaonline.org/nm/documents/BSLs/Bible_Translations.pdf. Based on sales through December 1, 2012.

According to Bible researcher Michael Marlowe, it "corrects the non-Christian interpretations of the RSV in the Old Testament and improves the accuracy throughout with more literal renderings ... The makers of this version undertook the work with the idea that there was a need for an evangelical version that was more literal than the New International Version but more idiomatic than the New American Standard Bible."[4]

The evangelicals who were desperately seeking an alternative to the re-gendered language of the NIV obtained the right to use the old RSV from the National Council of Churches in September 1998, allowing translators freedom to modify the original text of the RSV as necessary to rid it of de-Christianizing translation choices. Using it as a base, they removed the objectionable material, modified the translation, and presumptuously named it the English **Standard** Version.[5]

It's currently in 5th place in dollar sales and unit sales. It'll never take the top spot because it has to compete with the heavily promoted NIV. This "standard" changed its specs in about 360 places in 2007.

- Published in 2003, the **Holman Christian Standard Bible (HCSB)** is the latest wannabe. Broadman & Holman (the Southern Baptist Convention's publishing house) had been using the NIV. They knew the copyright holder of the NIV was preparing a politically correct "inclusive language" revision, which would make the NIV less accurate but more acceptable to feminists. They tried to buy the copyright to the NASB three times but were unsuccessful. Finally, they did their own translation based on the same Greek New Testament text behind the NIV and ESV.[6]

Looking for final authority in all the wrong places.

Everybody knows that one of the purposes of a *standard* is to eliminate all competition by showing the others' deviation from "the standard."

---

[4] Michael Marlowe, "English Standard Version," December 2007, http://www.Bible-researcher.com/esv.html.
[5] Ibid.
[6] Michael Marlowe, "The Holman Christian Standard Bible," revised August 2011, http://www.Bible-researcher.com/csb.html.

And yet it's not the name on the cover that makes a Bible God's standard. It's the history of victory.

Here's the thing; all new Bibles are really in competition with One Book. And they know it. The King James Bible has been God's standard for the past 400 years.

That's why men like Douglas Stauffer and William P. Grady write books highlighting this fact. It's all about which Bible has authority. And which one is the final authority.

Every church, Christian school, college, or university knows that they must appeal to a higher authority than their own opinion. That's why their statements of faith always include their belief in *"the Bible"* or *"the Word of God."*

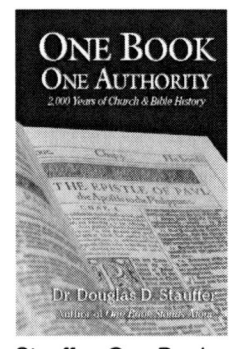

Stauffer, *One Book One Authority* ©2012

The only problem is that when they say *"The Word of God"* and *"The Bible,"* what they mean is *"The Original Bible,"* which (a) never existed, (b) they admittedly don't have, and (c) they claim to be their "final authority even though they aren't sure which or how many verses it contains, let alone what the actual wording is.

How dreadful.

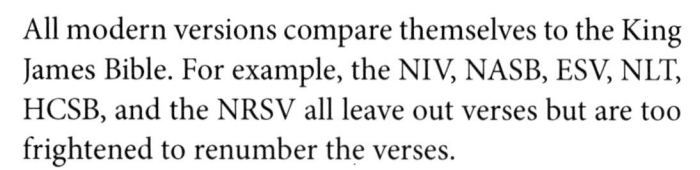

All modern versions compare themselves to the King James Bible. For example, the NIV, NASB, ESV, NLT, HCSB, and the NRSV all leave out verses but are too frightened to renumber the verses.

Most remove or question at least 16 verses and yet retain the verse numbering system. If the verses shouldn't be there, why don't they just "man up" and change the verse numbers. Not a chance. They're competing with **THE** standard.

Grady, *Final Authority: A Christian's Guide to the King James Bible* ©1993

The Lord took 160 years after the invention of the printing press to deliver THE standard printed Bible. Four hundred years and billions of copies later it's still the standard.

The KJB has outlasted all other pretenders to the title. Everyone is so anxious to take the crown that they presumptuously call themselves **"Standard"** as soon as they are published—only to be punished by Mr. Market in less than 50 years.

Even the guys that build them know that their "new" versions are outdated as soon as they hit the press.

Here is what NIV committee member Jack P. Lewis said:

> A translation starts to become outdated from the moment it is completed. Information from new manuscript materials, new insights into the languages in which the Bible was first written, and new data concerning biblical history need to be communicated to the reader. Changing ideas about translations and changes in the English language itself all outdate a version thus preparing the way for the process to be started all over again.[7]

So much for the certainty of the words of truth.

A new generation of Christian academics, scholars, and businessmen are even now working on a brand new "standard" before the ink is dry on the old new "standard" version. So how can you tell…

Which Bible the Lord considers to be THE Standard?

He's made that task a piece of cake.

It's the one he's been using for the past 400 years; the one that's been produced over an estimated 5 billion times; the one that's been translated into over 760 languages. Anybody can figure it out.

Before we wrap up, let's look at a big controversy over two little words…

---

[7] Jack P. Lewis, *The English Bible from KJV To NIV: A History and Evaluation with Indexes* (Grand Rapids, MI: Baker Book House, 1982), 363–364.

Chapter Twenty

The Revelation 16:5 controversy

> Heaven and earth shall pass away, but my words shall not pass away. (Matthew 24:35)

Did the Lord Jesus Christ drop a routine fly ball on Revelation 16:5?

A popular author thinks he did.

James White thinks two words in the Book of Revelation of the King James Bible that are not found in any known Greek manuscript are one of the best textual reasons to dump the concept of King James Bible supremacy.

And those famous words are…

"shalt be"

Let's look at the readings…

Wycliffe Bible 1395	…Just art thou, Lord, that art, and that were hooli,…
Tyndale New Testament 1526	…lorde which arte and wast thou arte ryghteous and holy…
Coverdale Bible 1535	…LORDE which art and wast, thou art righteous and holy,…

297

Matthew Bible 1537	...Lord which art & wast, thou art **righteous** & holy,...
Great Bible 1539–1540	...Lorde, whych arte and wast, thou arte ryghteous & holy,...
Geneva Bible 1557	...Lord, thou art iust, Which art, and Which wast: and Holy,...
Bishops' Bible 1568	...Lorde, which art, and wast, thou art ryghteous & holy,...
King James Bible 1611	...Thou art righteous, O Lord, which art, and wast, and **shalt be**...
NIV (©1984)	...You are just in these judgments, you who are and who were, the Holy One...
NASB (©1995)	...Righteous are You, who are and who were, O Holy One, because You judged these things...
ESV (©2001)	...Just are you, O Holy One, who is and who was, for you brought these judgments...

As you can see, all English Bibles before the King James have "**Holy**" instead of "shalt be." The new versions have "**O Holy One**" instead of "**shalt be.**"

Here's the thing. This verse has no current Greek manuscript support. That's caused some to discount the text of the King James Bible.

Here's James White's criticism...

> I would like to provide an expanded discussion of a textual error in the King James Version for those who demand a single example of "error in the KJV!" ... For the KJV only advocate, there is simply no way out of this problem ... the reading was created out of the mind of Theodore Beza, one unknown to the ancient church, unknown to all Christians until the end of the sixteenth century ... **quite simply, before Beza, no Christian had ever read the text the way the KJV has it today.**[1]

---

[1] James R. White, *The King James Only Controversy: Can You Trust Modern Translations?* (Bloomington, MN: Bethany House), 236–241. (emphasis mine)

You're the umpire; here's what happened on the play:

- ✓ James White is right, there is no currently known Greek manuscript support for the reading "**shalt be**" and it doesn't appear in a printed Greek New Testament until Beza's 1589 edition. But Beza defended his translation: "And so without doubting the genuine writing in this ancient manuscript, I faithfully restored in the good book what was certainly there."[2]

- ✓ All English Bibles printed before the King James do not contain those words. Modern versions (except the New King James Version) have "O Holy One" or some variation.

BUT, we need to review the play...

In which language did the apostle John write the Book of Revelation?

Some scholars believe the Book of Revelation was originally penned in Hebrew and only later translated into Greek. This theory makes sense because John was a Jew...

Robert B. Y. Scott (1899–1987), a clergyman of the United Church of Canada, Old Testament scholar, and former chairman of the Department of Religion at Princeton University[3] said:

> We come to the conclusion, therefore that the Apocalypse [Book of Revelation] as a whole is a translation from Hebrew or Aramaic...[4]

Charles C. Torrey (1863–1956) was an American historian, archaeologist, and scholar who taught Semitic languages at the Andover Theological Seminary (1892–1900) and Yale University (1900–1932). He founded the American School of Archaeology at Jerusalem in 1901.[5] Torrey said:

---

[2] Textus-Receptus.Com, "Revelation 16:5—Theodore Beza," last modified December 18, 2012, http://textus-receptus.com/wiki/Revelation_16:5#Theodore_Beza_2.
[3] *Wikipedia*, s.v. "Robert Balgarnie Young Scott," last modified November 21, 2010, http://en.wikipedia.org/wiki/R._B._Y._Scott.
[4] R. B. Y. Scott, *The Original Language of the Apocalypse* (1928), 6, as cited in James Scott Trimm, trans., "The Hebraic-Roots Version Scriptures" (South Africa: Institute for Scripture Research, 2005). (Available: http://www.isr-messianic.org/downloads/hrv_intro.pdf), xxi.

...the Book of Revelation was written in a Semitic language, and that the Greek translation ... is a remarkably close rendering of the original.[6]

The **Book of Revelation** itself says:

> And they had a king over them, *which is* the angel of the bottomless pit, **whose name in the Hebrew tongue** is Abaddon, **but in the Greek** tongue hath *his* name Apollyon. (Revelation 9:11)

Sounds like John may have written the book in Hebrew and, as a convenience, provided the word in Greek.

If it's true that the reading "shalt be" was "unknown to the ancient church, unknown to all Christians" as James White states, then how come it appears in a Latin commentary on the Book of Revelation by Beatus of Liebana in AD 786, which preserved the work of Tyconius, written around AD 380?[7] The Donatist writer Tyconius was "one of the most interesting and original minds among Latin theologians of the fourth century."[8]

Dr. Thomas Holland, author of *Crowned with Glory: The Bible from Ancient Text to Authorized Version,* said:

> [Dr. John] Wordsworth[9] also points out that in Revelation 16:5, Beatus of Liebana (who compiled a commentary on the book of Revelation) uses the Latin phrase *"qui fuisti et futures es."* This gives some additional evidence for the Greek reading by Beza (although he apparently drew his conclusion for other reasons). Beatus compiled his commentary in 786 AD. Furthermore, Beatus was not writing his

---

[5] *Wikipedia*, s.v. "Charles Cutler Torrey," last modified November 13, 2012, http://en.wikipedia.org/wiki/Charles_Cutler_Torrey.

[6] C. C. Torrey, *Documents of the Primitive Church* (1941), 160, as cited in Trimm, "The Hebraic-Roots Version Scriptures," xxi.

[7] Textus-Receptus.Com, "Revelation 16:5—Beatus of Liebana," last modified December 18, 2012, http://textus-receptus.com/wiki/Revelation_16:5#Beatus_of_Liebana.

[8] P. R. Aykroyd and C. F. Evans, eds., *The Cambridge History of the Bible, Volume I: From the Beginnings to Jerome* (New York: Cambridge University Press, 1970), 554.

[9] *Wikipedia*, s.v. "John Wordsworth," last modified December 13, 2012, http://en.wikipedia.org/wiki/John_Wordsworth. Dr. John Wordsworth (1843–1911) "edited and footnoted a three volume critical edition of the New Testament in Latin." (Thomas Holland, see note 10.)

The Revelation 16:5 controversy

own commentary. Instead he was making a compilation and thus preserving the work of Tyconius, who wrote his commentary on Revelation around 380 AD (Aland and Aland, 211 and 216. Altaner, 437. Wordsword, 533.). So, it would seem that as early as 786, and possibly even as early as 380, there was an Old Latin text which read as Beza's Greek text does.[10]

If the original was written in Hebrew and then translated into Greek and Latin, the original reading has just as much chance of showing up in Latin manuscripts as Greek. Besides, there are only 4 Greek manuscripts of Revelation 16:5 dated before the 10th century.[11]

There are an estimated 10,000 Latin manuscripts in existence. But no one's got the money, time, or inclination to discover their contents.

Early 20th-century textual critic Herman Hoskier cited the Ethiopic version as containing the phrase "shall be" in Revelation 16:5.[12]

Here's what Hoskier found…

"…Justus es, Domine, et Rectus qui fuisti et **eris**"	Ethiopian version as cited by Herman Hoskier in Latin
"…Just thou art, and Righteous that was and **will be**…"	Translation from Latin
"…Thou art righteous, O Lord, which art, and wast, **and shalt be**…"	King James Bible

Let's think about this…

---

[10] Thomas Holland, "Lesson Ten: Textual Considerations," SovereignWord.org, accessed January 2013, http://www.sovereignword.org/index.php/defense-of-the-traditional-Bible-texts-and-kjb/37-dr-thomas-hollands-manuscript-evidence-class/212-dr-thomas-hollands-manuscript-evidence-class-lesson-10.

[11] TheKing'sBible.com, "KJV Today: Beza and Revelation 16:5," accessed January 2013, http://www.thekingsbible.com/KjvToday/Revelation_16_5.aspx.

[12] Herman Hoskier, *Concerning the Text of the Apocalypse: Collation of All Existing Available Greek Documents with the Standard Text of Stephen's Third Edition Together with the Testimony of the Versions, Commentaries and Fathers*. 2 vols. (London: Bernard Quaritch, 1929).and footnoted a three volume critical edition of the New Testament in Latin." (Thomas Holland, see note 10.)

1. Dr. James D. Price, in his book *King James Onlyism: A New Sect*, has a heading titled "Ethiopic Version Preserved the Text [of the New Testament]."[13]

2. No one has ever collated all of the 10,000 Latin manuscripts, or for that matter any of the other versions. How can you come to any dogmatic conclusion until you've seen all the evidence?

3. The Lord can reveal as much manuscript evidence as he wants. But he has promised to preserve his words and his promises never fail.

In 1611 the King James translators had sitting on the table in front of them all the previous readings of seven earlier English Bibles and all the editions of the Greek New Testament. Plus, they had access to some manuscripts no longer available to us today. Nobody knows what evidence they had when they made the decision to go with the "**shalt be**" reading.

The King James translators made a choice. They chose to go with Beza's 1589 reading. Did the translators' **choice** slip by the Lord?

If the reading is **an error**, does the Lord become the village idiot by allowing a bogus reading (even if only two words) to be reproduced billions of times over a 400-year period and translated into over 760 languages? He could've easily moved the King James translators to stick with the old reading, **but He didn't**.

After all, if the Book of Revelation was originally written in Hebrew and there aren't any original Hebrew manuscripts, then any translation can contain the correct reading.

So why the rush to judgment?

Shouldn't **all** the evidence be examined before a verdict is rendered? Shouldn't the textual researchers at the Institute for New Testament Textual Research (Institut für Neutestamentliche Textforschung) in Munster, Germany,[14] get to work carefully checking not only the 10,000+ Latin manuscript evidence but also those in other languages as well?

---

[13] James D. Price, *King James Onlyism: A New Sect* (©James D. Price, 2006), 170.
[14] See Institute for New Testament Textual Research at http://egora.uni-muenster.de/intf/index_en.shtml.

Instead of rolling on the floor laughing because he thinks he found an error in the King James Bible, shouldn't James White consider **why** the Lord and the translators **purposely** placed a reading with little Greek manuscript support in the text when they didn't have to?

Maybe he should have gone Upstairs for a review of the play.

If you're interested in more data on this issue, visit http://textus-receptus.com/wiki/Revelation_16:5.

Chapter Twenty-One

Which Bible should you use?

Seek ye out of the book of the LORD, and read… (Isaiah 34:16)

First, you might want to look for the biggest stack. A graph of units sold pitting the King James Bible against the NIV might look something like this…

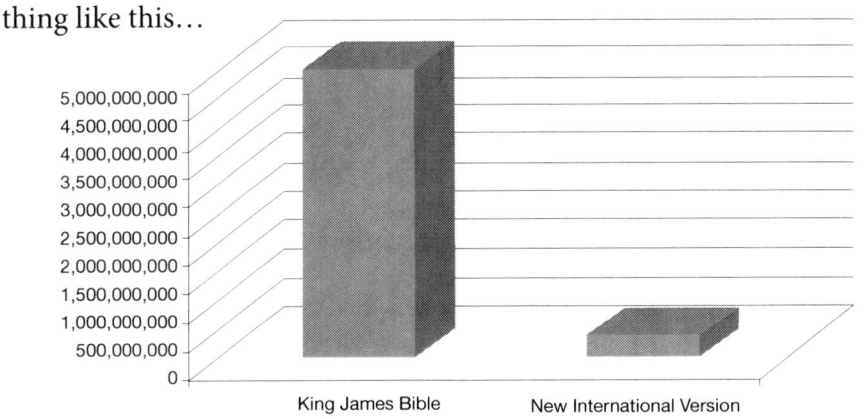

It's been claimed that more than five billion King James Bibles have been sold or given away.[1] The NIV has over 400 million copies in print.[2]

It's like comparing a 50-story skyscraper to a four-family tenement.

---

[1] Adam Nicholson, interview with Gwen Ifill, December 24, 2003, *PBS Online NewsHour*. (Available: http://www.pbs.org/newshour/bb/entertainment/july-dec03/nicolson_12-24.html.) Historian Adam Nicholson is author of the national bestseller *God's Secretaries: The Making of the King James Bible*. Also see:
http://www.huffingtonpost.com/timothy-beal/happy-400th-birthday-king_b_836538.html;
http://www.sltrib.com/sltrib/home/51258251-76/Bible-james-english-king.html.csp;
http://www.calvarychurch.com/site/files%5Clookingup%5CLU05-08-2011.pdf.

[2] Amazon.com, "Book Description," *Holy Bible: New International Version* (hardcover), accessed January 2013, http://www.amazon.com/The-Holy-Bible-International-Version/dp/1444701533.

Second, you might want to look for the one with a proven track record. If the Bibles were in NASCAR, and each year was a lap, you'd find that the King James Bible has made 400 laps around the track without a pit stop, unlike all the rest.

The King James Bible leads the field; 1611 to 2011 ... that's 400 laps (1 lap = 1 year). The text and translation have remained constant for over 400 years. The real revision was done in 1885. It was a separate entity known as the Revised Version.

400 laps and counting

The New, New International Version has been roundly rejected.

The NIV ©1984 ran 33 laps (years) until its owners decided it needed a pit stop. The major overhaul took place in 2011. The NIV ©2011's use of gender-neutral language was so controversial that the book was rejected by the Southern Baptist Convention,[3] the Lutheran Church–Missouri Synod,[4] and the Council of Biblical Manhood & Womanhood (CBMW).[5] If all these folks rejected it, would the Lord approve of it?

NASB had 14 complete verses added to its text in 1975.

The NASB had its first pit stop in 1975 having only circled the track four times since the first edition was published in 1971. What was the major overhaul? Fourteen complete verses **were added** to the text.[6] If that weren't enough, its owners turned in for another pit stop in 1995. It's now known as the Updated NASB, ©1995. The NASB is running out of fuel now anyway.

---

[3] Eryn Sun, "Southern Baptists Reject Updated NIV Bible," *Christian Post,* June 18, 2011. (Available: http://www.christianpost.com/news/southern-baptists-pass-resolution-rejecting-2011-niv-at-annual-convention-51288/#UIc0rZbevJ5AB6Yg.99.)

[4] Audrey Barrick, "Lutherans Latest to Reject New NIV Bible Over Gender Language," *Christian Post,* September 4, 2012. (Available: http://www.christianpost.com/news/lutherans-latest-to-reject-new-niv-bible-over-gender-language-81060.)

[5] Jared Moore, "NIV 2011: Rejected by the Council of Biblical Manhood & Womanhood (CBMW)" (blog), November 23, 2010, http://jaredmoore.exaltchrist.com/2010/11/23/niv-2011-rejected-by-the-council-of-biblical-manhood-womanhood-cbmw.

[6] BibleGateway.com, "Version: New American Standard Bible (NASB)," accessed January 2013, http://www.Biblegateway.com/versions/New-American-Standard-Bible-NASB.

The ESV went stealth and had a secret pit stop in 2007.

The ESV underwent a minor revision in 2007. The publisher has chosen not to identify the updated text as a second or revised edition; it is intended to replace the original ESV under the original name. At present, both revisions coexist on the market.[7]

Third, you might want to look for the Bible that was the base from which hundreds of translations were made. Even the famed *"Original Bible"* never exploded into over 760 languages.

But maybe your best bet is to...

Use the Bible the Lord would use if he came to your church.

It's the same one he's been using and blessing for the past 400 years. The question of which Bible is "the Bible" is not a hobby horse, it's not a game, it's not a debate to be won, and it's not something to be trifled with. What we're talking about is believing in **A Book** that contains the **pure words** of the living God.

It's the only hope you have of knowing "**whole** truth and **nothing** but the truth." Beyond that, you're open to the whims, suggestions, and opinions of men.

If that book isn't 100% true, then you need to find another religion. Unless you're a Roman Catholic, whose authority is vested in the pope and the men of the Magisterium (the teaching authority of the Church), you have no other source of authority.

One thing you'll **never** get from anyone that does **not** have that one book is **certainty**. They can't give it to you. They're still hunting for the *"Original Bible."* But you will get certainty from the Lord...

---

[7] *Wikipedia*, s.v. "English Standard Version," last modified January 8, 2013, http://en.wikipedia.org/wiki/English_Standard_Version.

> Have not I written to thee excellent things in counsels and knowledge, That I might make thee know **the certainty of the words of truth**; that thou mightest answer the words of truth to them that send unto thee? (Proverbs 22:20–21)

> **That thou mightest know the certainty** of those things, wherein thou hast been instructed. (Luke 1:4)

You don't have to learn a foreign language. You don't have to go to seminary. You don't have to study textual criticism. You can do any and all those things if you want, **but** the Lord has made **finding** his words easy. They are "nigh thee."

All you have to do is identify **The Book**. The Lord believes **you can have certainty** even if your teachers don't. Your pastor, your teacher, and your college professors have absolutely no authority beyond their own opinions. You need the truth. You need **A Book**. You need a book that's 100% Scripture and 100% **error-free.**

The Lord has provided such **A Book** for you. It's the one that's been bringing forth good fruit for over 400 years.

> Even so every good tree bringeth forth good fruit ... For every tree is known by his own fruit... (Matthew 7:17 & Luke 6:44)

It's the Authorized Version of 1611, popularly known as the King James Bible.

I have laid out the case for the King James Bible. In the end, you're free to make up your own mind and choose whichever Bible you wish. Nobody has the right to force-feed you what you don't want. It is my prayer that this text has helped you settle the "Bible Version Controversy" for yourself once and for all.

Buy the truth, and sell *it* not;
also wisdom, and instruction, and understanding. (Proverbs 23:23)

About the Author

Jack McElroy

Formerly an aimless and depressed ex-college house painter, Jack McElroy became a serial entrepreneur who found true happiness, success, and fulfillment through a personal relationship with the Lord Jesus Christ (in whose hand is the soul of every living thing, and the breath of all mankind), which began when he was born again in October 1978.

Raised as a Roman Catholic, McElroy attended a Catholic grammar school and a Jesuit high school. Once a believer in the Big Bang theory and Evolution, he now passionately extols the veracity of "The Book." He has read through the Bible 18 times (including the 1611 First Edition of the King James Bible twice). He has taught it to all age groups, from preschoolers to adults. He has served as a youth leader for over 20 years and as a deacon at a Baptist church for over 12 years.

He has been the president of McElroy Electronics Corporation for over 35 years. He is president of McElroy Publishing and McElroy Rare Bible Page Collections. He was Chief Manager of Minneapolis Cellular Telephone Company LLC and President of Dutchess County Cellular Telephone Corporation.

He holds a B.S. in Industrial Management from Lowell Technological Institute (now UMass Lowell). Jack and Susan have been happily married for 38 years. They have four children and three grandchildren.

For more information about Jack McElroy, visit:
http://jackmcelroy.com

Other Books by the Author

How I Lost My Fear of Death and How You Can Too is a new, unique, and universal soul-winning tool that you can give to anybody of any religion without fear of insulting them.

- Cuts to the chase–focuses on what 10 major religions say about what you must **DO** to get eternal life versus what Christ has already **DONE**
- Perfect for folks who want more detailed information before committing their lives to Christ
- An evangelistic tool that's suitable even for a funeral
- Universal appeal–everybody faces their own mortality; even Christians who want reassurance of eternal security should read this
- Over 110 Scripture references explain biblical truths
- 50 pictures and illustrations immediately connect with readers from ages 12 and up
- Clear gospel presentation
- Compact and convenient 5" × 7" size
- Inviting cover–intriguing text and image designed to make you think
- 168 easy-to-read pages

Available in Softback and Amazon Kindle.

Adoniram Judson, Jr. (1788–1850) said, "The motto of every missionary, whether preacher, printer, or schoolmaster, ought to be '**Devoted for life**.'"

Now for the first time, you can read and study the arsenal of soul-winning tools used by "The Father of American Foreign Missions."

Adoniram Judson's Soul Winning Secrets Revealed—An Inspiring Look at the Tools Used by "Jesus Christ's Man" in Burma is the only book in the world that contains an outstanding collection of the four most prominent tracts Judson used as well as the first translation of Judson's newly discovered fifth tract that he used as a primer on the Old Testament promises of a Savior.

Available in Hardback, Softback, and Amazon Kindle.

Bibliography

Ackroyd, P.R., and C.F. Evans, eds. *The Cambridge History of the Bible from the Beginnings to Jerome.* Volume I. New York. Cambridge University Press, 1970, 1984, 1989.

Adams, Bobby, Samuel C. Gipp, Eberhard Nestle, and Kurt Aland. *The Reintroduction of Textus Receptus Readings in the 26th Edition and Beyond of the Nestle/Aland Novum Testamentum–Graece.* Miamitown, OH: DayStar, 2006.

Aland, Kurt. "The Significance of the Papyri for New Testament Research." In *The Bible in Modern Scholarship,* edited by J.P. Hyatt. Nashville, TN: Abington, 1965.

Allen, Ward. *Translating for King James.* Nashville, TN: Vanderbilt Press, 1969.

American Bible Society. Committee on Versions. *Report on the History and Recent Collation of the English Version of the Bible. Presented by the Committee on Versions to the Board of Managers of the American Bible Society, and Adopted, May 1,1851.* Cornell University Library Digital Collections. Ithaca, NY: Cornell University Library, 1851.

Archer, Gleason L. *New International Encyclopedia of Bible Difficulties: Based on the NIV and the NASB.* Grand Rapids, MI: Zondervan, 1992.

Ballard, Peter. "The Bible Is Reliable Despite Textual Errors." Last updated July 19, 2008. Accessed January 2013. http://www.peterballard.org/catalog.html.

Barker, Kenneth. "The American Translations of the Bible." Helpmewithbiblestudy.org. Accessed December 2012. http://helpmewithBiblestudy.org/5Bible/Trans-TheAmericanTranslations_Barker.aspx.

Barna Research. "Data and Trends: Answers to Frequently Asked Questions." Data collated from several surveys through 1998. Accessed December 2012. http://web.archive.org/web/19990508110144/http://www.barna.org/PageStats.htm.

Barrick, Audrey. "Lutherans Latest to Reject New NIV Bible Over Gender Language." *Christian Post,* September 4, 2012. Available: http://www.christianpost.com/news/lutherans-latest-to-reject-new-niv-bible-over-gender-language-81060/.

Bauder, Kevin. "Now, About Those Differences, Part Twenty Three: Sinister Et Dexter." Central Seminary. Accessed December 2012. http://www.centralseminary.edu/resources/nick-of-time/in-the-nick-of-time-archive/100-now-about-those-differences/229-now-about-those-differences-part-twenty-three-sinister-et-dexter.

Beacham, Roy E., and Kevin T. Bauder, eds. *One Bible Only? Examining Exclusive Claims for the King James Bible.* Grand Rapids, MI: Kregel, 2001.

Beckman, Rick. "KJV 1611 vs. KJV 1769" (blog). March 24, 2007. Accessed December 2012. http://www.rickbeckman.org/kjv-1611-vs-kjv-1769.

———. "More Changes Between the 1611 and the 1769 Editions of the KJV" (blog). March 25, 2007. Accessed December 2012. http://rickbeckman.org/more-changes-between-the-1611-and-the-1769-editions-of-the-kjv/.

Bethel University. "Affirmation of Faith." Accessed January 2013. http://www.bethel.edu/about/faith.

Bible Research. "The Apparatus of a Critical Text." Accessed January 2013. http://www.bible-researcher.com/tisch02.html.

———. "Chicago Statement on Biblical Inerrancy with Exposition." Accessed January 2013. http://www.Bible-researcher.com/chicago1.html.

Bible.org. "Daniel B. Wallace." http://Bible.org/users/daniel-b-wallace.

BibleGateway.com. "Version: New American Standard Bible (NASB)." Accessed January 2013. http://www.Biblegateway.com/versions/New-American-Standard-Bible-NASB/.

Bob Jones University. "Statement about Bible Translations." Accessed November 2012. http://www.bju.edu/communities/ministries-schools/position-statements/translation.php.

Brake, Sr., Donald L. "World's Best-Selling Book." *Washington Times,* July 18, 2012. http://communities.washingtontimes.com/neighborhood/worlds-best-selling-book/2012/jul/18/bible-forbidden-book-banned-book/.

Bromiley, Geoffrey W., ed. *International Standard Bible Encyclopedia,* vol. IV. Grand Rapids, MI: Eerdmans, 1979.

Brown, David L. "More Proof the Traditional Text (Textus Receptus) Is of Apostolic Origin." King James Bible Research Council. Accessed November 2012. http://www.kjbresearchcouncil.com/Pages/Articles/More_Proof.htm.

Burgon, Dean. *The Traditional Text of the Holy Gospels.* London: George Bell and Sons, 1896.

Burgon, John William. *The Last Twelve Verses of Mark.* 1871. Reprint, Collingswood, NJ: Dean Burgon Society Press, 2008.

———. *The Revision Revised: A Refutation of Westcott and Hort's False Greek Text and Theory.* 1881. Reprint, Collingswood, NJ: Dean Burgon Society Press, September 2000.

Burkitt, F.C. *The Old Latin and the Itala.* Cambridge: n.p., 1896.

Bibliography

Cedarville University. "Biblical Heritage Gallery: The Revisions." Accessed January 2013. http://www.cedarville.edu/cf/advancement/cbts/heritagegallery/exhibits/celebrating-the-Bible.

Center for the Study of New Testament Manuscripts. "John Mill--Novum Testamentum." Accessed January 2013. http://www.csntm.org/printedbook/viewbook/JohnMillNovumTestamentum1707.

Central Baptist Theological Seminary. "Doctrinal Statement." Accessed January 2013. http://www.centralseminary.edu/about-central/foundational-documents/doctrinal-statement.

Central Baptist Theological Seminary of Virginia Beach. "Biblical Foundations Statement." Accessed January 2013. http://www.baptistseminary.edu/about/doctrine.html.

Christian Booksellers Association. "CBA Best Sellers." Accessed January 2013. http://www.cbaonline.org/nm/documents/BSLs/Bible_Translations.pdf.

Churchill, Winston. *Churchill's History of the English-Speaking Peoples.* 1958. Edited by Henry Steele Commager. Reprint, New York: Barnes and Noble Books, 1995.

Colwell, E.C. "Scribal Habits in Early Papyri: A Study in the Corruption of the Text." In *The Bible in Modern Scholarship,* edited by J.P. Hyatt. New York: Abingdon Press, 1965.

———. *Studies in Methodology in Textual Criticism of the New Testament Manuscripts.* Leiden, Netherlands: E.J Brill, 1969.

———. *What Is the Best New Testament?* Chicago: University of Chicago Press, 1952.

Combs, Bill. "Is the Preface to the King James Version Really an Embarrassment to the KJV-Only Movement?" *Theologically Driven* (blog). May 16, 2012. http://dbts.edu/blog/?p=2985.

Combs, William W. "Errors in the King James Version?" *Detroit Baptist Seminary Journal 4* (Fall 1999). Available: http://www.dbts.edu/journals/1999/Combs.PDF.

Comfort, Philip W. *New Testament Text and Translation Commentary.* Carol Stream, IL: Tyndale House, 2008.

Coptic Orthodox Church, Diocese of Los Angeles. "Orthodoxy: Holy Scripture." Accessed December 2012. http://lacopts.org/orthodoxy/our-faith/the-holy-bible/.

Crosby, Jonathan. "Why Does the Bible Contradict Itself? A Case Study of Ahaziah's Age." Accessed January 2013. http://www.letgodbetrue.com/bible/scripture/ahaziah-contradiction.php.

Dallas Theological Seminary. "DTS Doctrinal Statement." Accessed January 2013. http://www.dts.edu/about/doctrinalstatement.

Daniell, David. *The Bible in English: Its History and Influence.* New Haven, CT: Yale University Press, 2003.

Dean Burgon Society. "Who Was Dean John William Burgon?" Accessed December 2012. http://www.deanburgonsociety.org/DeanBurgon/whowasdb.htm.

Demy, Timothy. "James Hall Brookes." Pre-Trib Research Center. Accessed January 2013. http://www.pre-trib.org/data/pdf/Demy-JamesHallBookes.pdf.

Denver Seminary. "Our Statement of Faith." Accessed January 2013. http://www.denverseminary.edu/about-us/what-we-believe/.

DeRemer, Bernard R. "Church Builders: B.B. Warfield, Scholar." *Disciple Magazine,* vol. 3, no. 20 (October 24, 2011).

Doughterty, David L. "Non Existent Revisions in the King James Bible." Accessed December 2012. http://www.learntheBible.org/non-existent-revisions-in-the-king-james-Bible.html.

Ehrman, Bart D. *Lost Christianities: The Battles for Scripture and the Faiths We Never Knew.* New York: Oxford University Press, 2005.

Elders of Grace Community Church. "The Biblical Position on the KJV Controversy." Accessed December 2012. http://jcsm.org/StudyCenter/john_macarthur/KJV.htm.

English Standard Version Study Bible. Wheaton, IL: Crossway, 2008.

Epp, Eldon Jay. "It's All about Variants: A Variant-Conscious Approach to New Testament Textual Criticism." *Harvard Theological Review,* vol. 100, no. 3 (July 2007). DOI: http://dx.doi.org/10.1017/S0017816007001599.

———, and Gordon D. Fee. "A Continuing Interlude in NT Textual Criticism." *Studies in the Theory and Method of New Testament Textual Criticism.* Grand Rapids, MI: Eerdmans, 1993.

Freethinker's Books. Accessed August 2011. http://www.freethinkersbooks.com.

Funding Universe. "Thomas Nelson, Inc. History." Accessed December 2012. http://www.fundinguniverse.com/company-histories/thomas-nelson-inc-history.

Geerlings, J. *Family E and Its Allies in Mark.* Salt Lake City: University of Utah Press, 1967. Available: http://www.cspmt.org/pdf/Identity%20of%20the%20New%20Testament%20Text%20III.pdf.

Geisler, Norman. *Bible Translations: Which Ones Are Best?* Complete PowerPoint Library CD © 2008.

Geisler, Norman L., and Thomas Howe. *The Big Book of Bible Difficulties: Clear and Concise Answers from Genesis to Revelation.* Wheaton, IL: Victor Books, 1992.

Geisler, Norman L., and William E. Nix. *A General Introduction to the Bible.* Chicago: Moody Bible Institute, 1968.

———. *A General Introduction to the Bible, Revised and Expanded.* Chicago: Moody Press, 1986.

Goodspeed, Edgar J. *The Complete Bible: An American Translation.* Chicago: University of Chicago, 1923.

Gordon-Conwell Theological Seminary. "Statement of Faith." Accessed January 2013. http://www.gordonconwell.edu/about/Statement-of-Faith.cfm.

Grady, William P. *Given by Inspiration: A Multifaceted Study on the A.V. 1611 with Contemporary Analysis.* Swartz Creek, MI: Grady Publications, 2010.

Grossman, Cathy Lynn. "Bible Readers Prefer King James Version." *USA Today*, updated April 21, 2011. http://www.usatoday.com/news/religion/2011-04-21-king-james-Bible.htm.

———. "Update of Popular 'NIV' Bible Due in 2011." *USA Today*, September 1, 2009. http://www.usatoday.com/news/religion/2009-09-01-Bible-translation_N.htm.

Grossman, Ron. "For Some Christians, King James Is the Only Bible." *Chicago Tribune*, March 12, 2011. http://articles.chicagotribune.com/2011-03-12/news/ct-met-king-james-20110311_1_king-james-Bible-translation-Bible-study-class.

Hodge, Archibald, and Benjamin Warfield. "Inspiration." *Presbyterian Review* 6 (April 1881). Available: http://www.bible-researcher.com/warfield4.html.

Holland, Thomas. "Lesson Ten: Textual Considerations." SovereignWord.org. Accessed January 2013. http://www.sovereignword.org/index.php/defense-of-the-traditional-Bible-texts-and-kjb/37-dr-thomas-hollands-manuscript-evidence-class/212-dr-thomas-hollands-manuscript-evidence-class-lesson-10.

Holy Bible: The New King James Version. Old Time Gospel Hour edition. Nashville, TN: Thomas Nelson, 1982.

Holy See Press Office, College of Cardinals Biographical Notes. "Martini, Card. Carlo Maria, S.I." Updated January 9, 2012. http://www.vatican.va/news_services/press/documentazione/documents/cardinali_biografie/cardinali_bio_martini_cm_en.html.

Holypop. "What Does the Bible Say? New King James Bible Translation." Accessed December 2012. http://www.holypop.com/answers/New_King_James_Bible_Translation.

Hort, A.F. *Life and Letters of Fenton John Anthony Hort*, 2 vols. London: Macmillan, 1896.

Hoskier, H.C. *Codex B and Its Allies*, 2 vols. London: Bernard Quaritch, 1914.

Hoskier, Herman. *Concerning the Text of the Apocalypse: Collation of All Existing Available Greek Documents with the Standard Text of Stephen's Third Edition Together with the Testimony of the Versions, Commentaries and Fathers*, 2 vols. London: Bernard Quaritch, 1929.

International Council on Biblical Inerrancy. "The Chicago Statement on Biblical Inerrancy." 1978. Accessed January 2013. http://www.reformed.org/documents/index.html?mainframe=http://www.reformed.org/documents/icbi.html.

Jones, Floyd Nolen. Which Version Is the Bible? 17th ed. The Woodlands, TX: KingsWord Press, 1999. Available: http://www.3bible.com/books/Which%20Version%20is%20the%20Bible.pdf. Also at http://www.scribd.com/doc/14110607/111/ANCIENT-TRANSLATIONS-SUPPORT-THE-RECEIVED-TEXT.

Kayser, Phillip G., and Wilbur N. Pickering. "Has God Indeed Said?" *The Preservation of the Text of the New Testament*. Omaha, NE: Biblical Blueprints, 2009, 2004.

Keathley, Ken. "What I've Been Reading (6)—Creationism Is Evolving," *Between the Times*, September 7, 2012. http://betweenthetimes.com/index.php/2012/09/07/what-ive-been-reading-6-creationism-is-evolving/.

Kelly, Russell Earl. "The King James Bible Controversy." September 2011, Acworth, GA. http://www.tithing-russkelly.com/theology/id34.html.

Keylock, Leslie R. "The Bible That Bears His Name." *Moody Monthly* (July–August 1985). Accessed December 2012. http://www.theoldtimegospel.org/about/akjvb4.html.

Kinney, Will. "The Ever Changing NASBs." Accessed January 2013. http://brandplucked.webs.com/everchangingnasbs.htm.

———. "The Infallibility of Scripture: Are You a Bible Believer or a Bible Agnostic?" Accessed January 2013. http://brandplucked.webs.com/biblebelieveragnostic.htm.

Lewis, Jack P. *The English Bible from KJV to NIV: A History and Evaluation with Indexes*. Grand Rapids, MI: Baker, 1982.

Bibliography

Lighthouse Christian Bookstore. "NKJV Study Bible: Second Edition." Accessed December 2012. http://www.thelighthousechristianbookstore.com/product.asp?sku=9781418548674.

Logos Bible Software. "Overview: King James Version." Accessed January 2013. http://www.logos.com/product/8586/preachers-essential-library.

Loughran, David B. "Bible Versions: Which Is the Real Word of God?" Part 1. Stewarton Bible School, Stewarton, Scotland (June 1999). http://atschool.eduweb.co.uk/sbs777/vital/kjv/part1-4.html.

Malane, Daniel Joseph. The Bible: *"Word of God" or Words of Men? Truth Versus the Myths of Christian Fundamentalism.* Bloomington, IN: Xlibris, 2007.

Marlowe, Michael. "English Standard Version." December 2007. http://www.Bible-researcher.com/esv.html.

———. "The Holman Christian Standard Bible." Revised August 2011. http://www.Bible-researcher.com/csb.html.

Master's Seminary. "Statement of Faith--The Holy Scriptures." Accessed January 2013. http://www.tms.edu/AboutSOFTheHolyScriptures.aspx.

Maxey, Al. "A View of the Versions: The Revised Standard Version, a Critical Analysis." Accessed December 2012. http://www.zianet.com/maxey/Ver3.htm.

Metzger, Bruce M. *Textual Commentary on the Greek New Testament.* Stuttgart: German Bible Society, 1994.

Moody Bible Institute. "Doctrinal Statement." Accessed January 2013. http://www.moodyministries.net/crp_MainPage.aspx?id=334.

Moore, Helen, and Julian Reid, eds. *Manifold Greatness: The Making of the King James Bible.* Oxford, England: Bodleian Library, University of Oxford, 2011.

Moore, Jared. "NIV 2011: Rejected by the Council of Biblical Manhood & Womanhood (CBMW)" (blog). November 23, 2010. http://jaredmoore.exaltchrist.com/2010/11/23/niv-2011-rejected-by-the-council-of-biblical-manhood-womanhood-cbmw/.

Moorman, Jack. *Forever Settled: A Survey of the Documents and History of the Bible.* Collingswood, NJ: Dean Burgon Society Press, 1999.

Morris, Henry M. "A Creationist's Defense of the King James Bible." Institute for Creation Research. Accessed December 2012. http://www.icr.org/home/resources/resources_tracts_kjv/.

Nelson KJV. "About the Translation." Accessed November 2012. http://www.kjv400celebration.com/about_the_translation.php.

Nicholson, Adam. Interview with Gwen Ifill. December 24, 2003. PBS Online NewsHour. Available: http://www.pbs.org/newshour/bb/entertainment/july-dec03/nicolson_12-24.html.

NIV Study Bible, 10th Anniversary Edition. Grand Rapids, MI: Zondervan, 1995.

Norris, Rick. "Rick Norris Responds to the 'Spelling Changes Onlyism' Argument Offered By Many in the 'King James Only' Camp." King James Only Resource Center. Accessed January 2013. http://www.kjvonly.org/rick/norris_spelling.htm.

Norton, David. *A Textual History of the King James Bible.* Cambridge, England: Cambridge University Press, 2005.

Official King James Bible Online. "King James Bible News." April 12, 2011. http://www.kingjamesbibleonline.org/King-James-Bible-News/.

Old Time Gospel Ministry. "The Authorized King James Version of the Bible."

Omanson, Roger L. *A Textual Guide to the Greek New Testament.* Stuttgart: German Bible Society, 2006.

Oxford University Press (China). "In the Beginning Was the Word." OUP China 50th Anniversary Exhibition. April 18, 2011. http://www.oupchina.com.hk/50thanniversary/exhibition_press.asp.

Parvis, Merrill M. "The Nature and Tasks of New Testament Textual Criticism: An Appraisal." Journal of Religion, vol. 32, no. 3 (July 1952). Available: http://www.jstor.org/stable/1201165.

Pensacola Christian College. "Articles of Faith." Accessed January 2013. http://www.pcci.edu/GeneralInfo/ArticlesofFaith.html.

Pickering, Wilbur N. "In Defense of Family 35." Accessed January 2013. http://www.walkinhiscommandments.com/Pickering/Miscellaneous/In%20Defense%20of%20Family%2035.pdf.

———. *The Identity of the New Testament Text II.* Available: http://www.enigstetroos.org/pdf/PickeringWN_TheIdentityofTheNewTestament%20II.pdf.

———. *The Identity of the New Testament Text II,* 3rd ed. Eugene, OR: Wipf and Stock, 2003. Available: http://www.cspmt.org/pdf/Identity%20of%20the%20New%20Testament%20Text%20III.pdf.

———. *What Difference Does It Make.* Available: http://www.google.com/url?sa=t&rct=j&q=&esrc=s&source=web&cd=1&ved=0CD8QFjAA&url=http%3A%2F%2Fsomehelpful.info%2FNT%2FMajority-text%2FPickering-other%2FWhat_difference_does_it_make.doc&ei=ddHCUOuYNpTV0gHfmoCACw&usg=AFQjCNFk5tQQ5EGEYWc6uK11LL-FdR4VeQ.

Piper, John. "Good English with Minimal Translation: Why Bethlehem Uses the ESV." January 1, 2004. http://www.desiringgod.org/resource-library/articles/good-english-with-minimal-translation-why-bethlehem-uses-the-esv.

"Poll: Americans Have Contradictory Desires in Choosing Bibles." *Peninsula Clarion* (Alaska), May 4, 2001. http://peninsulaclarion.com/stories/050401/rel_050401rel0100001.shtml.

Price, James D. *King James Onlyism: A New Sect.* © James D. Price, 2006.

———. "A Response to D. A. Waite's Criticism of the New King James Version." September 1995. http://www.jamesdprice.com/newkingjamesversion.html.

Price, Randall. *Searching for the Original Bible.* Eugene, OR: Harvest House, 2007.

Rick Beckman Home Page. Accessed December 2012. http://www.rickbeckman.org/.

Riley, William B. *The Menace of Modernism.* New York: Christian Alliance, 1917.

Robinson, Maurice A. "The Case for the Byzantine Textform: A New Approach to 'Majority Text' Theory." Paper presented at the Southeastern Regional Evangelical Theological Society Meeting, Toccoa Falls, GA, March 8–9, 1991. Available: Theological Research Exchange Network, www.tren.com.

Ryken, Leland. *The Legacy of the King James Bible: Celebrating 400 Years of the Most Influential English Translation.* Wheaton, IL: Crossway Books, 2011.

Ryrie, Charles. *Basic Theology: A Popular Systematic Guide to Understanding Biblical Truth.* Chicago: Moody Publishers, 1999.

Salmon, George. *Some Thoughts on the Textual Criticism of the New Testament.* London: John Murray, Albemarle Street, 1897.

Sandeen, Ernest R. *The Roots of Fundamentalism: British and American Millenarianism, 1800–1930.* Chicago: University of Chicago Press, 2008. ©1970 by The University of Chicago. All rights reserved. Published 1970. Paperback edition 2008. Used by permission.

Sarah's Albion Blog. "The KJB Story 1611–2011, The Word of a King." February 5, 2011. http://sarahmaidofalbion.blogspot.com/2011/02/kjb-story-1611-2011-word-of-king.html.

Schaff, Philip. *A Companion to the Greek Testament and the English Version,* 4th ed. rev. New York: Harper & Brothers, 1903.

Scrivener, F.H.A. *The Authorized Version of the English Bible (1611): Its Subsequent Reprints and Modern Representatives,* 1884. Reprint, Wipf & Stock Publishers, Eugene, OR, 2004.

Simms, P. Marion. *The Bible in America: Versions That Have Played Their Part in the Making of the Republic*. New York: Wilson-Ericsson, 1936.

Sorenson, David. "The Most Influential Book in the World: How the King James Version Has Changed the World." Ministry 127. May 4, 2011. http://ministry127.com/christian-living/the-most-influential-book-in-the-world.

Staggs, Brandon. "Inspired Translation of Copies Required for Bible Study." The King James Bible Page. Accessed January 2013. http://av1611.com/kjbp/articles/staggs-inspired-translation.html.

Stewart, David J. "Is the King James Bible Inspired or Preserved?" Jesus-is-savior.com. Accessed December 2012. http://www.jesus-is-savior.com/Bible/inspired_or_preserved.htm.

Streeter, B.H. *The Four Gospels: A Study of Origins*. London: Macmillan, 1951.

Strouse, Thomas. "A Review of the Book *From the Mind of God to the Mind of Man*." StudytoAnswer.net. Accessed December 2012. http://www.studytoanswer.net/bibleversions/mind_review.html.

Sun, Eryn. "Southern Baptists Reject Updated NIV Bible." *Christian Post,* June 18, 2011. Available: http://www.christianpost.com/news/southern-baptists-pass-resolution-rejecting-2011-niv-at-annual-convention-51288/#UIc0rZbevJ5AB6Yg.99.

Talbot School of Theology, Biola University. "Biblical Inerrancy." Accessed January 2013. http://www.talbot.edu/about/biblical-inerrancy/.

Textus-Receptus.Com. "Revelation 16:5--Beatus of Liebana." Last modified December 18, 2012. http://textus-receptus.com/wiki/Revelation_16:5#Beatus_of_Liebana.

———. "Revelation 16:5--Theodore Beza." Last modified December 18, 2012. http://textus-receptus.com/wiki/Revelation_16:5#Theodore_Beza_2.

TheKing'sBible.com. "KJV Today: Beza and Revelation 16:5." Accessed January 2013. http://www.thekingsBible.com/KjvToday/Revelation_16_5.aspx.

Thomas Nelson Corporate web site. Accessed December 2012. http://www.thomasnelson.com/consumer/dept.asp?dept_id=1118916&TopLevel_id=100000.

Time for Truth. "The 'Whitewash' Conspiracy--Re: *The King James Only Controversy* by James White" (book review). Accessed January 2013. http://www.timefortruth.co.uk/content/pages/documents/1309647013.pdf.

Trench, Richard Chenevix. *On the Authorized Version of the New Testament in Connection with Recent Proposals for Its Revision*. New York: J.S. Redfield, 1858. Available: http://ia600308.us.archive.org/35/items/authorizedversio00trenrich/authorizedversio00trenrich.pdf.

Bibliography

Trimm, James Scott, trans. "The Hebraic-Roots Version Scriptures." South Africa: Institute for Scripture Research, 2005. http://www.isr-messianic.org/downloads/hrv_intro.pdf.

Trinity International University. "Statement of Faith." Accessed January 2013. http://www.tiu.edu/about/statement-of-faith.dot.

Union Theological Seminary, New York. http://www.utsnyc.edu/Page.aspx?pid=2526.

Vance, Laurence M. *Double Jeopardy: The New American Standard Update.* Pensacola, FL: Vance Publications, 1998.

———. "Excerpt from Double Jeopardy: The NASB Update." Chap. 1. http://www.Biblebelievers.com/Vance3.html.

———. "The NRSV vs. the ESV." Accessed December 2012. http://www.av1611.org/vance/nrsv_esv.html.

Wallace, Daniel B. The Majority Text and the Original Text: Are They Identical? Bible.org. Accessed December 2012. http://Bible.org/article/majority-text-and-original-text-are-they-identical.

———. "Why I Do Not Think the King James Bible Is the Best Translation Available Today." Bible.org. Accessed December 2012. http://Bible.org/article/why-i-do-not-think-king-james-Bible-best-translation-available-today.

Warfield, Benjamin. "Inspiration." From *The International Standard Bible Encyclopedia,* edited by James Orr, vol. 3. Chicago: Howard-Severance, 1915. Available: http://www.Bible-researcher.com/warfield3.html.

Watkins, Terry. "The Truth About the English Substandard Version." http://www.av1611.org/kjv/ESV_Intro.html.

Wegner, Paul D. *A Student's Guide to Textual Criticism of the Bible: Its History, Methods, and Results.* Downers Grove, IL: InterVarsity Press, 2006.

Wheaton College. "Statement of Faith and Educational Purpose." Accessed January 2013. http://www.wheaton.edu/About-Wheaton/Statement-of-Faith-and-Educational-Purpose.

White, James R. *The King James Only Controversy: Can You Trust Modern Translations?* Minneapolis, MN: Bethany House, 2009.

Williams, James B., and Randolph Shaylor, eds. *From the Mind of God to the Mind of Man: A Layman's Guide to How We Got Our Bible.* Greenville, SC: Ambassador-Emerald International, 1999.

Wong, Simon. "Which King James Bible Are We Referring To?" *Bible Translator*, vol. 62, no. 1 (2011). Available: http://www.ubs-translations.org/fileadmin/publications/tbt/technical/BT-62-1-Wong.pdf.

Woodbridge, John D., ed. *Great Leaders in the Christian Church.* Chicago: Moody, 1989. Available: http://www.disciplemagazine.com/www/articles/155.628.

WORDsearch. "New International Version (NIV)." Critical Reviews. https://www.wordsearchbible.com/products/12533.

Writing Center, University of North Carolina at Chapel Hill. "Revising Drafts." Accessed December 2012. http://writingcenter.unc.edu/handouts/revising-drafts/.

Wurmbrand, Richard. *Answer to Half a Million Letters,* 2nd ed. Faridabad, India: Dr. P.P. Job, 1988.

Index

Abraham, seed of, 139–140
adding to words of the Bible, 27, 29–30, 32, 286
Ahaziah, 279–284
Aland, Kurt, 66, 98, 291
Alexandria, Egypt, 39–41
Alexandrian (critical) textform. *See also* variant readings; verses, missing
    as basis of modern Bible versions, 49, 50, 54
    error-filled, 42–46
    history of, 35–41
    usage in the church, 47–49
Allison, Dale C., 61
American Bible Society, 125, 176–177
American Standard Version (ASV), 136, 143, 292
Amon (Amos), 59–60, 61
Antiochian text, 49. *See also* Received Text (Textus Receptus)
Apocalypse (Revelation), 297–303
Apocrypha, 163
Apostle Paul. *See* Paul
Archer, Gleason, 280–281
Arthur, Kay, 68
Asa (Asaph), 56–60
ASV (American Standard Version), 136, 143, 292
Augustine of Hippo, 40
authority of the Bible
    attacked by rationalism, 262
    as final, 1, 7, 8, 260, 287, 294
    as fundamental belief, 227
Authorized Version (AV). *See* King James Bible
authorship of the Bible, 1–2, 10, 120, 287
autographs. *See* original autographs ("Original Bible")

baptism, doctrine of, 29–32

Barker, Kenneth, 130
Barna Research Group, 124
Basic Theology (Ryrie), 109–110
Bauder, Kevin, 90, 211–213, 219–224
Beatus of Liebana, 300
Beckman, Rick, 180, 194–196, 200
"begotten God," 147, 152, 162
believer's baptism, doctrine of, 29–32
Ben Chayyim Masoretic Text, 136
Bengel, Johann Albrecht, 260–261
Bentley, Richard, 260–261, 280
Bethel University, 252
Beza, Theodore, 298–299, 300–301
Beza 1589 Greek New Testament, 299, 300–301, 302
Bible, "Original." *See* original autographs
Bible, The: "Word of God" or words of men? (Malane), 85–86
Bible as a book
    all of God's words contained in, 8, 11, 31, 159, 244, 273, 286–287
    as physical book, 2, 5–7, 11, 14, 86–87, 157–160, 158, 219, 308
    unified, 123, 138, 189
Bible in America (Simms), 94
Biblia Hebraica Stuttgartensia, 136
Biblica, 72
Biblical childbearing, doctrine of, 142
Biblical Position on the KJV Controversy, The (MacArthur), 31–32
Bishops' Bible, 158, 182, 184, 185, 187, 196, 200, 298
Bishops' Bible (Bodleian Library copy), 184, 187, 192, 196
Black, Matthew, 98
Blayney, Benjamin, 168
Blayney edition of KJV (1769), 10, 164, 168, 179, 217
Bob Jones University (BJU), 90–91, 95, 102–103, 253, 254
Bois, John, 165, 182, 200

323

book, the Bible as. *See* Bible as a book
Briggs, Charles Augustus, 270–271
Broadman & Holman, 293
Brookes, James H., 263–264, 268
Bunyan, John, 113–114
Burgon, John W., 41–43, 47, 48
Burkitt, F. C., 40
Byzantine textform, 49. *See also* Received Text (Textus Receptus)

Cambridge History of the Bible, 40–41
Cambridge University Press
    Cambridge Paragraph Bible, 163
    Cambridge vs. Oxford printings of KJV, 194, 201, 202–203, 205–210
    current printing of KJV, 185
    New Cambridge Paragraph Bible, 183
    reproductions of 1611 KJV, 164
Campbell, Gordon, 118
capitalization (God vs. GOD), 185–186
Catholicism, 98–99, 260, 307
Caxton, William, 157
Cedarville University, 216
Central Baptist Theological Seminary of Minneapolis, 253, 254
certainty of the words of truth, 32–33, 122, 295, 307–308
Chafer, Lewis Sperry, 234
Chicago Statement on Biblical Inerrancy, 247–248, 257, 271–272
childbearing, Biblical, doctrine of, 142
choosing a Bible, 9, 33, 102–105, 211, 305–308
Christian ethics, doctrine of, 140–141
Chronicles/Kings, discrepancies in, 275–278, 279–284
Churchill, Winston, 112
Clark, Gordon, 99
Clement of Alexandria, 153
Codex Aleph (Sinaiticus). *See* Sinaiticus and Vaticanus
Codex Alexandrinus, 223
Codex B (Vaticanus). *See* Sinaiticus and Vaticanus

cognitive dissonance, 258
Colwell, Ernest Cadman, 38–39, 53
Combs, William W., 89
Comfort, Philip W., 62, 121
Constantinopolitan text, 49. *See also* Received Text (Textus Receptus)
converts, 255
Coptic Orthodox Church, 49–50
corruption. *See* variant readings
Council of Biblical Manhood & Womanhood (CBMW), 306
Coverdale, Miles, 111
Coverdale Bible, 111, 158, 182, 184, 187, 194, 297
Critical and Exegetical Commentary on the Gospel According to Saint Matthew (Davies and Allison), 61
critical text, 49. *See also* Alexandrian (critical) textform
criticism. *See* textual criticism
Crosby, Jonathan, 282–283, 286
Cross, Paul, 117
Crowned with Glory (Holland), 300–301

Dallas Theological Seminary, 252
Danby, Keith, 72–73
Daniell, David, 92, 118
Darwin, Charles, 262
Davies, W. D., 61
Dead Sea Scrolls, 187–189, 223
deductive reasoning, 6, 220, 225
Demy, Timothy, 263
Denver Theological Seminary, 250–251
Detroit Baptist Theological Seminary, 253, 254
Diatessaron, 154
doctrine comparison tables (verse examples)
    believer's baptism, 29–32
    Biblical childbearing, 141–142
    Christian ethics, 140–141
    forgiveness, 23
    inerrancy, 23–26, 71–72
    of Jesus Christ, 72–73, 162
    man, 136–138

plenary inspiration of the Scriptures,
26–27
preservation, 238–239, 272
seed of Abraham, 139–140
sin, 22, 138–139
sinlessness of Christ, 68–70, 70–71,
73–75
tabernacle in the wilderness, 20–21
Trinity, 108–110
visions, 141
Douay-Rheims Bible, 98
Doughterty, David L., 207–208

ecclesiastical text, 49. *See also* Received
Text (Textus Receptus)
ecumenism, 98–99
editions of the KJV. *See* King James
Version, editions of
Egypt, 39–41
Egyptian textform, 49. *See also* Alexandrian (critical) textform
Ehrman, Bart, 53, 100, 261
Elhanan, 71, 162
Elohim vs. Jehovah, usage of, 184–189
English language, 123–124
English Revised Version (ERV), 38, 143,
163, 177, 215–216
English Standard Version (ESV) (2001)
Beersheba/Sheba wording, 207
discrepancies of numbering in OT,
277, 279, 281
endorsements of, 24–26, 28, 29
errors in gospels
Luke, 25–26, 63–65
Mark, 61–63
Matthew, 56–57, 59
history of, 292–293
original language of Revelation and,
298
verse examples related to doctrines,
22, 70–71, 109
English Standard Version (ESV) (2011)
compared to other "standard"
Bibles, 289–290
errors in Mark, 62–63
Matthew, missing verse in, 27

verse examples related to doctrines,
20, 23, 26–27, 29–30
Epiphanius, 223
Epp, Eldon J., 34
Erasmus, Desiderius, 86–87, 259
ERV (English Revised Version), 38, 143,
163, 177, 215–216
ESV. *See* English Standard Version
ESV Study Bible, 153–156
Ethiopic Bible, 223, 301–302
Eusebius, 223, 224
evolution, 262, 269–270
Ezra, 122–123

Faber, F. W., 118
faith, statements of, 118, 247–248,
250–253, 257, 271–272, 294
Falwell, Jerry, 89, 146–147
Fee, Gordon, 223
footnotes in NKJV/KJV, 147–149
forgiveness, doctrine of, 23
France, R. T., 61–62
freethinkersbooks.com, 74–75
fundamentalism, 254–255, 263–265

Gallup poll, 125
Gaussen, Louis, 233–234
Geerlings, Jacob, 48
Geisler, Norman L., 111, 124–125, 179,
275–280
genealogical errors in Matthew, 56–61
Geneva Bible, 158, 182, 185, 194, 200,
298
Gentile, usage of, 173–174
geographical errors in Luke, 63–65, 162
German theological rationalism, 262,
266
Gibson, Mel, 282
Glenny, W. Edward, 169, 212–213
God vs. Lord, usage and capitalization
of, 184–189
God's words, all contained in Bible, 8, 11,
31, 159,
244, 273, 286–287
Goliath, 71
Goodspeed, Edgar, 179

325

Gordon-Conwell Theological Seminary, 252, 253, 254
Grady, William P., 294
Great Bible, 158, 182, 184, 187, 194, 200, 298
Greek
    footnotes about, in KJV, 148
    not required for choosing a bible, 9, 33, 211
Greek New Testament. *See also* Alexandrian (critical) textform; Received Text (Textus Receptus)
    Beza 1589 edition, 299, 300–301, 302
    edited by Erasmus, 86, 259
    identical manuscripts of, 213–214
    John Mill's edition, 260, 262
    manuscripts, similarities between, 203
    modern, 57–58, 202
    text-types of, 47–49
    UBS4 (United Bible Societies) text, 49, 65, 66, 100, 239
    Westcott and Hort text, 46–52, 54
Greek Orthodox Bible, 223
Gutenberg Bible, 84, 157

HCSB. *See* Holman Christian Standard Bible
Hebrew
    footnotes about, in KJV, 148
    as language of Christ, 13, 273
    not required for choosing a Bible, 9, 33, 211
    as original language
        of Book of Revelation, 297–303
        of Epistle to the Hebrews, 224
        of Gospel of John, 13
        of Gospel of Matthew, 223–224
    standard texts of Old Testament, 136
Hendrickson Publishers, 164
Hodge, Archibald A., 263, 267, 268, 271, 272
Hodge, Charles, 267
Holland, Thomas, 300–301

Holman Christian Standard Bible (HCSB)
    compared to other "standard" Bibles, 289–290
    errors in Luke, 63–65
    history of, 293
    inspiration and, 238
    verse missing in 2 Corinthians, 255
Holy Ghost, 14, 45, 59
Hort, Fenton, 46–47, 50–54
Hoskier, Herman, 301
hyperbole, 15

Identity of the New Testament II, The, 155–157
imprimatur, 99
Incarnation, 162
inductive reasoning, 6, 220–221
inerrancy of Scripture
    Chicago Statement on, 247–248, 257, 271–272
    definition of, 268
    doctrine of, 23–26, 71–72
    modern Bible versions and, 138–139, 236–237
    Princeton doctrine, 267–272
    statements of faith, 118, 247–248, 250–253, 294
    supposedly inauthentic verses and, 108, 291
inspiration of Scripture
    Chicago Statement on, 247–248
    "God-breathed," 239–240
    meaning of, 13–14, 233–238, 241–246, 259, 267–272
    per 1 Corinthians, 242
    per 2 Timothy, 153, 235–236, 238, 241, 242
    per Book of Job, 241
    plenary inspiration, doctrine of, 26–27
Institute for New Testament Textual Research, 302
Introduction to the Bible (Geisler and Nix), 179
Irenaeus, 153, 154, 223

Isaiah, 62–63

Jehovah vs. Elohim, usage of, 184–189
Jerome, 153, 223
Jesus Christ
   authentic variants and, 122
   "begotten God," 147, 152, 162
   as Bible project manager, 9–10, 13, 287
   disciples, appointment of, 25–26
   doctrine of, 72–73, 162
   Hebrew as language of, 13
   Incarnation, 147, 162
   as living word, 14
   sinlessness, doctrine of, 68–70, 70–71, 73–75
   truthfulness of, 68–71, 75, 104, 161
John, Gospel of
   errors in, 69–71, 73, 151–152
   original language of, 13
Johnson, Samuel, 168
Jones, Bob, 102

Kayser, Phillip G., 98–99
Kent, Homer, 32
Keylock, Leslie R., 108
Kilpatrick, George Dunbar, 38–39
King James Bible (KJB)
   as a brand, 129, 195, 210, 212
   compared to NKJV, 132–136, 145–146
   discrepancies of numbering in OT, 275–278, 279–284
   footnotes in, 148
   as inspired book, 92–96, 214, 218
   most used and best-selling version, 112, 117–119, 124–125, 217, 305
   Revelation, original language of, 297–303
   revision of (see English Revised Version)
   as a standard-bearer, 158–160, 294
   textual basis of, 136, 214, 259
   translations into other languages, 112
   Translators' Preface to, 148–149, 158–159
   verse examples related to doctrines, 20, 23, 109, 136–142
   verses not in modern translations, 95–97, 100–101, 107–108
King James Only movement, 89–91, 120, 129, 143, 219–222
King James Version, editions of
   1611 edition, 163, 164, 177
   1629 and 1638 editions, 167–169, 181–183
   Blayney edition (1769), 10, 164, 168, 179, 217
   Cambridge Paragraph Bible, 163
   Cambridge vs. Oxford printings, 194, 201, 202–203, 205–210
   capitalization (God vs. GOD), 185–186
   compared to modern versions, 161–162
   editorial word choices in, 172–176, 190, 191, 193–194, 196–198, 199
   Elohim (God) vs. Jehovah (Lord), usage of, 184–189
   New Cambridge Paragraph Bible, 183
   Paris edition (1762), 164, 167–169, 193, 198, 217
   printing and typographical errors in, 165–167, 190–191, 193, 198
   spelling and grammar standardization in, 167–172, 189, 193
Kings/Chronicles, discrepancies in, 275–278, 279–284
Kinney, Will, 36

Lake, Kirsopp, 53
Latin Vulgate, 22
Lazarus, 137–138
Leningrad Manuscript B19a, 136
Lewis, Jack P., 143, 280–281, 295
Liebana, Beatus of, 300
Lindsell, Harold, 234
literary devices, 15–16

Lockman Foundation, 67
Logos, 217
Lord vs. God, usage and capitalization
    of, 184–189
Loughran, David, 47
Lowry, Robert, 208–209
Luke, Gospel of
    errors in, 25–26, 63–65, 162
    "scripture," use of, 257
    story of Lazarus in, 137–138
    textual variants in, 121
Lutheran Church-Missouri Synod, 306

MacArthur, John F., 31–32
Majority text, 49. *See also* Received Text
    (Textus Receptus)
Malachi, 62–63
Malane, Daniel Joseph, 85–86
man, doctrine of, 136–138
manuscripts. *See also* Sinaiticus and
        Vaticanus
    comparison of text-types, 49
    judging as evidence, 202
    Latin, 156, 301–302
    oldest vs. best, 35–41, 66–68,
        100–101, 156, 214
Mark, Gospel of
    ending of, 153–156
    errors in, 61–63, 72–73, 74
    three versions of in Alexandria,
        40–41
Marlowe, Michael, 293
Martini, Carlo Maria, 97–98
Masoretic text, 136, 188
Master's Seminary, The, 252
Matthew, Gospel of
    genealogical errors in
        Amon-Amos, 59–60, 61
        Asa-Asaph, 56–60
    Hebrew as original language of,
        223–224
    verses or words missing in, 27, 74
Matthew's Bible, 158, 184, 185, 187, 194,
    200, 298
McElroy, Jack
    Bible background, 10–11

life history, 8–9
reasons for writing this book, 16–17
McGrath, Alister, 117
Mencken, H. L., 117
The Message, 287, 292
Metzger, Bruce M.
    on corruption of the NT, 53, 100
    on errors in gospels
        Luke, 63–65
        Matthew, 56–57, 59–60
    on inconsistencies, 70, 73
    as member of UBS committee, 98
Mill, John, 260, 262
missing verses. *See* verses, missing
modern English Bible versions. *See also*
        specific version names
    Alexandrian textform as basis of, 49,
        50, 54
    inerrancy of Scripture and, 138–139,
        236–237
    inferior quality of, 6, 178
    as personal versions, 290
Mohler, R. Albert, Jr., 24–25, 68
Moody Bible Institute, 252
Moody Monthly, 108
Moore, Sam, 129–131, 132, 146
Morris, Henry, 113
Moses, 3, 76–77, 197, 230–231

NA27. *See* Nestle-Aland text
NASB. *See* New American Standard
        Bible
National Council of Churches, 143, 193
Nelson, Thomas, Inc., 113, 142, 143, 164
Nestle-Aland text (NA27), 49, 100. *See
        also* Alexandrian (critical)
        textform
Neutral textform, 49. *See also* Alexan-
        drian (critical) textform
New American Standard Bible (NASB)
    additions to in 1975, 306
    Beersheba/Sheba wording, 207
    compared to other "standard"
        Bibles, 289–290
    discrepancies of numbering in OT,
        277, 279, 281

Index

endorsements of, 24–26, 28, 32, 68
errors in gospels
    John, 69–71
    Luke, 25–26, 63–65
    Mark, 61–63
    Matthew, 27, 56–57, 59
original language of Revelation and, 298
Revised Standard Version and, 143
verse examples related to doctrines, 20, 22–23, 26–27, 29–32, 68–70, 109, 136–137
New Cambridge Paragraph Bible, 183
New International Version (NIV) (1984)
    Catholic version of NIV Psalms, 99
    contradicting the 2011 version, 71, 72–73
    discrepancies of numbering in OT, 277, 279, 281
    errors in gospels
        John, 69–71, 73
        Luke, 63–65
        Mark, 61–63, 72–73
        Matthew, 56–57, 59
    original language of Revelation and, 298
    Revised Standard Version and, 143
    sales of, compared to KJV, 305
    verse examples related to doctrines, 20, 23, 68–73, 136
New International Version (NIV) (2011)
    contradicting the 1984 version, 71, 72–73
    errors in gospels
        John, 73
        Mark, 72–73, 74
        Matthew, 56–57, 59, 74
    pronouns in, 175
    rejection of, 306
    verse examples related to doctrines, 20, 29–32, 71–75, 109
New Jerusalem Bible, 97
New King James Version (NKJV)
    compared to KJV, 132–136, 145–146
    errors in gospels
        in Mark, 61–63
        in Matthew, 74
    footnotes in, 140, 141, 147–148
    Lord vs. God, usage of, 187
    reasons for producing, 127–132
    Revised Standard Version and, 142–144
    textual basis of, 130, 136
    verse examples related to doctrines, 73–75, 136–142
New Living Translation (NLT), 175, 277
New Revised Standard Version (NRSV), 57, 290, 292
newspaper reporting, 25–26, 53
New Testament. *See* Greek New Testament
New Testament in the Original Greek, The Byzantine Textform (Westcott & Hort), 46–52
New Testament Text and Translation Commentary (Comfort), 62, 121
Niagara Bible Conference, 263–264
Niagara Creed, 264–265, 268, 272
NIV. *See* New International Version
Nix, William E., 179
NKJV. *See* New King James Version
NLT (New Living Translation), 175, 277
Norris, Rick, 205
Norton, David
    on KJV 1611 and 1769 edition differences, 181–184, 190–193, 196–197, 199–200
    on literalness, 174
    on typographic errors in KJV, 164–165
NRSV (New Revised Standard Version), 57, 290, 292
NU text (NA27 and UBS4), 49, 65. *See also* Alexandrian (critical) textform

Old Testament, Masoretic text, 136, 188
Omanson, Roger L., 60–61
One Bible Only? (Glenny), 169, 212, 220–222, 224
On the Origin of Species (Darwin), 262

Origen, 153, 223
original autographs ("Original Bible").
    See also variant readings;
    verses, missing
  autographic text, 249–250, 267
  disagreement of experts on, 5–6, 34,
    203
  as final authority, 153, 250
  God's words and men's words, mixture of, 2, 3, 4, 81
  language of, 212, 222
  lost or destroyed, 75–77, 79, 81,
    84–85
  modern versions as personal versions of, 290
  percentage of identical text in,
    81–83
  real vs. imaginary, 230, 257–258
  Vaticanus and Sinaiticus as representatives of, 36, 46
Orthodox Corruption of Scripture, The
  (Ehrman), 52–53, 100
orthodox scribes, 52–53, 62, 100–101
orthography, 167, 177, 216, 217, 229
Orwell, George, 53
Oxford University Press, 118, 164, 177
Oxford vs. Cambridge printings of KJV,
  194, 201, 202–203, 205–210

Papias, 223
Paris, F. S., 168
Paris, Thomas, 164
Paris edition (1762) of KJV, 164, 167–
  169, 198, 217
Parvis, Merrill M., 55–56
Patterson, Paige, 28
Paul
  Galatians, 139
  Hebrews, 224
  inspiration and, 235–236, 242
  journeys of, 39
  quoting from poets, 240
  Romans, 256
Pensacola Christian College, 253, 254
Phelps, William Lyon, 118

Pickering, Wilbur N., 39, 48, 54, 98–99,
  155–156
Piper, John, 29
plenary inspiration of the Scriptures,
  doctrine of, 26–27
political events in Bible, counting years
  from, 284–285
polls about preferred Bible versions,
  124–125
Presbyterians, 270–271
preservation, doctrine of, 238–239, 272
Price, James D., 133–134, 302
Price, Randall, 2–3, 81–82
Princeton inerrancy doctrine, 267–272
printing errors in KJV, 165–167, 190–
  191, 193, 198
printing press, 84, 112, 151
proof texts
  for Incarnation, 147, 162
  for Trinity, 108–110, 147, 162
Psalms, 99, 168–169, 223, 243

Queen Victoria, 114
quotation source errors in Mark, 61–63

rationalism, German, 262, 266
reasoning, deductive and inductive, 6,
  220–221, 225
Received Text (Textus Receptus)
  basis of King James Bible, 214, 259
  basis of Reformation Bibles, 49, 100
  compared to Alexandrian textform,
    47–49
  freedom from errors, 47
  Hort, rejection by, 50–51
  manuscripts, similarities between,
    203
recension, 50–51
Reformation Bibles
  printing technology and, 158
  Textus Receptus as base of, 49, 100
Revelation, Book of
  date of completion of NT, 231
  Ethiopian version in Latin, 301–302
  Hebrew as original language of,
    297–303

Index

Revised Standard Version (RSV), 142–144, 292
Revised Version (English Revised Version), 143, 163, 177, 215–216
revision, 50–51, 175–176, 215
Revision Revised, The (Burgon), 42–43
Riley, W. B., 93
Robinson, Maurice, 82–83, 151, 203
Rogers, John, 111
Roman Catholicism, 98–99, 260, 307
RSV (Revised Standard Version), 142–144, 292
Ruckman, Peter S., 209
Ryken, Leland, 117
Ryrie, Charles Caldwell, 109–110

Salmon, George, 45–46
Sandeen, Ernest R., 267, 268–270
sarcasm, 15–16
Schaff, Philip, 92, 94
Scofield, C. I., 263–264
Scofield Study Bible, 263
Scott, Robert B. Y., 299
Scripture. *See also* inerrancy of Scripture; inspiration of Scripture
 copies and translations of, 255–258
 understanding, 233, 241–244
Scrivener, Frederick H. A., 38, 163, 193
Searching for the Original Bible (R. Price), 2–3, 81–82
seed of Abraham, doctrine of, 139–140
Septuagint, 22
Simms, P. Marion, 94
sin, doctrine of, 22, 138
Sinaiticus and Vaticanus. *See also* variant readings; verses, missing
 basis of Westcott and Hort Greek text, 46–49
 errors in, 42–46
 history of, 35–36, 100–101, 112
 Psalms in, 223
 as representatives of original autographs, 36, 46
 usage in the church, history of, 47–49

sinlessness of Christ, doctrine of, 68–70, 70–71, 73–75
Smith, Miles, 148–149, 158–159
Smith, Morton, 40
Some Thoughts on the Textual Criticism of the New Testament (Salmon), 45–46
souls, 84–85, 136–138
Southern Baptist Convention, 306
spelling standardization in KJV, 167–169, 189, 193
Sproul, R. C., 68
"standard" Bibles, 289–295
Stanley, Charles, 68
statements of faith, 118, 247–248, 250–253, 257, 271–272, 294
Stauffer, Douglas, 294
Stowell, Joseph, 68
Streeter, B. H., 41
Studies in the Theory and Method of New Testament Textual Criticism (Epp), 34–35
Sumner, Robert, 89
Swindoll, Charles, 71
Syrian text, 49. *See also* Received Text (Textus Receptus)

tabernacle in the wilderness, doctrine of, 20–21
taking away from words of the Bible, 27, 29–30, 286
Talbot School of Theology, 252
temple of the Lord, 183–184
Tertullian, 40
Text of the New Testament, The (Metzger), 53, 100
text-types (textforms) of Bible manuscripts, 49. *See also* Alexandrian (critical) textform; Received Text (Textus Receptus)
Textual Commentary on the Greek New Testament (Metzger), 60

textual criticism. *See also* original autographs; variant readings
- corruption in manuscripts, 37–43, 52–54
- dirty secrets of, 44–46
- not a science, 33–34
- supposedly inauthentic verses, 108, 291
- Westcott/Hort text vs. Received Text, 46–52

textual errors vs. translational errors, 94, 120, 216–217

Textual Guide to the Greek New Testament, A (Omanson), 61–62

Textual History of the King James Bible, A (Norton), 182–200

textual variation. *See* variant readings

Textus Receptus. *See* Received Text (Textus Receptus)

Theissen, Henry C., 234

theological rationalism, German, 262, 266

theoretical Bible. *See* original autographs

Thomas Nelson, Inc., 113, 142, 143, 164

Torrey, Charles C., 299–300

Towns, Elmer, 132, 149–150

traditional text, 49, 51. *See also* Received Text (Textus Receptus)

translational errors vs. textual errors, 94, 120, 216–217

Translators' Preface to KJV, 148–149, 158–159

Trench, Richard Chenevix, 92–93

Trinity (triunity of God), 109–110, 162

Trinity International University, 252

Trump, Donald, 128–129

Twain, Mark, 180

Tyconius, 300, 301

Tyndale, William, 111, 158

Tyndale Bible, 111, 187, 194, 200, 297

typographical errors in KJV, 165–167, 190–191, 193, 198

UBS4 (United Bible Societies) text, 49, 65, 66, 100, 239. *See also* Alexandrian (critical) textform

UBS (United Bible Societies) translation committee, 66, 98–99

understanding Scripture, 233, 241–244

University of North Carolina at Chapel Hill, 175–176

USA Today, 72, 124

Vance, Laurence M., 142–143

variant readings
- in 2 Samuel, 71–72
- authentic vs. fake, 120–122, 202, 220–221
- estimated numbers of, 84, 107–108, 260
- in gospels
  - John, 69–71, 73, 151–152
  - Luke, 63–65
  - Mark, 61–63, 72–73, 74, 153–156
  - Matthew, 56–61, 74
- grading of, 239
- oldest manuscripts vs. best, 35–41, 66–68, 100–101, 156, 214
- Protestant doctrine not jeopardized by, 85, 122, 154, 257, 260–262, 280–281
- in "standard" Bible versions, 289–290
- types of errors in, 11–12, 45–46, 54
- in Vaticanus and Sinaiticus
  - collated by Burgon, 42–44
  - compared to Received Text, 47
  - disagreement between, 41, 44, 154
  - as "God's mistakes," 45
  - origin of, 35–41
  - as text of "Original Bible," 36, 46

verse comparisons. *See* doctrine comparison tables (verse examples)

verses, missing
- in 2 Corinthians, 255
- in Acts, 29–32
- critics' disagreement about, 34
- in Matthew, 27
- from modern translations, 95–97, 100–101, 107–108
- numbering/renumbering of, 294
- in "standard" translations, 289–291

Victoria, Queen, 114
visions, doctrine of, 141
Vulgate, 22

Wallace, Daniel B.
    on inferiority of Received Text, 107–108
    on missing verses, 95–96, 100, 115
    on textual percentages, 81, 82
Ward, Samuel, 165
Ware, Bruce A., 68
Warfield, Benjamin B., 234–235, 263, 265–267, 268–269, 271, 272
Webster, Noah, 246
Wegner, Paul, 188–189
Westcott, Brooke, 46–47
Westcott and Hort Greek text, 46–52, 54
Wheaton College, 250
White, James R., 90, 297–299, 300, 303
Wikgren, Allen, 98
Williams, James B., 90
"Word of God," 248–251, 254–255, 272–273
word of the Lord, 80, 86–87, 103–105, 224–225
words of the Bible, adding to or taking away from, 27, 29–30, 32, 286
words of truth, certainty of, 32–33, 122, 295, 307–308
Wordsworth, John, 300
Wurmbrand, Richard, 281–282
Wycliffe Bible, 184, 185, 187, 297

Yahweh (Jehovah), 184–189
Young's Literal Translation (YLT), 185

Zondervan, 164

Scripture Index

Old Testament

Genesis

2:7	136, 137
6:5	185, 187
13:15	139
13:18	208
15:6	189
15:18	170
21:14	207
21:25	207
21:30	207, 208
21:31	207
22:33	208
22:19	208
26:15	208
26:18, 32	208
26:20, 21	208
26:25	208
26:28, 31	208
26:33	208
32:28	140
39:16	175

Exodus

29:43	19
34:20	170
34:25	170
36:19	20
38:11	165

Leviticus

11:10	170
15:33	170
24:11-16	103
26:40	165

Numbers

7:55	170
9:13	170
23:19	104
23:23	107
35:1-7	208

Deuteronomy

4:2	27, 286
12:32	27
26:1	196
29	209

Joshua

3:11	181, 183, 196
13:29	197
17:8	208
19:2	201, 206, 208
19:2-6	207

Ruth

3:15	174, 196, 197

1 Samuel

15:29	104
17:29	1
18:1	166
24:13	240

2 Samuel

5:19-25	188
15:7	23, 249
21:19	71, 162

1 Kings

4:26	275, 277, 278
4:32	240
16:6-8	284
16:15	283
16:23	284
16:29	283, 284
18:27	16
22:41	283
22:51	283, 284

335

2 Kings

3:1	283, 284
8:17	280
8:26	279, 281
9:29	283
11:10	181, 183
24:8	285
24:12	285

1 Chronicles

14:10	189
14:11	189
14:15	189
14:16	189
21:16	170

2 Chronicles

9:25	275, 276, 277, 278
13:6	166
16:1	285
18:1	283
19:1-3	283
21	281
22:2	279, 281, 284
22:7	284
23:9	184
23:11	173
28:11	186, 187
33:19	201, 206, 209
36:9	285

Ezra

2:22	166
2:62	122
2:63	122
3:5	166
6:3-5	240
7:12-26	240, 242

Nehemiah

2:17	170
2:20	170

Job

1:1	144
3:7	144
3:8	144
6:8	170
13:8	144
27:5	170
30:29	144
31:21	170
32:8	233, 241, 243, 246
34:14-15	137
38:36	243

Psalms

10:5	138
12:6-7	80, 224
15:4	259
19:7	173, 289
23	68, 168-169
33:11	80
68:11	161, 210
69:32	166, 196, 198
73:25	170
93:5	205
100:5	80, 101, 272, 275
107:43	170
111:7-8	224
116:16	170
117:2	225
119:98-100	286
119:140	172
119:152	225
119:160	80, 151, 225
138:2	103

Proverbs

2:6	244
2:9	244
3:11-13	243
8:5-8	244
15:32	243
18:8	140, 141
19:18	142
22:1	104
22:20-21	308

Scripture Index

22:32	308
23:23	308
24:21	245
25:1	240
29:18	141
30:5	27, 172
30:5-6	27
31:1	240

Ecclesiastes

3:21	137
8:10	22
8:17	166
12:7	137
12:12	158

Song of Solomon

1:9	278

Isaiah

6:8	166
3:17-18	188
7:14	143
9:3	138
28:4	170
28:9	243
29:8	170
29:14	170
34:16	305
40:3	62
40:8	225
49:13	181, 184, 187

Jeremiah

15:7	170
17:15	219
20:9	16
23:36	105
31:14	181, 189
34:13	209
34:16	194, 200, 201, 206, 209
36:23	3, 79
48:36	171
49:1	166, 196, 198
51:30	181, 190
51:63	76, 79

Ezekiel

1:2	285
5:1	166
6:8	166, 181, 190
8:1	285
11:24	166
20:1	285
24:5	181, 191
24:7	166, 181, 191
26:14	166
34:31	166
36:2	166
42:17	166
46:23	166
48:8	181, 191

Daniel

1:12	166
3:15	181, 192
6:13	167
6:3-4	160

Nahum

3:16	201, 206, 209

Zechariah

6:4	167

Malachi

3:1	62
3:16	3

New Testament

Matthew		27:35	291
1:7-8	56, 59, 251	27:52	171
1:7, 8, 10	12, 148, 162, 282, 283, 284	**Mark**	
1:10	59, 60	1:2	12, 61, 63, 251
1:11-12	285	1:35-39	65
1:18-2:20	61	1:39	64, 65, 162
4:4	80, 104	1:41	12, 72, 162
4:23	64, 65, 162	3:5	74, 147, 162
5:18	80	7:16	96, 291
5:22	74, 147, 162	9:44	96, 291
5:29	15	9:46	96, 291
5:44	291	10:7	291
6:13	291	10:18	196, 199
7:17	308	10:21	291
9:34	171	10:24	291,
11:25	282	14:68	291
11:27	199	11:26	96, 291
12:47	27, 28, 44, 254, 290	12:26	265
13:6	171	12:36	265
14:9	181, 192	12:37	92
16:2	291	13:11	265
16:3	291	13:31	80, 272
17:21	291	15:28	96, 291
16:16	196, 198	16:9-20	142, 153, 154
16:26	136, 137		
17:21	96	**Luke**	
18:11	96, 291	1:4	308
18:22	22, 23	4:4	291
20:16	291	4:17	22
20:22-20:23	291 291	4:21	257
19:5-6	123	4:38	171
21:42	256	4:44	12, 63, 64, 65, 162, 251
21:44	290	6:44	308
22:32	286	8:5	171
22:43	286	8:43	291
23:14	96, 291	9:26	35
23:19	15	9:54-56	291
23:24	15, 179	10:1	25
23:27	15	10:32	44
24:35	44, 80, 103, 272, 297	13:35	121
25:13	291	14:26	15
		16:22	137

338

Scripture Index

17:35	44	28:16	291
17:36	96, 291	28:29	97, 291
21:33	80, 272	**Romans**	
22:43-44	291	1:25	145
23:17	44, 96, 100, 291	2:9	173
23:34	44	2:14	173
24:12	290	3:4	55
24:40	290	4:3	189
24:42	291	4:25	145
John		7:13	171
1:18	12, 147, 151-152, 162	9:5	142
1:46	16	14:10	16
5:3	291	15:4	256
5:4	96, 291	16:24	97
6:63	13, 272	**1 Corinthians**	
7:7, 8, 10	12, 69, 70, 73, 147, 161	2:13	265
7:17	127	2:15	44
7:53-8:11	142	4:9	196, 199-200
8:58	286	7:12	242
9:38	44	7:32	167
10:28	199	12:28	181, 182
10:35	286	13:1-2	44
16:15	44	13:2	171
17:17	104, 272	13:4	227
Acts		15:6	167, 181, 193
1:16	265	**2 Corinthians**	
2:4	265	2:17	105
4:27	145	10:5	145
5:34	171	11:26	171
8:9	145	11:32	167
8:32	256	12:13	16
8:36-38	29	13:14	255, 289
8:37	30, 97, 291	**Galatians**	
15:23	171	3:6	189
15:34	97, 291	3:16	139, 286
17:11	256	4:9	286
17:28	240	5:7	16
18:5	171	5:12	16
19:19	171	**Philippians**	
22:8	171	2:9	103, 117
24:6b-8	97, 291		
26:22	171		
27:18	167		

339

Colossians		**2 Peter**	
3:2	145	1:21	265
		3:16	105
1 Thessalonians		**1 John**	
5:22	145	4:3	171
1 Timothy		5:7	108-110
2:4	211	5:7-8	109, 147, 162
3:16	147, 152, 162	5:12	181, 193
		Revelation	
2 Timothy		9:11	300
1:12	171	13:6	167
2:2	194	16:5	297-298, 300, 301
2:15	145, 282, 284, 286	22:2	171
2:19	123		
3:15	235, 256		
3:16	234, 235, 237, 238, 241, 242, 243, 246, 265		
3:17	265		
4:13	167		
Titus			
1:2	104		
3:10	145		
Hebrews			
4:12-13	209		
6:18	104		
8:13	286		
11:6	79, 80		
11:23	167		
12:27	286		
13:13	89		
James			
1:7	290		
3:10	255		
5:4	171		
1 Peter			
1:23	104, 224, 273		
2:2	171		

Image Credits

Introduction: Randall Price, *Searching for the Original Bible,* Harvest House Publishers © 2007. **Chapter 1:** Sea Cow, Copyright Liquid Productions, LLC, 2013. Used under license from Shutterstock; Porpoise, Copyright Serg Zastavkin, 2013. Used under license from Shutterstock; Badger, Copyright Meoita, 2013. Used under license from Shutterstock; Goat, Copyright Nataliia Antonova, 2013. Used under license from Shutterstock; Sofa, Image Copyright ponsuwan, 2013. Used under license from Shutterstock; Dr. R. Albert Mohler, Jr., http://commons.wikimedia.org/wiki/File:Al_Mohler.jpg; Dr. Paige Patterson, by Btwebster86, http://en.wikipedia.org/wiki/File:Paige_Patterson_with_a_student_in_2009.jpg; John Piper, by Micah Chiang, Micah_68, http://www.flickr.com/photos/micah_68/5170297736/sizes/o/in/photostream/; Dr. John F. MacArthur, by Grace to You via Flickr, http://farm5.staticflickr.com/4009/4612672096_7994c6a9ba_o.jpg; Sir John Tenniel Lewis, Lewis Carroll's *Alice's Adventures in Wonderland,* 1865. **Chapter 2:** Dean John Burgon, Used by permission, Christian Research Press, Ankeny, IA; Fenton Hort, Used by permission, Christian Research Press, Ankeny, IA; Bart D. Ehrman, *The Orthodox Corruption of Scripture: The Effect of Early Christological Controversies on the Text of the New Testament* © 1993 by Oxford University Press; Bruce M. Metzger and Bart D. Ehrman, *The Text of the New Testament,* 4th ed. © 1964, 1968, 1992 by Oxford University Press; George Orwell's *1984,* Secker and Warburg © 1949. **Chapter 3:** Bruce Metzger, Charles Fields, 2003, http://en.wikipedia.org/wiki/File:Bruce_Metzger.JPG; Roger L. Omanson, *A Textual Guide to the Greek New Testament,* p. 57; Map of Israel, http://www.bible-history.com/maps/samaria_central_palestine.html; Kurt Aland, Tobias Aland, personal collection, http://en.wikipedia.org; Bruce M. Metzger, *Textual Commentary on the Greek New Testament,* p. 185; Charles Swindoll, © Roger Ressmeyer/CORBIS. Used by Permission. **Chapter 4:** Daniel Joseph Malane, *The Bible: "Word of God" or Words of Men?* Bloomington, IN: Xlibris, 2007. **Chapter 5:** Carlo Martini, SJ. Used with Permission © Marco Longari, Getty Images; Greek NT Committee, TA (Personal Collection), Wikimedia Commons; *The Psalms New International Version* © 1996 Catholic Book Publishing Corp., NJ; James B. Williams and Randolph Shaylor, *From the Mind of God to the Mind of Man* © 1999 James B. Williams and the committee on the Bible's Text and Translation. **Chapter 6:** Dr. Jack Moorman, *8,000 Differences Between the N.T. Greek Words of the King James Bible and the Modern Versions* © 2008; Charles C. Ryrie, *Basic Theology: A Popular Systematic Guide to Understanding Biblical Truth* © 1986, 1999 Charles C. Ryrie, Moody Press, Chicago; www.Institute For Creation Research.org; John Bunyan, BunyanMinistries.org. **Chapter 7:** Moon Stamp, US Postal Service 1969; Philip W. Comfort, *New Testament Text and Translation Commentary* © 2008 Philip W. Comfort, Tyndale House Publishers, Inc. Carol Stream, IL, p. 213. **Chapter 10:** Spelling icon, Alexander Moore, Findicons.com; Proofreader icon, Alessandro Rei, Findicons.com; "Book and glasses" by Natis [ID 349000095] Fotolia (us.fotolia.com). **Chapter 11:** Dead Sea Isaiah Scroll, © John C. Trever, PhD, digital image by James E. Trever. 1QIsa Col. 3 3:16–24. Used with permission. **Chapter 12:** Roy E. Beacham and Kevin T. Bauder, *One Bible Only.*

Grand Rapids, MI: Kregel, 2001. **Chapter 13:** White Mountain Puzzles, Great Events of the Bible. **Chapter 15:** Aland, Aland, Karavindopoulos, Martini, Metzger. *The Greek New Testament* (4th ed., 1993) United Bible Societies. **Chapter 16:** *Webster's 1828 Dictionary,* Foundation for American Christian Education, San Francisco, CA; Humpty Dumpty, Used with permission, http://www.clipartof.com/; Zenith TV, Used with permission, Dan Schumann. Photo by Karin R. Schumann, 1995. **Chapter 17:** Richard Bentley, by Arthur Thomas Malkin via Wikimedia Commons; Charles Darwin, *On the Origin of Species.* G Books 2011. **Chapter 18:** Norman L. Geisler and Thomas Howe, *The Big Book of Bible Difficulties: Clear and Concise Answers from Genesis to Revelation* © 1992 Norman L. Geisler and Thomas Howe. Baker Books, Grand Rapids, MI; Richard Wurmbrand, *Tortured for Christ* © 1967 The Voice of the Martyrs. Published by Living Sacrifice Book Company, Bartlesville, OK; Three glasses, Used with permission. Artist: Alexey Stiop, ImageDirekt.com. **Chapter 19:** Douglas Stauffer, *One Book One Authority* © 2012 Douglas Stauffer; William P. Grady, *Final Authority: A Christian's Guide to the King James Bible* © 1993 William P. Grady. **Chapter 20:** James R. White, *The King James Only Controversy, Can You Trust Modern Translations?* © 1999, 2009 James R. White, Bethany House Publishers, Division of Baker Publishing Group, Grand Rapids, MI. **Chapter 21:** "Blue sports car," Prosetisen [ID 50477272] Fotolia (us.fotolia.com).

CPSIA information can be obtained at www.ICGtesting.com
Printed in the USA
BVOW07s0759021214

376762BV00003B/3/P